the jews

Books by Howard Fast

the jews

story of a people

by Howard Fast

The Dial Press, Inc.   New York, 1968

Printed in the United States of America

Design by Thomas Clemens

ISBN 0-440-50506-8 (pbk)

BVG 01

CONTENTS

Illustration sections facing pages 86, 166 and 246

About the Author

Howard Fast was born in 1914 in New York City, where he lives today. Educated in the public schools, he published his first novel, *Two Valleys*, at the age of nineteen. Since then he has written twenty-four books, among them *Citizen Tom Paine*, *The Unvanquished*, *Freedom Road*, *Spartacus*, *April Morning*, and *Agrippa's Daughter*. Over twenty-five million copies of *Freedom Road* have been printed, and it is said to be the most widely read novel of this century.

Mr. Fast is married to the painter Bette Cohen and they have two children, Rachel, born in 1944, and Jonathan, born in 1948.

To the memory of:

Ida Yerushalayim
Baruch Ben Aaron
Isaac ha Cohen
ava shalom

PART ONE

the Desert

The desert was cruel and hard and dry, and these were the people of the desert. They were herdsmen; their wealth was in sheep and goats and they moved often, from one sparse pasture to another, from one water hole to another. Their community was tribal, and their chief was the patriarch of the tribe, the ruler absolute, the dispenser of justice and lord of life and death. He had many wives—possibly the right to sleep with any woman in the tribe who was unmarried and make her pregnant. His power was very great but it was limited by three harsh adversaries: poverty, hardship, and hunger.

The size of each tribe varied, perhaps from a minimum of a hundred to a maximum of a thousand. Hardly ever more than a thousand, for the water holes have not changed much in the three and a half thousand years since then, and we know that if a tribe increased to over a thousand, neither water nor pasture would support it.

The tribesmen lived in tents. They wove cloth from the wool of their beasts and worked leather from the skins. They worked copper into weapons, and when they were fortunate enough to trade their wool or cheese for some of the rare and precious tin, they made tools out of bronze. As yet they knew no iron, and their progress from place to place was on foot.

Their range of wandering and grazing was about three hundred miles in length from south to northeast in a ribbon fifty or sixty miles wide, from the southern part of the Sinai peninsula through the Negeb, and then in a sort of crescent through the area known as Jordan today. This is not to imply that all the tribes grazed over the entire area. Most likely, each tribe had grazing rights in a limited area. If the grass and water were good, then the particular tribe would cling to their place; but since the grass and water were like as not less than good, the tribe would look for a better place, and since another tribe had the better place, it meant war and bloodshed.

Life was hard, demanding, and bitter; but the air was clean and the night sky was filled with the presence of the universe, and herdsmen have time to contemplate and dream.

Three and a half thousand years ago, there must have been hundreds of these tribes in the vast desert that stretched from the Red Sea to the Syrian highlands. Since it would have been difficult if not impossible for a band of herdsmen to exist alone, the tribes were linked into loose confederations, binding themselves to a common if distant ancestor, and a common history-mythology, often a wonderful quilt of stories, transmitted verbally from generation to generation.

The confederated tribes would call themselves the children of the common ancestor, but this was merely a generic means of identification, which the desert herdsmen used for any and all nations. Our own interest is focused upon a singular group of tribes who called themselves the Children of Israel, or in their own tongue, the *Beni-Yisrael*.

———————

Exactly how many of these Children of Israel tribes—how many minor clans and gens and subfamilies—there were, we do not know. Records centuries later talk of the twelve tribes of Israel, but 12 was a magic number, a symbol-number, and even if we do a simple count out of the Bible, we come up with fourteen—Reuben, Simeon, Levi, Judah, Issachar, Zebulun, Dan, Gad, Naphtali, Asher, Joseph, Ephraim, Manasseh, and Benjamin. This was reduced to twelve by eliminating the "Joseph" designation entirely, and then taking the two so-called Joseph tribes, Ephraim and Manasseh, and counting them as half-tribes. Possibly there were a number of other "Joseph tribes" that history and the Bible forgot, and possibly the Amorites, another grouping of desert tribes, were so closely connected with the Beni-Yisrael, that there was a shifting back and forth.

Certainly, the Midianite tribal grouping, whose livestock grazed over the wild and sparse badlands of southern Sinai, were intimately connected with the Israelites, for out of their tribe of Ken came Moses' bloodline if not Moses himself. And since the Kenites were unquestionably absorbed into the Israel grouping, we have fifteen tribes.

Some hold that Abraham, the ultimate ancestor in the strange and beautiful mythology of these desert tribesmen, was an Amorite, since the Amorites told the same wonderful

stories of the Patriarchs, Abraham, Isaac, and Jacob—but the
mythology was shared by the Midianites, and possibly even
by the fierce Amalekites, who were a common enemy of the
Beni-Yisrael.

All we know of these tribes with any degree of certainty
is that generation after generation they shared alike the bitter desert existence, squabbling among themselves, fighting
each other on occasion, wandering in the wilderness—not just
for forty years but for hundreds and hundreds of years—and
always with a window open to gaze upon milk and honey. For
always within sight of their own dry rock and sand were the
pastures of Eden, the green meadows of the Jordan Valley;
the lush pasturelands of the Nile Delta; the fig trees and the
date palms, the golden fields of wheat and barley, the fat
milk-cows, the great, snow-topped peaks of the Lebanon
Range; the cedar-topped mountains of Galilee.

How their mouths watered, how their hands shook with
frustration, how their women wept in hunger and thirst when
they looked upon these riches! The riches were there, but not
for the taking; the riches were well guarded indeed, by
mighty walled cities, by disciplined armies of thousands of
mail-clad spearmen and bowmen, by brazen power beyond
the wildest dreams of these desert herdsmen.

As for the Canaanites, the well-fed, well-dressed, well-pro-
tected, cultured, and civilized people who were so secure behind the mighty walls of their cities—they strolled upon the
ramparts, shaded themselves against the hot sun with para-
sols, gazed at the distant desert, saw the black tents of the
wanderers, and made a name for them, a word, a designation:
They called them the "Hebrews," or in the language of the
time and place, the *Ivrim,* which means "those who come
from the other side of the river."

Periodically, when thirst and hunger drove the Beni-Yisrael to desperation, they crossed the Jordan River or moved
up out of Sinai and matched their bronze-tipped spears and
copper knives against the disciplined ranks of armored soldiers; and on those rare occasions when desperate courage
carried the day, they were halted by the stone walls.

And again, weakened, half-dead of thirst and hunger, they put their courage aside and pleaded for help—and sometimes their plea was granted. At times when the king of Egypt was moved either by need for slave labor or by other needs, he would allow the herdsmen to bring their stock into the Nile Delta; and again, possibly in exchange for women, this or that petty Palestinian king would give them water rights and grazing privileges.

Since these moments of desperation recurred again and again throughout their history, references to them were woven into the Beni-Yisrael's mythology. All over the land of milk and honey there were places that their ancestors, Jacob, Isaac, and Abraham, had touched or rested on; caves where their dead lay; stone altars they had built for worship. Though the land was forbidden, they were not strangers to it.

After endless years of gazing upon paradise and enduring for the most part the barrenness of the desert, three changes took place, channeling the lives of these herdsmen—shepherds, creatures of the range—in a different direction.

First, iron reached them, coming from the west, from a people called the Hittites who had learned that a man with an iron sword and iron helmet is not to be faced or halted by a man armed with copper and bronze.

Second, the horse appeared. The Beni-Yisrael were drovers; shepherds who trudged slowly, painfully, endlessly across the burning badlands; who hid themselves in the shade of the arroyos from the murderous noonday sun; who gazed across the stony wasteland of the Negeb and Sinai and Jordan with hopeless resignation, for in the desert the man on foot is at best a gambler with a lucky throw and at worst a sojourner in hell.

We are not sure where the Children of Israel first found horses; most likely the horse entered their lives with the chariot—the two together, an incredible invention of man that was to change not only ancient warfare but the whole ancient way of life. Some hold that the Hittites brought the chariot with the iron sword, while others suspect that the chariot came from Crete or Greece, across the sea to Egypt, and from Egypt into Palestine. However it was, the chariot appeared in the whole eastern Mediterranean basin at more or less the same time, about twelve hundred years before our era.

The iron sword and the horse and chariot were the great equalizers; they catapulted the herdsman into history. Desert-parched, bitter with longing, the footbound wanderer of the desert and the badlands was suddenly mobile, just as the Plains Indian who captured the first wild Spanish horse became mobile. In one day, the herdsman could cross an area that took three days on foot. Before his wild horses and bronze-clad chariot, the once-disciplined foot soldiers broke and fled. The great walled cities could still resist him, but the fertile valleys in which they stood were his for the taking. The pent-up longing of the Bedouin Beni-Yisrael exploded into motion. The patriarchs were replaced by war chiefs; they stood in their chariots with brazen helmets and colored feathers and they swept under the walls of the cities and hurled their nine-foot spears in defiance. They cut out their footholds, first on the east bank of the Jordan River, and then across the river and into Palestine proper.

Fierce, wild, merciless, their war banners embroidered with the totemic gods they worshipped—the bull, the unicorn, the snake, and the lion—they terrorized the more or less cultured Palestinians. These people, the Canaanites of Palestine, closed the gates of their cities, and sent messengers to their great protector, the king of Egypt, pleading for help. "The Hebrews, the barbarians from the desert, from across the river, are upon us. Help us."

But the king of Egypt had his own problems—barbarians with chariots and iron swords cutting into his own land.

Thus two of the changes, the iron sword and the horse—and then a third, a man called Moses.

———•◦•—◦———

Without Moses, the Jews are unthinkable, unimaginable;

and here I talk of Jews specifically, in both the historical
and contemporary sense. Not the Children of Israel—the
Beni-Yisrael—not the desert tribesmen, not the Bronze Age
and Early Iron Age barbarians who swept into Palestine from
the desert and overwhelmed the Canaanites; they were not
the instrument of Moses and neither was Moses their instrument. His instrument was the Jew, and in due course this
will be explained. Moses *was* the Jew. He stepped into history
as the Jew, and so the Jew stepped into history, and became
so much a part of it.

In all of history, there is no one quite like Moses, no other
man who put this kind of stamp on a handful of people, and
in a sense gave them to eternity. He looms through the ages
as a giant, not only as a man but as a force and as a memory.

For over a hundred years now, critical scholars in the field
of the Old Testament have played a game which might be
entitled "Who was Moses, if—" or conversely, "Who wasn't
Moses, if—" But all of them, apparently, appear to have over-
looked a very important fact: that two thousand years ago, in
the time of Philo—a wise and learned Jew of Alexandria—
there were also critical scholars of the Old Testament; yet
neither Philo nor any of his contemporaries doubted the existence of Moses. The likely reason for this is that in the
great libraries of Egypt, particularly the one in Alexandria,
there was ample material on Moses. Subsequently, all libraries were destroyed, just as every Jewish library in Jerusalem
was destroyed. So while we have references to books about
Moses, the actual books no longer exist. When books must
be inscribed by hand on parchment, both the number of copies and the availability are limited. Jews, as the interested
party, felt no need to document the existence of Moses; their
own existence was proof sufficient of his.

Yet the plain fact of the matter is that we do not know who
Moses was in terms of his origin. Few scholars still question
the fact that his name is Egyptian, and that the mode of the
name is either of the aristocracy or of the royal house. *Moysha*
is the Hebrew pronunciation, and in Egyptian this means
"a child is given." Still, *Moysha* is only half a name; the other

half was usually the name of the god who gave the child—the method of naming reaching back to the time when Egyptians believed that gods fathered favored children. Thus Ramses, the Egyptian king of the time of Moses, was properly called *Ra-Moysha,* or "Ra [the sun god] has given a child." So with other royal names.

Then was Moses actually of the Egyptian royal house, as the Bible specifies? Was he plucked from the water by the king's daughter? Was he a cast-off child of the Levites? Or was he a Kenite, as were his wife and her people—which would make him a Midianite? Was he in all truth a great lord of the Egyptian foot soldiers and chariots? (This last is a rabbinical legend, yet the rabbis of two thousand years ago did not spin their legends from thin air.) Did he marry a princess of Ethiopia, or of Kush, and if he did, where was the Land of Kush?

Was he indeed, as the ancient Greek-Egyptian historian Manetho wrote, a despised upstart who led the "lepers" out of Egypt at the command of the Egyptian gods? This last claim is filled with interest and excitement. But the word *leper* is a mistranslation. The meaning of Manetho's label was "unclean," a leper being one who is deemed unclean in the physical sense; Manetho's use of it applied to those Moses led was in the religious sense, unclean, ritually defiled.

Then whom did Moses lead out of Egypt? Who were these people? What had they done to offend the gods of Egypt? Why were they unclean? Were they the Levites? And who were the Levites, that curious tribe of the Beni-Yisrael who received no land in conquered Palestine for their lot, but only the right of priesthood? And why did the Levites alone, among all the tribes, have Egyptian names, such names as Merari, Meriam, Assir, Putiel, Phinehas, Hophni, Pashur, Hur?

As of today, there are no answers to these questions. We know only this, that sometime in the thirteenth century before our era, probably during the long reign of Ramses II, a man called Moses led his followers out of Egypt. This happened concurrently with the transition of the Beni-Yisrael into chariot men and iron sword bearers. While Moses led

his people out of Egypt, hundreds of miles away the desert
herdsmen were swarming into Palestine.

———————•◦•◦•◦•———————

Ramses II, the Pharaoh of the exodus, was a great builder.
His father began and he completed that sprawling palace on
the bank of the River Nile that the Egyptians called "The
Great House," or in their own language, *pharaoh*. In time the
kings of Egypt, being inseparable from this great house, took
on its name and thus became the Pharaohs.

Ramses' lust for stone, size, and rock-ribbed immortality
knew no limits. He built that giant statue of himself in the
desert that Shelley describes in "Ozymandias." He built
walled cities, colonnaded temples, and even islands in the
Nile. He carved tombs out of the red rock of the Nile escarp-
ment; until he was well into his eighties, he built with fury,
frenzy, and unremitting compulsion.

And out of this compulsion to build came his insatiable
need for labor. Never before had a king of Egypt employed
the number of slaves that worked on the projects of Ramses
II. He had agents in every slave market in the Near East; he
sent expeditions into the highlands of what is today's Ethiopia
to find him slaves; he instituted savage indebtedness laws to
force his own people into slavery; and he enslaved many
tribes that lived on the fringes of fertile Egypt, the seagoing
fisherman tribes of the North African coast, the nomads of
North Africa—when they were pressed by hunger and thirst,
they came to the Nile for water and to the Egyptian markets
for fodder—and the nomads of Sinai who were allowed on
occasion to graze their flocks in parts of the Delta.

So we have a historical background for that admonition that
echoes and re-echoes through Jewish history: "—lest you forget that once you were slaves in Egypt." We are fairly certain
the king who enslaved them was Ramses II. His reign was
long enough to span the time the Bible tells of, and in that
time he fathered dozens of children. There were enough
royal progeny out of his loins to account for a Moses born to
one of his wives or to allow for a Moses plucked from the

rushes. There was constant war during his reign, so the rabbinical legends of the soldier Moses may have a basis in fact; and there was a tribe or a group or a cult of people called "Levites," whom this same Moses led out of Egypt.

—————•◦•◦•◦•—————

The Levites are as intriguing a mystery as one finds in all the rich life of antiquity. The Bible speaks of a vast concourse of people led out of Egypt by Moses, literally hundreds of thousands, but by now almost every scholar agrees that this notion was a subsequent interpolation, ascribing the population figures of the time of King David to the throng led by Moses. The route of the exodus has been explored, the water holes charted, the amount of grazing calculated, and there is agreement that less than a thousand people were involved in the exodus—and probably no more than five or six hundred. How incredible that these few hundred should have made the impression they did upon mankind's memory!

Yet they made that impression, and in a sense they, along with Moses, were the makers of the Jew and of Judaism. Who they were, where they originated, and what precisely their relationship was to the Beni-Yisrael we do not know and possibly will never know. We do know that at a given point Moses joined them (or appeared out of them), that he challenged Ramses II in their behalf, and that he led them out of Egypt to the desert where they would worship their own God. We know that Moses was a man to be remembered, a man beloved and feared and hated, but a man of majesty, of enormous human dignity, and a man who began the process of law, without which the particular development of the Jews would have been impossible. We know too that he was a prophet of God, a priest of God who spoke in God's name.

But what god? The Levites who were led by Moses were not monotheists; monotheism was still far in the future, and as we go on with our story we will trace out the fascinating process that brought the Jews eventually to monotheism, to the ultimate concept of God joined to man; but at the moment we have many gods.

We mentioned before the totemic animal gods of the
northern Beni-Yisrael tribes, and years later at the time of
exodus the images of these gods survive on their war banners.
A dragon spat fire from the banners of the Reubenites. Issachar worshipped the sun and the moon and embroidered
them on a black banner. In Numbers, the command is "Ev-
eiy man of the Children of Israel shall pitch by his own
standard, with the flag of their father's house." A far cry from
the injunction against images. In the forefront, the yellow
lions of Judah; and the gods of Judah were those lions with
women's heads, called sphinxes, which crouched centuries
later in the holy temple of Solomon. The Joseph tribes worshipped the bull, just as did their distant relatives on the Isle
of Crete and their near relatives on the Phoenician coast of
Palestine.

Most curiously, on the war banners of the Danites—a tribe
of the Beni-Yisrael—there was the god Nehushtan, the snake,
the serpent, he who gave knowledge to man in the Garden
of Eden, even as the Greek Prometheus gave fire to man and
incurred the eternal hatred of Zeus, the thunderer. There
was another thunderer, Yahweh, the god of Horeb in Sinai,
the fierce, proud, jealous god of the high places—and he
was the enemy of Nehushtan, the serpent. (Like the sphinx
gods of Judah, Nehushtan was placed in Solomon's Holy Temple of Yahweh, and his great brazen form sat there until
King Hezekiah cast him out and had his valuable bronze
melted down for more constructive purposes.)

We add to this the wolf god of the Benjaminites, and then
turn to the Bible to see how these same Benjaminites were
hated—almost to the point of extermination—by the other
tribes. And then to complete even a brief survey of the various gods the Beni-Yisrael worshipped, we remember the
Asherites—the tribe of Asher—who had given up the art of
the herdsman to till the fertile fields of southern Galilee, who
raised temples to their mother goddess, Ashtoreth, and worshipped her by sexual intercourse with the temple priestesses
—a practice found so attractive that its allure spread all over

Palestine, so that again and again the angry priests of Yahweh cry out: "Thou shalt not whore after strange gods!"

But to return to the Levites—who was their god and the
god of their leader Moses?

On this score, the Bible is thoroughly confusing. When
first Moses sees the burning bush, we are told that this is a
manifestation of an angel of God. But the modern concept
of angels did not exist then; they were only other lesser gods.
Then we are told that the Lord Yahweh is in the burning
bush—Yahweh, the thunder god of the high places, the god of
vengeance and jealousy. Then, when Moses asks for God's
name, God replies, *"Ehyeh-Asher-Ehyeh,"* Hebrew words
meaning, "I am that I am," a beautiful, profound, and mystical concept of a universal God—a concept impossible to the
world of Moses, and not to mature until centuries later.
Then, a line or two later, God changes his name and specifies
that he is Yahweh, the thunderer, stating, "This shall be my
name forever,/ This my appellation for all eternity," and incidentally using the poetic form of the Psalms, the twice-
stated picture-image, a form in popular use seven hundred
years later. And in between, God states to Moses that he is
also "the God of your fathers, the God of Abraham, the God
of Isaac, and the God of Jacob."

But what could that have meant to Moses, who was either
out of the royal Egyptian line, or one of the mysterious Levites with their Egyptian names, or else a Kenite herdsman?

Then, in the course of this confusion of gods and the names
of God, Moses begs, "What if they do not believe me and
do not listen to me, but say: The Lord did not appear to
you?" Whereupon Yahweh the thunderer, the enemy of Nehushtan the serpent, tells Moses to cast his rod upon the
ground, and the rod promptly turns into Nehushtan, the serpent.

But the serpent, as a thing worshipped, is always connected with agriculture, with fertility rites; and in spite of
the frequent references to the magic rod of Moses, it is unlikely that Nehushtan was the god of Moses or the Levites.

Eventually, all the tribes of the Beni-Yisrael adopted and embroidered the great Moses-exodus saga, and they intertwined their own gods and rites and legends with it until the entire text turned into a sort of patchwork; but the single bold line of events, the story of how Moses, the leader and lawgiver, brought a people out of Egypt and put a stamp upon them that was never to be lost, remained.

The Levites, whoever they were, could not have been a peasantry. For one thing, they inhabited an area of grasslands—wet, often swampy, but grasslands nevertheless—and for another, peasants would have perished after a few days in the desert. So we can draw certain more or less accurate conclusions about the mysterious Levites: they were herdsmen, and therefore not Egyptians, for there were no tribal herdsmen who were part of the body-Egypt; they had some connection, however vague, with the Beni-Yisrael, otherwise their subsequent merging into the tribes of Simeon, Judah, and Ken would have been less peaceful; they had been resident a long time in Egypt, as witness their Egyptian names; they accepted Moses, either because he was of them or of the royal Egyptian line; and they worshipped a particular god.

This god was *their God,* and they eventually constituted themselves as a tribe of priests because *their God* conquered all other gods—not foreign gods, but the gods of the Beni-Yisrael. It was *their God* who gave that awful and stunning command to their leader, Moses:

"I, the Lord [Yahweh] am your God who brought you out of the land of Egypt, the house of bondage: You shall have no other gods beside Me."

Their god then was Yahweh, the thunderer, the jealous and just god, whose name, as the holy tetragrammaton, would eventually appear over seven thousand times in the history and philosophy of a people not yet formed—a book to be called the Bible.

———•◆•———

It is terribly important that we understand this question of the god of the Jews and how he began the long process of evolution which was to result not simply in monotheism but in an ethical outlook which prompted the Rabbi Hillel to sum up the Jewish religion and what it asked of a man in a single line: "Love thy neighbor as thyself."

Moses and the people he led were not monotheists, and only the most metaphysical interpretation of history could make them so. Not even among their own related clans of the Beni-Yisrael was there monotheism or anything resembling it.

The Levites had a god who by his own word was first among all the gods. He was a desert god, for he could not be worshipped as all other gods were in the households or temples of the towns. The Levites had to go out into the desert to serve him properly—but why? Why into the desert, unless it was because without going a very considerable distance into the desert, they could not see him. And if they did see him, the God Yahweh, what then did they see? Again, Exodus is specific:

They set forth from Succoth and encamped at Etham, at the edge of the wilderness. The Lord [Yahweh] went before them in a pillar of cloud by day, to guide them along the way, and in a pillar of fire by night.

Smoke by day, fire by night—could there be a more specific description of a volcano? A god who lived upon a mountain (Sinai or Horeb, both mountains, perhaps two names for the same mountain, and Yahweh was god of these mountains) whose location has been forgotten except that it was in Sinai, a god who would permit no graven image—for how was his form to be sculptured? A hot, consuming god: "Beware of going up the mountain or touching the border of it," Exodus in the Torah informs us. "Whoever touches the mountain shall be put to death." The mountain itself is even more deadly than the god. Again, from Exodus, "Now Mount Sinai was all in smoke, for the Lord [Yahweh] had come down upon it in fire; the smoke rose like the smoke of a kiln, and the whole mountain trembled violently."

A volcano on the edge of eruption—a god to be most feared.

We have a better picture now—and the story can continue. There was a tribe or a clan of desert herdsmen who had once left the bleak badlands of Sinai to find pasture in the Nile Delta. They were there either by invitation or by tacit permission. By language and perhaps by common mythology—the Abraham, Isaac, and Jacob theme—they claimed kinship with other desert tribes who called themselves the Beni-Yisrael, or the Children of Israel. Once, perhaps in the long past, they had worshipped a fiery volcanic god whose name was Yahweh (although we shall never truly know the name or how it was pronounced, only an approximation).

Possibly a time came when the volcano fell into a period of passivity. Then, in the comprehension of these barbaric desert wanderers, the God would have failed them, died, departed. Perhaps that happened before they found refuge in Egypt—or perhaps they, like other tribes, had found refuge in Egypt many times, since the Egyptians set high store upon nomads, valuing the woolen cloth they wove and the cheese and meat of their flocks.

Sometime about twelve hundred and fifty years before the beginning of the Christian era, these herdsmen were enslaved by Ramses II, probably to work upon warehouses he was building at the edge of the grasslands. They were cruelly used, and as nomads the whole notion of forced labor was abhorrent to them. Concurrently, two things happened. The volcano burst into new activity and a leader appeared, a man remembered as Moses.

Moses led these tribesmen out of Egypt—no more than a thousand of them and most likely only five or six hundred. He accomplished this manumission not by violence but by the force of his personality—and by this same force of personality he led the herdsmen to Mount Sinai and back to the worship of the Lord God, Yahweh.

In the course of this, Moses instituted a code of laws, the basis of what would become the Ten Commandments as we now know them. They were not then, at the beginning, the ethical pronouncements they finally became, but as with all things Mosaic, a foundation was laid—and this is the key to

Moses, a mighty personality that pointed in a single direction.

Most likely, there were, excluding the Levites, four tribes of the Beni-Yisrael who grazed their flocks in the eastern half of the Sinai peninsula and in the Negeb, which is geographically a part of Sinai—the Judahites, the Simeonites, the Calebites, and the Kenites. Of these four, the tribe of Judah was the center of power and population, probably by count the largest of all the tribes of the Beni-Yisrael. Simeon was a small tribe, and was eventually absorbed into Judah, as were the tribes—or clans, as some hold—of Caleb and Ken. These were the tribes that Moses joined together with his own Levites, and since the main center of power—Judah—immediately set its imprint on all of them, even then they began to be known as the *Yehudim,* or Jews. We must see them in this tight amalgam under the leadership of Judah—as opposed to all the other tribes of the Beni-Yisrael.

In a sense, they were a people entirely different from the northern tribes, the Beni-Yisrael of the Transjordan grazing lands. The Yehudim were still chewing the bitter cud of the dry desert, whereas the northern tribes had cut their way into Palestine, occupied Gilead, built or taken over cities there, tasted the sweet taste of milk and honey.

In another way, too, the Yehudim were different. It is quite true that they worshipped the woman-headed lions, the winged sphinx, but these were small gods of small power when set against their mountain god, Yahweh of the fire and the thunder.

It was to these tribes that Moses came with his Levites, and possibly it was Moses who forged the southern confederation that was based upon Jewish power. In any case, Moses was their prophet, and for all time they made themselves into the image of Moses—and Moses into their image as well.

It is they, the Judahites, the Yehudim, who venerated the Levites, who accepted them as a clan holy to Yahweh, and who put at their service their iron Hittite swords, their horses and their chariots—but why this was, we do not know. We can only speculate on the relationship between the Levites

and Yahweh, on its beginnings and on its history; but it must
have been such as to still any question on the part of the Yehudim of the Levites' right to be first in the service of Yahweh,
the special guardians of his ritual and the speakers with his
voice.

When finally all of Palestine was conquered by the desert
tribes of the Beni-Yisrael and the land was divided among
the tribes, the Levites received no portion of land as such,
but only the right of priesthood and the right to collect taxes
in forty-eight villages. (The number 48, 4 times 12, was a
magic number, and it is doubtful that the Levites ever, in fact,
had this right. In any case, it was long after the time of
Moses.) This, of course, only deepens the mystery of who
they were. If they were in actuality a tribe of the Beni-Yisrael, then it is inconceivable that they could have been satisfied without land; but if they numbered only five or six hundred souls at the time of Moses, which would mean less than
a hundred adult males of vigorous age, it is conceivable that
they could be supported by some sort of tithing, even during
the transition from the desert to southern Palestine.

By the time of King David, incidentally, the Levites had
spread all over Palestine, nor were they all still in the service
of Yahweh. Like the common folk of the Beni-Yisrael, they
found other gods attractive; but we will deal with that
later.

———•—•—•———

So we make a picture for ourselves of how it was in the beginning—not a beginning of a particular day or month or
year, but a beginning that was spread out over two or three
generations.

The time was some thirty-three hundred years ago, but
uncertain, so that it could be half a century in either direction. The rich, beautiful rectangle of Palestine lay warm in
the Mediterranean sunlight. It was a land of cities and cultures—but in the desert that surrounded it there were twelve,
fifteen, twenty tribes of fierce nomads who had chewed the
bitter cud of thirst and hunger for far too long. On foot, they

had been helpless; but suddenly they stood in chariots, drove prancing horses, cast iron-shod spears. Now they began to hack and bite at the land which their mythology had assured them was theirs by right of first usage—the *Eretz-Yisrael,* Hebrew for the "land of the Beni-Yisrael."

In the north, at a given moment of their surge into Palestine, the tribes made a confederation, which was led by a mighty warrior-leader, a war chief whose name was Hoshea. (Later, Jewish scribes prefixed this name with the first syllable of their God's name, *Yah,* and Hoshea became *Yehoshua,* or Joshua, the son of Nun, the Levite slave, servant and armorbearer of Moses, and thus incorporated into Jewish legend. But in his actual life, Joshua may have lived a generation before Moses, and may well have died without ever hearing the name of Moses.)

In the south, at a given moment, another confederation of the Beni-Yisrael began to claw and hammer their way into Palestine. They were led by a man who was a prophet and lawgiver, rather than a warrior, and whose name, Moses, remains one of the mysteries of history. But they were no less fierce, indeed far fiercer and more merciless, than their northern relatives. They were led by Levites, roaring the battle cry of the war god Yahweh, and probably beating a martial tattoo on their breastplates, upon which were fixed their magic stones of divination, the Urim and Thummim. "Red was Levi," the Bible tells us—red with blood or red with the fiery locks that still crop up so often among the Jews.

PART TWO

the Land

"The land of Israel," *Eretz-Yisrael*, is as old as time and man's memory and man's written history, and the place where the first true alphabet was formed, so that men might put down their memories, and possibly the place where the first walled town was raised up by man. And paradoxically, it was the land of Israel long before the barbarian chariot-warriors of the Beni-Yisrael invaded and conquered it.

The rationale behind this apparent paradox lies in the amorphous coverage of that curious tribal umbrella—the Beni-Yisrael. But who were and who were not the Beni-Yisrael is most difficult to say. As we shall see.

The land was called Canaan, except for the seacoast south of where Tel Aviv is today. For about forty miles south of this city, on the rich coastal plain, sea raiders, possibly from Crete, had landed, put down their roots, and were in the process of building five walled cities. This was more or less concurrent with the invasion of the Beni-Yisrael from the south and the east. The cities the sea raiders built on this fertile strip of Eretz-Yisrael were called Gaza, Ashkelon, Ashdod, Ekron, and Gath. (Note the prefix *Ash*, signifying the mother god, Ashtoreth, the god of the Beni-Yisrael tribe of Asher.)

These sea people were called Philistines, and eventually their name, somewhat changed, was given to the whole of the country—Palestine. The regrettable anti-Semitic bias of so many Christian scholars has led to a general acceptance of the fact that the Philistines were "Aryan," whatever that may mean, and that they spoke an Aryan language; but nowhere in the Bible is there any indication that the Philistines and the Beni-Yisrael had difficulty understanding each other, and their verbal intercourse appears to have been so constant and natural that common sense would indicate the Philistines spoke either a dialect of Hebrew or a Semitic language so closely related that no interpretation was required.

The rest of Canaan was inhabited by the Amorites (sometimes called Canaanites), a people that had absorbed a good many Egyptians and Hittites.

These Canaanites were also Beni-Yisrael, which means simply that the Abraham-Isaac-Jacob cycle was their mythology as well as the mythology of the desert raiders. They claimed Abraham as their original patriarchal ancestor, and

pointed to the fact that he and his progeny were actually
buried in Canaan. They spoke Hebrew, the same language
as the Beni-Yisrael, and they worshipped variously the same
gods, the mother god, the bull, the snake, and the sun and the
moon. But there was one god they did not worship—the
Lord Yahweh.

Interestingly, they were divided into eleven tribes—or
city-states, since they were a walled-city people by then—
and if one were to accept the Philistines as a related stock, we
would have the magic number 12.

One way to understand the seeming contradiction of Beni-
Yisrael inside Palestine and Beni-Yisrael outside Palestine
is to remember that the number 12 as applied to the tribes
of Israel was symbolic, that the Beni-Yisrael, historically
speaking, were a comparatively large language-grouping
(comparable to the Greeks), and that the Jews were essentially a single, large, powerful tribe of this grouping—the
Yehudim, or Judahites—and that their invasion of Palestine
and their subsequent history within Palestine were unique,
separate and apart from all the other tribes of the Beni-
Yisrael; even though in the course of the centuries in Palestine the Jews absorbed into their own body politic thousands
and thousands of Beni-Yisrael who were not originally Jewish, or Yehudim.

———•◦•———

Topographically and climatically speaking, the land of
Israel thirty-five hundred years ago was very different from
Israel today, even with all the reclamation efforts of the new
Jewish state. On its hillsides and in its valleys, millions of
olive trees thrived, and there were forests of cedar and pine.
For over three thousand years, every war, every battle, every
invasion took its toll of trees. In the Roman wars with the
Jews, the olive trees were cut down by the hundreds of thousands. The hills were denuded, and with no root system to
hold the soil, erosion became a continuous process. The running soil choked the valley outlets, captured water, and pesti-
lent swamps appeared. And with the disappearance of the

forests and with the erosion, the water table shrank and the climate itself changed.

But see the land as the Beni-Yisrael saw it. The wind itself was fragrant with the smell of the pines and the cedars. Everywhere there were brooks, icy springs, precious water that bubbled out of the earth into lovingly constructed catch basins, ponds that swarmed with freshwater fish. The orchards were numberless, groves of olive and fig and almond and pomegranate and citron, and on every slope a vineyard; for all over the Mediterranean world, Israel was known as the land of the wine. On the plains, the golden grain, and on the uplands, the grazing sheep, and even in the dry lands that reach south from Jerusalem, there was far more fertility than exists today. Reaching from Sidon in the north to Beersheba in the south, it was one of the richest and most fruitful places in all the ancient world.

———•••———

So we see the land and its people, Beni-Yisrael in Canaan and Beni-Yisrael outside Canaan—in all truth, Eretz-Yisrael, the land of Israel. Yet why, we must ask, if there were Children of Israel inside Canaan as well as in the desert, does the Bible separate the invaders from the invaded, and why is the Bible biased for the invaders and against the invaded? The answer is obvious: it was the invaders who wrote the Bible, and they wrote it from the point of view of the conquering tribes—and in the end, the Bible is the history of Moses and the God Yahweh, from the point of view of the single powerful tribe that gained ascendancy over the rest of the Beni-Yisrael, the Tribe of Judah, the Yehudim, the Jews.

To understand this properly, we must consider three invasions of Palestine, or Canaan; and all three as invasions of the Beni-Yisrael, specifying the Beni-Yisrael as nomad herdsmen who spoke a common language, Hebrew, who shared a common mythology and a common patriarchal history, claiming a common ancestor, Abraham, a common hero-cycle, Abraham, Isaac, Jacob, and Joseph, and a common racial-national designation.

The first invasion began about four thousand years ago, and speaking in the most general sense, this story is told in the final thirty-eight chapters of Genesis. But only in the most general sense, since most of the Genesis story was written over a thousand years after the events described. We can say that the first invasion continued for almost five hundred years. It began with the entrance of nomad Beni-Yisrael into unused grasslands in Palestine. The numbers increased. On occasion, they fought each other, and again they combined to fight against the older inhabitants of the land.

The Beni-Yisrael of this first invasion learned to till the soil. They became farmers and they learned to build walled cities and to live in them. The Lord God Yahweh they never knew. In time they forgot their nomad animal and sun and moon gods and turned to the worship of the mother god, Ashtoreth. All over the land, they raised up groves of trees sacred to her and to her male symbol, the bull consort. Women served the mother god in the temples, giving their virginity to worshippers. The land was rich and the people multiplied.

The second invasion must have begun about thirty-five hundred years ago, and it continued for at least a hundred years and possibly longer. This is the invasion that we read about, again most confusingly, in the books of Joshua and Judges. Most likely, portions of Judges are much older than Joshua. The Judges, those tribal heroes such as Gideon, Ehud, Jephthah, Tola, Samson, and Ibzan, were war chiefs who led either their own tribe or some combination of tribes. Possibly the time between this barbarian invasion and the earlier invasion of the Beni-Yisrael into Palestine was bridged by what is called the half-tribe of Manasseh and the tribes of Reuben and Gad. These three tribes had already built walled cities on the east bank of the Jordan. They were alternately threatened and shamed into aiding the invaders.

The later stage of this second invasion was, as we mentioned before, led by the war chief Hoshea. (In Numbers 13:16: "Moses changed the name of Hoshea son of Nun to Joshua.") But as we noted, it is unlikely that Moses and

Joshua ever heard of each other. Hoshea brought together enough of a confederation of the nomads-turned-chariot-warriors to make a decisive crossing of the Jordan River and a permanent penetration into Palestine. Whether he actually brought down Jericho we don't know. Certainly he was powerful enough to lay siege to the walled cities, and probably many of them surrendered to him.

It is of Joshua's northern confederation that the Bible speaks most specifically. Anywhere between six and twenty tribes may have participated in it, and in the course of the next several centuries, they conquered most of the walled cities, occupied them, rebuilt them, learned urban ways and culture, found the worship of Ashtoreth and the bull most engaging, fought each other on occasion, but were for the most part held together by the threat of two unshakable power centers in the south, the league of five Philistine cities and the mighty rock fortress city of Jerusalem.

From then in the very beginning until today, the city of Jerusalem has been a central factor in Jewish history, in the Jewish mind, and in the Jewish dream. The city itself is very ancient, built first as a city at least five and a half thousand years ago and possibly as an urban dwelling place a thousand years before then. It sits on a high place so commanding and so defensible that it was said that he who rules Jerusalem rules the land. The name of the city goes back four thousand years to two ancient Semitic words, *yarah*, "rock," "foundation laid down," and *Shalem*, the name of a Semite god. Curiously, in one of those sections of Genesis that must be ancient indeed (14:17), Jerusalem is referred to as Salem (note *Shalem*); and Abraham and the king of Jerusalem, Melchizedek, have a relationship to each other that makes it unlikely that they were not of the same generic group.

In any case, the Jebusites who lived in Jerusalem and the land around it during the chariot invasion of Joshua were of the Beni-Yisrael. Although Joshua could defeat them in the open, as he did, he could not even begin the conquest of their city—any more than he could move against the five Philistine cities.

And this—this impasse, this constant threat from the Philistines and the Jebusites—was what brought Joshua's northern confederation and the Sinai-Negeb confederation of Moses together, although this probably did not happen until
after Joshua's death.

The third invasion of the Beni-Yisrael into Eretz-Yisrael
began about 3,250 years ago, in its inception at least, under
the leadership of Moses. It differed from Joshua's invasion
in that one tribe of the Beni-Yisrael dominated the invasion,
the tribe of the Yehudim; that this tribe in all likelihood
made up more than two-thirds of the invading group; and that
this tribe worshipped a god unknown to the rest of the Beni-
Yisrael, the Lord God Yahweh. In other words, the Mosaic
invasion from the south into the land of Israel was an invasion of the God Yahweh, served by his Levite priests and supported by the Jewish Beni-Yisrael, at the head of a league
of small tribes, clans, and Bedouin families.

And of this invasion, strangely, we know practically nothing.

———————•◆•◆•———————

The first five books of the Bible, known to the Christian
world as the Pentateuch, are called by the Jews *The Torah,*
which is Hebrew for "the teaching," or "the law"—both translations being acceptable since there is no precise or exact
rendition of *torah* into English. They are also known as
"The Five Books of Moses," since legend has it that Moses
wrote these books by his own hand under the direct inspiration of God. Curiously enough, the books of Joshua and
Judges, the sixth and seventh books of the Bible, have sections that predate the Torah, while the preceding five books
were all put together in their present form long after the
death of Moses. Deuteronomy, the fifth book of the Torah,
was written at least six hundred years later, while the others
were edited and pieced together into a coherent whole from
many ancient sources. An entire school of scholarship has

arisen during the past hundred years, concerned—sometimes to the point of childishness—with unraveling the sources of the Torah; the results are a maze we have neither the space nor the time to investigate.

But simply to continue the tale of the invasion of Eretz-Yisrael by the many tribes of Israel, and to make sense of the historic emergence of the Jewish people, we must examine some of the Torah rather carefully—since it is practically the only source we have for the life and deeds of Moses.

Four books of the Torah—Exodus, Leviticus, Numbers, and Deuteronomy—deal with Moses; but the curious story of the death of Moses and his burial in a forgotten tomb exists only in Deuteronomy—that book written by one writer (the only one of the five to come from a single hand) six centuries after the time of Moses.

Exodus breaks off with Moses in the prime of life. It treats only of the man alive. Leviticus finishes with Moses receiving God's instructions on Mount Sinai. Numbers, like Leviticus, has Moses as the lawgiver—and thus we leave him. But Deuteronomy, flowing from the hand of a masterly storyteller, has this to say:

Moses went up from the steppes of Moab to Mount Nebo, to the summit of Pisgah, opposite Jericho, and the Lord showed him the whole land; Gilead as far as Dan; all Naphtali; the land of Ephraim and Manasseh; the whole land of Judah as far as the Western Sea; the Negeb; and the Plain—the valley of Jericho, the city of palm trees—as far as Zoar. And the Lord said to him; this is the land of which I swore to Abraham, Isaac, and Jacob, "I will give it to your offspring." I have let you see it with your own eyes, but you shall not cross there.

So Moses the servant of the Lord died there, in the land of Moab, at the command of the Lord. He buried him in the valley in the land of Moab, near Beth-Peor; and no one knows his burial place to this day.

Why does no one know his burial place, when burial places were graven into the memory of the Beni-Yisrael? They knew where Abraham was buried, where Isaac and Jacob were buried—is it possible that they did not know the burial place of this giant of a man who was the symbol of the people? And why did he not die in Eretz-Yisrael? And how did he come to Moab and the Acacia woods of the Jordan Valley, when his life was in Sinai, serving Yahweh, the God of Sinai?

No one knows the answers to these questions for certain, but we can draw some conclusions. Firstly, ancient people used the burial location of a hero as a basic claim to land, and if Moses had been buried in the vicinity of Beersheba, it would tend to weaken the subsequent claim of the Jewish kings to the more fertile northern half of Palestine. Secondly, the Deuteronomist was determined to make an absolute link between Moses and Joshua, and to do this, Moses had to be in the north, where Joshua crossed over into Eretz-Yisrael. Thirdly, when God showed Moses the promised land, he gave him Ephraim and Manasseh, the rich heartland of the Kingdom of Israel-Samaria, the historic enemy of the Jews.

Obviously written for political reasons, the story in Deuteronomy placed Moses, the Jew and Levite, in a position where he and his descendants could lay claim to all of Israel.

———————•—•—•—————

There is good reason to believe that the Yehudim and their allies invaded Eretz-Yisrael from the south rather than from the east. Whether Moses led the invasion or not is of less importance than the fact that he forged a cohesive unit out of the Jews and the Levites, established the primacy of the Lord God Yahweh, and led these people—his people—onto the stage of history. It is entirely possible that in the time of Moses' leadership the Jews were driven back into the Negeb several times, that they made several attempts to reach the Judean hills and failed—and thus the story of the forty years wandering in the desert might well have had roots in reality. It is equally possible that Moses was buried in some rocky tomb in the Sinai desert, perhaps at the Mountain of

Yahweh, which was called on different occasions Mount Sinai and Mount Horeb. (There is a Mount Sinai rising seven and a half thousand feet out of the southeastern corner of the peninsula but no one knows whether this was the Mountain of God.)

As I said before, we know little if anything of the Jewish invasion into the south of Palestine—except that by a hundred years after the death of Moses, the Jews were in the land, the most powerful of all the tribes of the Beni-Yisrael, and the Levite priesthood had spread as far north as Galilee.

The forging of a great alliance between the Yehudim and the many other tribes of the Beni-Yisrael must have been a response to the menace of the Philistines. Probably a Semitic people, speaking a tongue kindred to Hebrew, the Philistines were not of the Beni-Yisrael. They were a warlike people, with a large population and a disciplined army, and they had built five fortress cities on the southern coastal plain of Eretz-Yisrael. There are indications that at the time of Moses and during the next hundred years, they manned desert outposts stretching well into the Negeb—built no doubt to halt the incursions of the Jews.

The skirmishing and fighting between the Jews and the Philistines must have been constant, and unquestionably this was the major factor in causing all the tribes of the Beni-Yisrael to come together. The second factor was that great unconquerable rock looming over all of Eretz-Yisrael, the mountain fortress of Jerusalem. But Jerusalem was very much the lesser of two problems.

A hundred years passed, and the Jews were in the land now. A century of fighting the Philistines had turned them into the most warlike of all the Beni-Yisrael, and their Lord God Yahweh had become a god of war and vengeance and justice. They were a hard people, hardened by being the have-nots, hardened by the dry badlands of the northern Negeb, hardened by the demands their God made of them. Because of their power, they were able to claim grazing rights north to the Lebanese mountains, and they installed their Levite

priesthood throughout Eretz-Yisrael. Among the other tribes
of the Beni-Yisrael and among the Philistines, they had a new
name: Judah (*Yehuda*), "the lion's whelp."

———•◆•———

The history of the Jew is the history of his God, his belief,
his philosophy, and his unique role on the stage of human affairs. There are those who would have it that Moses established monotheism by proclamation with the word of God,
but this is a wholly metaphysical point of view, and somehow
it robs the truth. The truth is far more splendid. Yahweh,
the Lord God of Moses, was one god among many. Moses
knit him to a people, the Yehudim, a tribe of a numerous
and widespread Semite people called Beni-Yisrael. This contract between Yahweh and a people was called in Hebrew a
berit—and this *berit,* or covenant, remained with the Jew. "I
am the Lord [Yahweh] your God who brought you out of the
land of Egypt, the house of bondage," Yahweh thundered.
"You shall have no other Gods beside Me." Every tribe of
the Beni-Yisrael had its own gods. There were altars in every
olive grove, in every cedar clump in Eretz-Yisrael. North to
south, there were temples to Ashtoreth, the mother, and
the temple prostitutes (or priestesses) gave themselves to the
worshippers.

But these were the gods of others. The god of Moses and
the god of Jew and Levite was Yahweh. For a time now,
Yahweh and the other tribal gods will lead an uneasy existence, side by side—but always uneasy.

PART THREE

the Kings
and the prophets

S amuel was a Levite, a priest of Yahweh, so far as we know, who had the confidence of the northern confederation and very possibly served an altar of Yahweh among them. He lived at a period when the Philistine confederation reached its maximum strength, and such were the dangers of total Philistine hegemony over Eretz-Yisrael that he managed to unite those two almost irreconcilable enemies, the Jewish Yahweh worshippers and the northern confederation of Joshua (or Hoshea) tribes. The northerners had by then come under the influence of the Levites, leading to acceptance of Yahweh worship along with their worship of Ashtoreth, Nahushtan, and the bull cult, and they were therefore open to Samuel's influence.

(Since the power of this northern or Joshua confederation was centered in the fertile midland of Israel, north of Jerusalem to Galilee, and will be historically known as Samaria, we will for the sake of convenience also speak of the confederation as Samaria. In the Bible, however, the anti-Jewish tribes of the north are called "The Kingdom of Israel" as opposed to "The Kingdom of the Jews," or Yehudim. But it is far less confusing to speak of the northern kingdom as Samaria, which will be its official title in later historic times.)

In uniting Judah and Samaria, Samuel had a thorny problem—that of choosing a warlord—for that was the meaning of the initial post—who would command the respect and loyalty of both the northern and southern tribes. The northern tribes feared and hated the Jews, whom they looked upon as barbarians. On the other hand, the Jews, fierce, proud desert people, who still regarded war as a sacred calling in the service of Yahweh, had only contempt for the northerners. The Jews despised the bull cult, treated the temple priestesses as whores, and demanded the right of their Levite priests to establish altars to Yahweh everywhere in Eretz-Yisrael, meanwhile denying a similar right to the cult of Ashtoreth. At the slightest provocation, the Jews were ready to take up arms against any of the northern Beni-Yisrael and particularly those powerful tribes of Ephraim and Manasseh, who formed the hard core of Samaria; and only the Philistine on his flank prevented Judah from moving north in force against the confederation.

However, there was one tribe of the northern confederation that was hated by the other tribes of the confederation
even more than the Jews; and this was the tribe of Benjamin.
The Benjaminites, like the Levites, are one of the numerous
fascinating mysteries of Jewish history. They appear to have
been of the Beni-Yisrael, yet not of the Beni-Yisrael. They
spoke Hebrew, and by every indication they appear to have
been Yahweh worshippers. Their lot of land was the driest,
the meanest, and most dangerous of all the northern confederation. They were given the wild valleys and hills between Jerusalem and the Philistine plain, and here, in an area
about ten miles by ten, they grazed their sheep, tended their
olive trees, and fought daily skirmishes with the Philistines
and the Jebusites. The tribe existed as a warrior cult, dedicated to war, feared by friend and foe alike—strangely like
the Spartans, who centuries later played a curious role in
Jewish history.

The Benjaminites were a small tribe. At best, they could
muster a thousand fighting men, including boys above the
age of thirteen, and during past years they had been cruelly
decimated by the Philistines. It was out of this tribe, quite
logically, that the priest Samuel chose the first great war chief
of all the Beni-Yisrael, Saul. Saul was a Joshuaite who could
command the respect of the Jews. His own tight following of
Benjaminites were the best fighting men in all the confederation. He was of the north, yet he hated the cult of Ashtoreth
and persecuted it cruelly while he was in power. He considered himself a servant of the Lord God Yahweh, and in his
campaigns he depended upon the Jewish fighting men after
his Benjaminites.

At first, Saul was able to halt the Philistines—and for a time
it even appeared that he would defeat them. But his own
dark, brooding nature and his almost insane persecution of
religious cults crumpled the confederation. Finally, he
repelled even Samuel, who had anointed him war chief, and
when Saul and his three sons fell in battle, the old priest gave
his blessing to a young Jew whose name was David. It was
David who took the step from war into peace, and made him-

self the first true king over all the tribes of the Beni-Yisrael.
This hegemony of the Yehudim over the Beni-Yisrael lasted
for only two reigns, that of David and of his son Solomon.
When Solomon died, the kingdom, kept together through
the personal force of these two men, father and son, split
apart—the northern confederation separating itself from the
Jews permanently.

----·—•—•—·----

By any measurement, David, king of the Beni-Yisrael, was
an extraordinary man. He had personal beauty, charm, wit,
courage, and a sense of destiny and a feeling for history. He
had the gift of helping circumstances. He married Saul's
daughter.

He was also an opportunist, ambitious beyond conscience,
cruel, callous, and not without that paranoid streak that had
tortured Saul. Legend has it that he killed a pituitary freak
called Goliath, a Philistine from the city of Gath. If indeed
there is substance in this, the Philistines must have been
grateful for Goliath's demise, for when Saul tried to do
away with David and his band of Jewish freebooters, Achish,
the Philistine king of Gath, gave David refuge. Later, when
David had assumed the role of war chief and king, he went
back to his old friends the Philistines, and talked them into
an alliance against the Jebusites, who held Jerusalem. Jerusalem was David's dream, his plum, the focus of his almost
unlimited ambition. He had no need of the Philistines to fight
the Jebusites; this he was perfectly capable of doing with his
own Jewish warriors, not to mention the thousands of auxiliaries he could call upon from the Joshua tribes. But the
Philistines were city people, well equipped with the scientific
achievements of the time, and they provided the machines to
breach the walls.

Once in Jerusalem, David made peace with the Jebusites—
incorporated their army into his, called upon levies from the
northern tribes; and with this great army turned the Philistines' own breach engines upon them.

He conquered the five cities of Philistia, smashed the Phi-

listine military might once and for all, annexed their lands
into the *Eretz-Yehudim*, or land of the Jews, made Jerusalem
his capital, hired architects from the Phoenicians—with
whom he had established friendly relations, and who were
possibly also of the Beni-Yisrael—began to draw up plans for
a great temple to the Lord God Yahweh, and established Yahweh worship not only throughout Israel but also among the
Philistines.

He had *élan* and verve, and he was enough of a poet to
understand the gods of others. His dedication was to Yahweh,
who had carried him and his Jewish *gibborim* (mighty warriors to whom war was a sacred trust of Yahweh) to victory
after victory, but he did not share Saul's malignant hatred of
Ashtoreth, the mother. He allowed the Joshua tribes to have
their sacred groves and their temple prostitutes, just as he
allowed the Philistines to maintain their bull cult. Let there
be many, David said, but among the others, Yahweh was first.

At the same time, David was ruthless in war. He led his
gibborim into the Negeb and broke the back of the Edomite
tribes there; even though they also were most likely of the
Beni-Yisrael, he brooked no opposition among them; either
all acknowledged the Jewish hegemony or he destroyed
them. Probably because the Phoenician seacoast cities would
exact too great a toll if he tried to take them, and also because
he needed Phoenician seamanship to manage the trade of the
mighty empire he was creating, he made a pact with the
Phoenicians, and elements of this pact were to endure over
the next five hundred years. From the time of David onward,
Jewish supercargoes would ride on the Phoenician ships, Jewish sailors would be among the Phoenician crews, and Jewish
colonies all over the world would maintain with the Phoenicians a network of trade and credit.

A word about David's reputation as a psalmist: traditionally, all of the books of Psalms are attributed to David;
but even Orthodox scholars admit that when analyzed on a
historical basis the great majority of the psalms were written
in a later period. There is little doubt, however, that David
played upon a stringed instrument, and that he composed

certain of the psalms and popularized other existing psalms, for, remembering that his time was not too far removed from the Homeric times, we can state that all such instrumentalists were both poets and singers. But which psalms can be directly attributed to David, we do not know.

As with Moses, David and the Jews acted and reacted upon one another. Where Moses was a giant, larger than life, noble and beyond lust, David was lust itself, flesh of flesh, talent and brilliance and shrewdness, the smallest of men and the largest of men, the most gifted and the least noble, the pure singer to the Lord, who whored and raped and lied and cheated. David was flesh and man was flesh—that most important of lessons, that beginning to humility and wisdom, which the Jew learned and wove into his very being. When he put down the story of this beloved and glorious king in his holy book, the Bible, the Jew minced no words. It was all there. "This is man," the Jew said. "I would not have him otherwise than as he is."

David is a part of the Jewish verve and viability; but if the great, sprawling empire put together by him and his son Solomon had lasted longer than their lifetimes, there would have been no Jews as such, no Jews as history knows them. Empires that endure produce Romans, not Jews.

The *gibborim*, like the Viking *berserkers*, could not endure, and would not outlast the two empire builders. Solomon found it simpler to hire mercenaries than to deal with the *gibborim*. He was rich. His father had sacked a dozen great cities. The gold and jewels of the whole Philistine confederation lay in the strong rooms of Solomon. He continued his father's relationship with the Phoenicians, and he and King Hiram of Tyre entered into what was the first historic business partnership. Solomon built a fine seaport town at Elath on the Red Sea, and there Hiram sent his shipwrights to build a great fleet of cargo ships, and Phoenician crews to man them. With Jewish soldiers and supercargoes, thus began one of the great successful commercial enterprises of history—shrewd traders, fine sailors, and a monopoly entry into the markets of Babylon and India. The profits were fabulous beyond belief,

and with the help of Tyrian craftsmen, Solomon built and
completed the splendid temple to Yahweh that his father had
planned. This was the first Temple, built upon the Temple
Mount in Jerusalem, where David had raised up an altar of
uncut stones to the Lord God. (A word must be said about
"the wisdom of Solomon." It seems superfluous to remark
that no man who gathers unto himself a thousand wives par-
takes of wisdom. Solomon was the second generation of
wealth. His father robbed and killed and conquered until he
had put together a great empire; Solomon inherited the
wealth but neither the verve nor dynamic quality of David.
It must also be said that he showed no evidence of David's
brilliance and creativity. In other words, Solomon was not
very wise, nor was he the author of that book of the Bible
which is called "The Wisdom of Solomon." The book was
written long after Solomon's death; and the actual "Wisdom
of Solomon" was the Jewish personalization of the quality of
wisdom itself. Throughout history the Jews have revered
wisdom with a constancy unmatched by any other people.
Once we emerge from the semimythical age of heroes and
demigods, the Jews tend to ennoble only the scholar, the wise
man, the sage, the rabbi, whose virtues are those of wisdom
and loving kindness. So deep and so important was this in
the mind of the Jew that he had to create the wise Solomon
after the fact. It should be noted that the beautiful love poem
titled "The Song of Songs which is Solomon's" was not
written until hundreds of years after the death of Solomon.)

Then as now, there was little that money could not buy,
and what gold would buy, Solomon bought—great armies of
thousands of chariots and tens of thousands of mailed mercenaries. He had no need now for the few thousand fanatical
gibborim; they were more of a burden than an asset. The
very feeding of his army required more produce than was
produced by all Judah in olden times. His stables at Megiddo
were one of the wonders of the world. Whole cities were built
to store barley and wheat. A thousand wives were insufficient
to titillate his jaded appetite, and from all the world over

came travelers, diplomats, even kings to gaze upon the wonders of his court.

But all of this rested on the back of the people, and most of the people were not Yehudim—who remembered David and would not deny the glory of his son—but Beni-Yisrael of the north. Even Solomon's wealth was not limitless. He had to resort to taxation—a new thing in Eretz-Yisrael. When he died, the people of the Joshua tribes presented a plea to his son that the taxation be lifted. The year was 933 before this era. Both the founding of Rome and the glory that would be Greece still lay far in the future. Rehoboam, Solomon's son, new to the throne of empire, haughtily rejected the plea of the northern tribes. With this, the old northern confederation rose in revolt against the Jews and set up Jeroboam ben Nebat as their king.

The empire of the Jews, which had lasted through the time of David and Solomon, was over forever. The Jews had discovered that their Lord God Yahweh was wider than Sinai and a mountain of thunder and fire. He led hosts, and then he washed his hands of hosts, because the hosts were unworthy. He built an empire and he destroyed it—and he had fared forth on the high seas to the most distant lands of the earth.

And most important of all, ascribing the end of the empire to the will of Yahweh, thoughtful Jews were able to see that the results were in keeping with the product. Heretofore, Yahweh had been a fierce and jealous god of war. Now there arose a new kind of man, the prophet, or in Hebrew *nabi*, to make the point that Yahweh was also just.

———•—•—•———

All ethical concepts represent a point of view. "The poor man's good is the rich man's evil" is as old as time, and in every society the controlling force makes the ethic. Throughout history, the taking of human life legalized as war is not simply permissible but admirable as well—the term *hero* given most often to the man who kills best in a cause con-

doned. Even the Mosaic injunction "You shall not murder"
was an internal, tribal matter, concerned with Judahites,
Levites, Simeonites, Kenites, and the other clans that made up
the southern confederation. It did not even apply to the whole
Beni-Yisrael, much less to such a non-Israel force as, for instance, the Amalekites. So it is understandable that in almost
any society, the ethic satisfies those who hold power and rule.

Among the Jews, a curiously different process took place.
The ethic, as it developed, was not the result of the power
center, the king and the aristocracy, but of the antithesis of
that power center, the *nabi* or prophet who spoke for the
people in the name of God.

This process of prophecy laid the basis for modern Judaism
and defined the Jew's role in history. It took place concurrently with the rule of the kings—indeed, the kings
provided the dynamic in which prophecy flowered—and without comprehending prophetic Judaism, its cause and meaning, it is impossible to comprehend the forces that made the
Jew.

———•—•—•———

The prophet spoke for mankind, for the poor, for the
oppressed, for the weak, the sinful—for the flesh as it was. He
had no illusions. His voice was clear, direct, and to the point.
He spoke with the voice of Yahweh, but most nobly he spoke
with the voice of man.

Moses was the first *nabi*, the first prophet, and thus the
prototype. Just as the stamp of Moses the man was placed on
the Jew, so the stamp of Moses the *nabi* was placed on the
form of prophetic Judaism. So important is this that we must
return to the Torah and listen to Moses the *nabi*, Exodus 32:7:

> The Lord [Yahweh] spoke to Moses, "Hurry down, for your
> people, whom you brought from the land of Egypt, have acted
> basely. They have been quick to turn aside from the way that
> I enjoined upon them. They have made themselves a molten calf
> and bowed low to it and sacrificed to it, saying, 'This is your
> god, O Israel, who brought you from the land of Egypt!' "

The Lord [Yahweh] further said to Moses, "I see that this is a stiffnecked people. Now, let Me be, that My anger may blaze forth against them and that I may destroy them, and make of you [Moses] a great nation."

Remember, this above is at the beginning of things Jewish, thirty-two hundred years ago, and Yahweh is the very model of an angry, jealous war god. So fierce is his bloodlust that he would exterminate a whole people, man, woman, and child —because they have quite understandably made a god, the bull god, to quiet their fears. Nor is it important whether or not this actually happened; we are quite certain that the original Yahweh was a volcano in Sinai; but this jealous, angry Yahweh of Exodus was God as the priests of the time presented him to the people, a paranoid war god who could be appeased only by the stink of burning meat on the altar stone.

Let us see how Moses the *nabi* deals with Yahweh (Exodus 32:11):

But Moses implored the Lord [Yahweh] his God, saying, "Let not Your anger, oh Lord [Yahweh], blaze forth against Your people whom You delivered from the land of Egypt with great power and with a mighty hand. Let not the Egyptians say, 'It was with evil intent that He delivered them, only to kill them off in the mountains and annihilate them from the face of the earth.' Turn from Your blazing anger, and renounce the plan to punish Your people. Remember Your servants, Abraham, Isaac, and Jacob . . ."

And Yahweh relents. Moses the man and the *nabi* treats the god Yahweh like a spoiled and murderous child, reasons with him, pricks at his vanity, and shames him into sparing the Jews. Moses the man can join with the people, understand them, pity them, love them; Yahweh cannot. In this cruel and nonhuman callousness, Yahweh was no different from the other gods of his time, no different from the gods of the Greeks, of the Egyptians, of the Babylonians. They were all of them incarnations of the forces of nature, and the forces of nature are moved by neither pity nor humanity.

What created the Jew as a singular part of mankind was not

the god but the prophet, not Yahweh but Moses the *nabi:*
Moses the man, bringing into being that strangely Jewish concept, that God is only proven in man's relations with his fellow man.

————•—•—•—————

"Power tends to corrupt; absolute power corrupts absolutely." The kings had power; the prophets had no power;
and of truly good kings, there were few if any. The prophets'
relation to the people is not to be confused with that of the
Roman tribunes. The tribunes had political power and represented the people; the prophets had no political power,
and they represented only Yahweh. But Yahweh was the god
of all the people; therefore the prophets defied the kings,
challenged them, denounced the aristocracy, and called for
justice. And since they spoke in the name of God, as their
sense of justice grew, so did the god Yahweh change.

This change in the Jew's concept of Yahweh—the evolu-
tionary process that began with a volcanic war god thirty-two
hundred years ago and had become a highly civilized and
gentle humanism twelve hundred years later—is the key to
Jewish history. The insane and bloody battles and adventures
and killings of all the various kings of Judah, a tiny country
divorced from the northern tribes of Israel and confined to
the hills around Jerusalem, are neither more nor less important than the bloody adventures of the kings of a hundred
other countries. The Jewish kings were no better, no worse
than other kings. They had power, and power corrupted
them—as it must corrupt all who hold it. But the difference is
that the kings of the northern confederation and of Judah
gave rise to the prophets—and out of the minds of the prophets came Judaism.

The first three great prophets of Israel came out of the
northern confederation, after the time of David and Solomon
and the break between the northern kingdom and the
southern kingdom. They arose in the time of Samaria's
greatness and power, for in the northern kingdom lay the
rich and fertile areas of Palestine, the wooded mountains and

fruitful valleys—the choice plum of the united empire of David and Solomon.

The prophets were a response to power and evil, and even more, a response to the rejection of the Lord Yahweh. Remember, Yahweh was the god of the Yehudim, the Jews of the south. Their Levite priests brought Yahweh worship to the north, but it prevailed only so long as the strength of the Jewish kings backed up the priests.

When the separation between Samaria and Judah occurred, the northern tribes repudiated the priests and worship of Yahweh and turned to their own gods. But here and there, fierce, proud, jealous of the fact that his god was the first among all the gods, a man would stand forth for Yahweh.

Most prophets were puritans, for the essence of Yahweh was puritanical, the god of the desert, of the dry, hard land; such a man was the prophet Elijah, who went away from the corruption and luxury—as he saw it—of the court of the "wicked" King Ahab, to find his God in the desert, where Moses had found Him. The very name of Elijah (in Hebrew *Eli-Yah*, which means "Yahweh is my God") speaks for Elijah's mission. He stood witness for Yahweh against Ashtoreth, against the bull, against the willing priestesses of the temples; and when there was famine in the land, Elijah, the lean, bearded, skin-clad prophet of the desert, confronted Ahab with his iniquity—for what better proof of Yahweh's wrath than the hunger in Samaria?

Elijah left no written preachments, as did the later prophets; but there must have been sufficient fire in his words to make him a legend. He joined the mythology of Judaism. Like Moses, he ascended living to the side of Yahweh. He became the most beloved presence among the Jews. For him, the extra silver goblet of wine at every Jewish Passover, for him the open door, for him the marvelous cycle of legends.

One of the most delightful of the Elijah legends bears retelling here, for it is very much to the point of Jewish philosophy and religious belief. It concerns one of Elijah's periodic journeys on earth, on some mission for God. On these journeys one or another pious man was permitted to accompany the prophet—as a reward for good deeds.

Here a gentle rabbi is chosen, and with a heart bursting with happiness, he sets out as the prophet's companion.

On the first evening of their journey, they seek shelter against the cold and the rain in the hut of a poor peasant. This peasant is an elderly man who shares his hut with his wife. They love each other deeply, and they have been married as long as time—almost to become part of one another. They have one cow, which gives them milk and butter and cheese, the nourishment of their being, aside from a small patch of vegetables.

So hospitable are they that they wash the feet of the visitors, give them their own small dinner and their own bed, themselves sleeping on the floor. Their hospitality is so full of natural love and tenderness that the rabbi finds his eyes brimming with joy as he falls asleep; but when he awakens, both old people are weeping bitterly. During the night, their single cow has died.

The prophet and the rabbi set out again on their journey, and when hours pass without the rabbi saying a word, the prophet asks gently:

"Do you doubt God's justice, rabbi?"

"Frankly, I do," the rabbi replies. "Here we have met two of the purest and kindest human beings I have ever known. Not in my entire congregation are there two such saintly people. And how does God reward them? By destroying their prime source of life and sustenance."

"Then you judge God, rabbi?"

"I judge what I see."

"And do you see God's justice?" the prophet asks.

"I see what I see."

"I think not. I will explain God's justice, but only once, rabbi. During the night, God spoke to me and asked me of my mission, and I told him of two people who were like saints. Then God wept, for his compassion is greater than yours and mine, rabbi, and he told me that already the Angel of Death was sweeping down to earth to do his necessary work, and that among those marked in his book was the old woman who welcomed us to her house. I pleaded with God to spare her, and while the Angel of Death can never be turned from his mission, God has the power to deflect him. Whereupon, God deflected his mission of death from the old woman to the cow —and in God's time, the old woman will die the same evening her husband dies. But now they are not alone, even though the cow is dead."

So filled with remorse is the rabbi when he hears Prophet Elijah's explanation that he bows his head in shame for the rest of that day. It rains and it is cold, and when evening comes, the two men are soaked and shivering. Then they see before them the imposing house of a very rich man, and the rabbi knocks at the door to ask for shelter.

The rich man who owns the house opens the door himself, curses the prophet and the rabbi as beggars, and finally in response to their pleading gives them a leaking and damp corner of his stable in which to spend the night. Unable to sleep for the damp and cold, the rabbi remains awake all night, and at the first hint of dawn, he sees the prophet steal out of the stable. He follows the prophet down to the village, watches Elijah engage and pay a mason and lead the mason back to the house of the rich man. There, before anyone in the house is awake, the mason repairs a corner of the foundation that was crumbling, making it as good as new.

Again, when they set off, the rabbi preserves an angry silence and again Elijah asks him whether he doubts God's justice. The rabbi, being an honest man, must perforce admit that he does; whereupon Elijah says:

"Twice you doubted, therefore we can journey together no longer. But I will explain, for you are a good man. Last night, I told God of this rich man's heart of stone, and God was happy that I did so. Many years ago, this evil man's great-grandfather buried a chest of jewels in the foundation of the house, and now the foundation is crumbling and would have revealed the chest. So God told me to go into the village and hire a mason—"

The rabbi interrupts the prophet, pleading for another

chance; but it is too late. The rabbi finds himself back in his synagogue and never again does he speak with Elijah. . . .

This is only one of a long and enchanting cycle of tales about the Prophet Elijah—composed, of course, many centuries after his death, and some of them as late as the Middle Ages.

———•◆•◆•———

After Elijah, the first of the literary prophets—Amos. His time was about 760 years before our era, and the object of his anger and indignation was another king of Samaria, Jeroboam II.

During his reign, which was the height of the power of the northern kingdom, Jeroboam fought a series of bloody and merciless wars with the Syrians, crushing them, killing without mercy. The poor were oppressed, bled unmercifully by the greed of the rich. Amos, like Elijah, spoke for Yahweh. Yahweh, above all, was a just God, and what does a just God require but righteousness—not this savage bloodletting, but righteousness? Could Yahweh witness this without wreaking vengeance?

"Hear this," Amos thundered, "you who swallow up the needy and strike down the poor, asking, 'When will the new moon be gone, that we may sell corn; the Sabbath over, so that we may offer wheat for sale?' You make the measure small, the price great, and you weigh on a crooked scale. You buy the poor for silver, the life of a hungry man for a pair of sandals, and you sell them not the grain but the chaff of the wheat. By the good life of Jacob, Yahweh has sworn, 'I will not forget what they have done.' "

About fifteen or twenty years after Amos, there appeared Hosea, the last of the Samaritan prophets—the last of those who addressed the Joshua tribes with the memory of the time when Yahweh, the god of the Jews, was God over all of the Beni-Yisrael.

Hosea, like so many of the prophets, had an acute sense of history, an almost inspired awareness of what man made inevitable. He saw the power and glory of Jeroboam and his court ending under a new power, Assyria, that military machine out of the east that no people could resist. To Hosea, there was no clearer evidence of Yahweh's just anger than Assyria. It was clear to Hosea that Assyria would destroy the northern confederation, the Kingdom of Jeroboam. Could there be any other reason than Samaria's faithlessness to Yahweh?

But with Hosea, there was a new step in the evolution of Yahweh. Unlike Amos and Elijah, Hosea could not be content with Yahweh's anger and justice. Yahweh was also a god of love—and the fate that would overtake Israel (Samaria) could bring no joy to Yahweh, only sorrow and grief. This, then, was a new development—a god who cannot entirely alter the course of history. The nonhuman, inhuman Yahweh with whom Moses pleaded, the Yahweh that was an incarnation of senseless nature, now had become a god who could know pain and suffering, who could weep for the fate of Israel.

> *I loved him then, when Israel was child,*
> *And up out of Egypt, I called my son.*
> *They heard my voice and came from there.*
> *They sacrificed to Baalim,*
> *They burned incense to graven images.*
> *I taught Ephraim also to go out of that place,*
> *Taking them by their arms.*
> *But they knew not that I had healed them.*
> *I drew them with cords of a man,*
> *With bands of love,*
> *And I was with them when they took off the yoke of slavery,*
> *And I gave them food to eat.*

For Israel—the Beni-Yisrael of the north—was lost. Assyria smashed it forever, and so arose the legend of the ten lost tribes that were taken into captivity by the Assyrians. But with the downfall of Jeroboam's kingdom, no ten tribes were taken into captivity, only the aristocracy of Ephraim, Manasseh, and Gad. In Galilee, the aristocracy of Asher and Naphtali could take refuge in the impregnable cities of

Phoenicia. The peasants and slaves were robbed and degraded. Cities were destroyed, homes burned. The aristocracy
disappeared, not from the world but from the Jewish horizon
—for they had never been Jews, only racially and linguistically connected under the umbrella of the Beni-Yisrael. These
aristocrats would be absorbed into the populations where the
Assyrians settled them; and then gradually, out of the im-
poverished and beaten peasantry remaining in Palestine, a
new culture would slowly arise—memories of the God Yahweh and what had befallen them when they turned their
back upon Him. They would find His Law, His Torah, and
where once was the great tribal spread of Palestine-Manasseh,
there would arise the kingdom of Samaria—a Samaria that
would trace a thin, futile thread through all of history, even
to today, where in Israel a few dozen Samaritans exist as the
last remnant of the Joshua tribes and the kingdom they built.

———————

Now we turn to the south, to the Kingdom of Judah, the
land of the Yehudim, or Jews. The once mighty empire of
David and Solomon had shrunk to a few hundred square miles
of the Judean hills, the bare environs of the city of Jerusalem.
Between sunrise and dusk, a man on foot could walk from
one end of the kingdom to the other, but perhaps its insignifi-
cance was a factor in its survival. Already, it had a peculiar
and singular character; the numerous clans and petty tribes
that had made up the following of Moses—the Judahites, the
Kenites, the Calebites, the Simeonites, the Perizzites—had
merged with the Benjaminites, the Jebusites, and the Philistines. The Hittite and Egyptian sections of Jerusalem had
disappeared into the body of the population. The Jew had
emerged, and he had only one definition—his relationship
to the Lord God Yahweh, his *berit,* his agreement, his contract—his beginning feeling that perhaps he was not separate
from the God but a part of a whole. This is the essence of the
three hundred years during which the Kingdom of Judah
existed—and, of course, of the exposition set forth by the three
great prophets of that time, Isaiah, Habakkuk, and Jeremiah,

all of them Jewish prophets, that is, prophets of the Kingdom of Judah. In retrospect, the kings appear only as the background against which the voice of the prophet sounds, the stimulus of petty greed and evil which calls forth the anger and judgment of Yahweh. There were a few exceptions, very few.

The three-hundred-year list of the Jewish kings pricks at the memory of anyone who has read the Bible—which details minutely their paranoid personalities, their bloody aggressions, and their tawdry kinship with all the thousands of dreary kings who have plagued mankind throughout history. We list their names only for the record, beginning with Rehoboam, the son of Solomon (933–917), Abijah (917–915), Asa (915–875), Jehoshaphat (875–851), Jehoram (851–844), Ahaziah (844–843), Athaliah (843–837, this one a queen-mother), Jehoash (837–798), Amaziah (798–780), Uzziah (780–740), Jotham (740–736), Ahaz (736–720), Hezekiah (720–692), Manasseh (692–638), Amon (638–637), Josiah (637–609), Jehoiakim (609–598), and finally, Jehoiachin (598–597). (Some might consider Zedekiah as the last king of Judah in that period. He was the uncle of Jehoiachin and ruled during a brief rebellion against the Babylonian conquerors.)

Such was the line of Jewish kings, who ruled over the Yehudim during the time between the fall of Solomon's empire and the conquest of Jerusalem by the Babylonians. It was during their time that there arose among the Jews those three mighty voices who spoke for the Lord God Yahweh.

———•—•—•———

Isaiah: We know little about him, the memory of the prophets being in what they said and not in who they were, but he seems to have been a member of a wealthy family, part of the aristocracy of Yehudim ancestry. It was he, if anyone, who first brought forward the concept of monotheism, that singular Jewish notion of God without a symbol. Yahweh, the God of Moses, was the first god among many gods—but Yahweh did not interdict all other gods. Ashtoreth and the bull were offensive to Yahweh and his Levite priests, but they tolerated the worship of Nehushtan, the snake (some scholars believe he was the ancient god of the Levites and that Yahweh was the ancient god of the Kenites), and of the lion-mothers of the Yehudim. The Yehudim also called themselves *gurya*, which means "the lion's whelp." Indeed, in the Talmud, out of ancient memory, it is noted that the Temple at Jerusalem was built in the shape of a crouching lion, even as Yahweh's voice is likened to a lion's roar. In Solomon's Temple, the lion-mothers (the sphinx) of the Yehudim crouched on either side of the great bronze serpent, the snake, Nehushtan. And there were even certain allowable bullock-gods that the Philistines had brought from their ancient place in Crete and which were tolerated in the Temple as a part of the inclusion of the Philistines into the body of the Yehudim.

These Isaiah destroyed. He put forward a new stage in the Jewish conception of Yahweh. For the first time, a voice indicates that there are no other gods—that Yahweh is the holy name of the one god, the only god. What the enemies of the Jews, particularly the Assyrians, will do is precisely what Yahweh desires them to do, for he is as much the God of Assyria as he is the God of the Jews. And when, after the conquest of the northern kingdom, a plague strikes down the great armed host of Sennacherib, the Assyrian king, this is proof evident of the mighty hand of Yahweh, who reached out to preserve his people—the people he brought out of Egypt. He, Yahweh, is the God of all, but the Yehudim are the chosen ones, the ones who bear the great responsibility.

So with Isaiah's urging and support, King Hezekiah has Nehushtan dragged out of the Temple, smashed with mallets, and then publicly melted down, so that Jews and Levites may see that the god Nehushtan is overthrown and of no consequence. So are the lion-mothers and the bullocks dragged in the dust, shattered, until in the Temple, for the first time, there is no graven god but only the unseen presence of Yahweh.

Not without the hatred and opposition of thousands was this accomplished, and there is a hint that Isaiah was murdered for his destruction of the gods. Yet the kings and the gods are forgotten, and the voice of Isaiah, witness for Yahweh, sounds down through the centuries.

For fear of Yahweh and the glory of his majesty
When he stands and the earth shakes with terror—
In that day, men will hurl aside the images of silver
and the images of gold,
Which each of them made, himself to worship,
Gifts to the moles and the bats,
Hiding them in caves and holes in the rocks—
Doing this for fear of the Lord,
And for the glory of his splendor.

The next great prophetic figure to appear on the Jewish scene is Habakkuk. We know almost nothing about the prophet himself, and some hold that it was under his influence that the Book of Deuteronomy was written, to restate the Law of Moses. Other scholars feel that Deuteronomy was written somewhat before Habakkuk; and all this is less important than Habakkuk's definition of Yahweh.

The political scene in the Middle East was changing now, about 600 B.C.E. The Assyrian power had waned, and the new force on the horizon was Chaldea, or Babylon, as it is most often called; a people curiously knit, by both language and historic memory, to the Beni-Yisrael. Habakkuk, like most thoughtful people of his time, could see that whenever a great power arose in the Middle East, it would find the commanding rock of Jerusalem and the Jews a thorn in its side.

He anticipated the clash between the Babylonians and the Yehudim, and the outcome was inevitable. A sort of miracle —if one is disposed to see a plague as a miracle—had saved the Jews from Assyria. But no one actually expected a miracle to save them from Babylon.

Habakkuk was a seer and a philosopher. Possibly he was under Babylonian influence; most likely, he had traveled to Babylon, for he used Babylonian methods of reading the stars. His universe was wide and sophisticated, and he deemed the Babylonians, as surely as the Jews, to be the children of the God Yahweh. Yahweh was a righteous god; he was also a loving god. If he equated the universe with a universal justice, it was inconceivable that he should love or honor war. The Jews transgressed Yahweh's Law, but so did the Babylonians. God's justice and power were universal, and to think that he used armies for his purpose was folly.

Such was the preaching of the prophet Habakkuk—and again we see the enormous ethical progress of Yahweh. No longer was he a fierce war god, using the Jews as his personal army and weapon of revenge. No longer did he march at the head of his barbarian warriors. Isaiah made the presence of God an invisible and pervading thing, ridding God's temple of the snake and the sphinx. Habakkuk liberated Yahweh from the Temple and from the Judean hills, pronouncing him the God of all men.

Now finally the Jews were on the verge of monotheism—not monotheism vulgarly conceived as a battle between Yahweh and the pantheon of Middle Eastern gods (such contests between the strong gods and the weak gods went on all over the Mediterranean world for centuries) but monotheism in its most thoughtful and pervading sense, the concept of God in a unity of all things.

———————

With Jeremiah, Jewish prophecy reached its high moment of understanding and universality—a level which produced the sublime prophecy of the Unknown Prophet and, much later, the marvelous wisdom of the Rabbi Hillel.

Jeremiah and Habakkuk must have known each other, and it seems impossible that Jeremiah did not listen to Habakkuk, learn from him, and develop his philosophy. Both men were deeply concerned with comprehending the will of Yahweh, the universality of God and the purpose of God. Possibly both of them were under the influence of Isaiah, and certainly Jeremiah must have played a role in the exclusion of the images of Nehushtan and the sphinx from the temple. Jere-

miah was a Levite, and already by then many thoughtful
Levites considered themselves members of a community
with a wider horizon than the Judean hills. After all, they
retained a memory of a time when they had been priests to
all of the Beni-Yisrael, and they tended to reject the tribal
parochialism that would set the Yehudim against the entire
world.

This was Jeremiah's point of view. He came by nothing
easily. He was a man tortured by doubt and fear, a man
driven to seek out the truth and state it, no matter what the
cost. Isaiah and Habakkuk had stated the infinite dimensions
of the God Yahweh. The Temple had been cleansed, and only
an invisible presence was there—but in the talk and thought
of the time, that same invisible presence was everywhere. The
Jews had made a contract, a covenant with that invisible
presence which they called the Lord God Yahweh. The
essence of that *berit* or contract was something new on earth,
something almost unknowable, and Jeremiah had to define it.
It was not easy. The strongest memory of the Jew had been his
role as a warrior in the service of a war god; and the immediate, half-hysterical reaction among the Jewish population to
the threat of the mighty power of Babylon was to fight—to
take up their arms and defend the city of Yahweh. It was this
position that Jeremiah had to face and repudiate, and his
own reply—which was to become the beginning ethical basis
for Judaism—was more or less as follows:

There is only one holy, unshakable agreement that a Jew
can make—the *berit,* the contract between himself and the
Lord God Yahweh.

Yahweh is the only God, the God of all men.

What is right is what Yahweh wills. Yahweh does not will
war, the murder of some of his children by others of his
children. When the tribe or the country is wrong, a Jew must
oppose tribe and country and serve Yahweh's will.

In the words of Amos: "The Lord Yahweh does nothing
unless He has revealed His secret to His servants the Prophets."

Politically, Jeremiah recognized the inevitability of Babylon, and called upon the Jews not to oppose Babylon and turn Jerusalem into a slaughterhouse under the impression that they were thus doing the will of Yahweh—who was equally the God and father of the Babylonians.

However, to one degree or another, the Jews opposed Babylon. Jerusalem was taken by the troops of Nebuchadnezzar, but the Jews were neither slaughtered nor enslaved. (Remember that the population of Jews at that time, in Jerusalem and its environs, is placed at about a quarter of a million or less by most historians.) Instead, the walls of Jerusalem were destroyed, and the entire aristocracy of the Jews was taken into exile. The Biblical reports of how many people actually were included in the captivity vary. In the Book of Jeremiah, we have the following figures: 3,023 Jews deported to Babylon in 597 B.C.E., 832 in 586 B.C.E, and 745 in 582 B.C.E. This adds up to 4,600 but most likely enumerates only men over the age of thirteen years. The numbers in Kings are somewhat larger, and the figure most often used as plausible is 35,000 including men, women, and children.

These were the aristocracy, the craftsmen, the physicians, and priests—indeed practically all of the skilled and educated people in the population. In the war-ravaged valleys of the Judean hills, there remained only poor peasants. The Jewish nation was a tired and sick body, from which the head had been severed.

Thus were the Jews, already an ancient people, taken away into captivity—at a time when Rome and Athens were still villages and civilization had not yet touched the dark forests of central Europe where the painted Teutonic tribesmen lived.

PART FOUR

the Exile

Of the series of events that shaped the Jewish people during their history, certainly none was more important or decisive than the Babylonian captivity. The Jews went into captivity in Babylon as provincial representatives of an insignificant and almost unknown tribal confederation that held the city of Jerusalem and the hills adjacent to it. Seventy years later, freed from the captivity by the Persian emperor Cyrus, the Jews of Babylon had become the first of the modern Jews. During the same period, the Lord God Yahweh became the unseen presence that was the God of all men. How this came about is one of the most fascinating stories in all history.

In the first place, Babylon was no more strange or alien to the Yehudim than England is to the Australians or the Canadians. The Jews regarded Babylon as the cradle of civilization, the original home of man, the place of the Tower of Babel, Noah, the Garden of Eden—indeed the place of origin of the most beloved of their myths. From here had come Abraham, the overall father of all the Semitic tribes west of the Euphrates River, the ancestor of Yisrael, who had fathered the Beni-Yisrael. The Babylonians spoke a language only slightly different from the Hebrew of the Jews, and in certain cities of Babylon the language was identical.

In every period of Jewish development, there had been Jews who traveled to Babylon and brought back stories of the beauties of that wonder-city, the fifty-five miles of walls, the wide, splendid avenues, the brilliance of the tile-covered palaces, the hanging gardens—indeed, here and there in Jerusalem, the Jews had attempted to duplicate the beauty and decor of Babylon, building not only houses but pools and garden terraces in the Babylonian manner.

On their part, the Babylonians must have regarded the Jews with deep respect. It is true that Nebuchadnezzar, the Babylonian king, had been merciless in his treatment of those who led the resistance against Babylon when he went up against Jerusalem; but Jerusalem had been surrendered to him and a pact was made; Zedekiah, one of the royal Jewish household, had been made king by Nebuchadnezzar; they signed an agreement, and then Zedekiah broke the agreement and led a revolt that in turn caused Nebuchadnezzar to besiege and take the city. Zedekiah was forced to watch his two sons put to death. Then he was blinded and put in prison for the rest of his life, and about eighty of those Jewish noblemen involved in the revolt were executed.

But this was the extent of Nebuchadnezzar's barbarism. No measures were taken against the thirty-five thousand Jewish people who were his captives, nor were they treated as the enemies of Babylon. Nebuchadnezzar wanted them out of Jerusalem; he wanted no Jewish fortification of that mighty rock that ruled the road between Egypt and Asia; so he turned it into a dead and empty city, its houses abandoned, its walls leveled.

The Jewish captives, however, were treated with kindness and consideration. The caravans that took them across the desert to Babylon were well stocked with food and water, and the Jews suffered no great privations. In Babylon, houses were built for the Jews and tracts of good land were given to them for farming. They were given fruit trees and vineyards, and they were allowed to keep what gold and jewels they brought from Jerusalem.

As one unravels out of Josephus and the Bible the facts of their treatment by the Babylonians, one has the impression that the Babylonians regarded them with not a little awe. The awe, however, was lost on the Jews. Nothing could buy off their bitterness at being uprooted from their beloved Jerusalem and taken into exile, and nothing the Babylonians could do short of total freedom could mollify the Jews. The first Diaspora (dispersion of the Jews) had taken place, and the Jews responded to it by becoming more intensely Jewish than ever before.

———— ·•·•·• ————

During those seventy years of exile in Babylon, the modern Jew came into being, or more accurately a "beginning-being." Patterns were established that have endured until today and which may well endure for many generations to come, including those two peculiarly Jewish concepts—*galut*, which in English means "exile," and *aliyah*, a Hebrew word that originally meant "ascent," or the climbing of a mountain of God, and which in Babylon, during the exile, took on the colloquial meaning of "return to Jerusalem," a meaning which it still carries today.

These two words, in a most singular sense, began the definition of the Babylonian Jew. Within their framework and during those seventy years, a number of interesting things happened.

It must be understood that until the exile, the Jews, like all other ancient people of the Mediterranean world, believed in an identity of god and place, god and city. Every ancient city in this area had a mystical identity with its god, and while the earth mother Ashtoreth had a wider area of worship, as Demeter in the Greek world and Ceres in the Roman area, the godhood was quite different. The earth mother's power was the power of growth, reproduction, fertility; the godhood of the great mountain gods of thunder and anger, as Zeus and Yahweh, was direct and overall, but the god was limited to his mountain, his city, his high place. The *temple* was not only a place of worship and sacrifice, it was also the dwelling place of the god—and unless one could approach the temple, one was without worship. (A whole population of the ancient world, slaves, foreigners, migrants, were without worship, curiously damned in a manner almost impossible for modern man to comprehend.)

We have been tracing the development of the Jewish concept—widening and deepening constantly with the experience of the people—and while a monotheistic universality had been in the process of development for many years before the exile, it had not been put to the hard test of reality. It is one thing to philosophize, for both ideas and exhortation may be accepted by people who are only partly ready to believe: it is something else entirely to be confronted suddenly by the actualization of the philosophical position.

This is what happened to the Jews. The 10 or 15 percent of their nation who were the most thoughtful, the most skilled, the most powerful—including a higher proportion of Levites—were suddenly removed from the presence and dwelling place of their God Yahweh. The caravan road from Jerusalem to Babylon was about six hundred miles long—a great distance even today but a greater distance in ancient times; out of sight and hearing of Yahweh, if Yahweh indeed dwelt in the Temple; even out of the memory of God.

Unless, of course, God was omnipresent—as much in Babylon as in Jerusalem. Unless worship of God was beyond distance or denial.

(So intimately is the history of the Jews bound up with the Jewish concept of God, that a word more must be said at this point about the Lord God Yahweh. Yahweh is a rendering of the four Hebrew letters *YHWH*. This is called the holy tetragram, or in Hebrew *shem hamephorash*. This name, YHWH, occurs somewhat less than seven thousand times in the Bible, and, anglicized with the insertion of vowels, the *Yehovah* becomes Jehovah—God of the Protestant Reformation. Here I use *Yahweh* because that is accepted as a more likely pronunciation than *Yehovah*. In ancient times, all names were considered magically effective, and in many cultures, people were given two names, one of which—the real name—remained secret, lest another use the name to gain power over the person. It is highly possible that in the early stages of Yahweh worship, the name *Yahweh* was used to influence and control the god. Quite naturally, as monotheism developed and broadened, the magical use of God's name became increasingly objectionable. So while the name *Yahweh* remains written in Jewish liturgy, at a certain point in time—possibly during the exile and possibly later—Jews stopped the use of the name and instead read YHWH as *Adonai*, which is the Hebrew word for "Lord," *adon*, in the possessive case. This resistance to the verbal use of a name for an unseen, omnipresent part of reality increased until at a time some three hundred years after the exile the use of the name was virtually forbidden, and it was spoken aloud only once during the year, by the High Priest during the Day of Atonement. Today, among the Jews, *Yahweh* or *Jehovah* is never used in liturgy, but only the words *God* or *Lord* or *Most High* or *Holy One,* and so forth.)

The problem was one that the Jews had to come to grips with, namely: when one lives in the land of the stranger, what else is one to do but turn to the gods of the stranger? The Jews were not the first to face this problem; the forced displacement of population was a part of ancient society—sometimes in the manner of the Babylonian exile, sometimes in the direct and brutal method of enslavement. Enslaved people were without worship; all gods turned their faces away from them; but the case of the Jew was different. He was not enslaved in Babylon; he had land, home, and position; but where was his God, and what was his alternative to the gods of Babylon?

It was this crisis in Jewish thought and practice that broke the prison of Yahweh once and forever, that firmly established His universality, and that led to the magnificent preaching of the Unknown Prophet. For the Jew's response to this crisis was simple yet profound: "The Lord Yahweh is my shepherd: I shall not want." Though the Temple would be rebuilt, in effect its day was over; and very quietly, the Jews undertook a revolution in religious practice and concept.

They built a synagogue, a place where people would gather to worship God, and which could be anywhere, large, small, elegant or drab, for ten or for a hundred or for a thousand, in any shape or form, out of any material, with no other definition than that it should be a place where Jews could come together to praise God. Increasingly, it was God or the Almighty; less and less was it Yahweh. Nor was it obligatory in the synagogue, as in the Temple at Jerusalem, that a priest should lead the worship. The priesthood—and the connected burning of animal flesh as an offering to God—was of the Temple, not of the synagogue.

(The priesthood, once a function of all the Levites, had, since the isolation of the Jews from the northern Beni-Yisrael, been preempted by and limited to the House of Zadok. Zadok, King David's favorite Levite, claimed descent from Aaron, the brother of Moses. With David's support, he put forward singular right to the priesthood, and managed to establish this right for his descendants. The Hebrew word

for "priest" is *cohen* or *kahan*, depending on how one trans-
literates it, and most Jews today who bear the names Cohen,
Kahan, Cahan, Cohan, Kahn, or related names, are descendants of one or another of the ancient priestly families that
served the Temple at Jerusalem. The family name Katz is
an abbreviation of Cohen-Tzedek, *tzedek* being the Hebrew
word for "righteous.")

Thus with the priest *(cohen)* clinging to his ancestral
temple function—possibly he scorned the humble synagogue
—there came into being in Babylon the first of those men
who would guide and comfort the Jews through the two and
a half thousand years—so often difficult and frequently hell-
ish—that lay ahead of them. These were the rabbis—the lay
religious and community leaders, a group of men whose
function was wholly new upon the earth. At that time, in
Babylon, they were not yet called rabbis. *(Rabbi* is a Hebrew
word in the possessive case, meaning "my master." It came
into popular communal use during the first century of our
era, as a title for Sanhedrin members; but long before then
it was applied to lay leaders of ethical Judaism.) The rabbinical concept did not spring full-blown from a given moment
in history; it began and it matured slowly, over a long period.
It began first with those who grappled with the enormous
religious problems of the detached Jewish community, with
the communal leader, the *nasi,* which is the Hebrew for
"prince," or more properly "duke" or "count"—since no
royal significance was attached to it. The synagogue leader
partook of it, as did the teacher, the keeper of the memories
of Judah and Jerusalem. Most importantly, it satisfied a need
of the Jewish people—and they maintained it from then on,
as we shall see. It was a part, a key part, of the Diaspora, and
from here on, the history of the Jews was inseparable from
the Diaspora.

———— · •◦• · ————

When at the end of the seventy-year period of exile, the
Persian Cyrus granted the Jews the right of return to Jerusalem, only part of them took advantage of his offer, and while

this part was a majority, a very important minority elected to remain in Babylon, which became one of the great Jewish (in Diaspora) centers of the ancient world.

The reason why this group elected to remain is another interesting effect of the exile—and one that played a decisive role in subsequent Jewish history.

In Israel, the basis of the economy of the tiny Jewish state was agriculture. The Judean hills were hardly suggestive of great fertility or abundance, but we must remember that for five hundred years the Jews had lovingly cultivated them, terraced them, brought the very soil from the valley bottoms, and had succeeded in turning the dry, sunbaked mountains into a garden of fertility that astonished travelers. We have tales in the Talmud of the olive groves, the vineyards, and the grain fields, and of their productivity, that are difficult to believe, but unquestionably true. The Jewish aristocrats, like the Greek aristocrats, were almost all farmers, excepting the Levites, who served in the Temple as priests, guards, and attendants; but transported to Babylon, the Jews could have taken no more than the barest subsistence out of the land the Babylonians gave them. Also, it was alluvial bottom land— the very opposite of their high terraces in Israel.

They had to live and they could not live as farmers. Perhaps they were unable to love a strange soil. The soil of Eretz-Yisrael was holy; there was nothing holy to them in the muddy flood canals of Babylon.

Whereupon, they found another way to live. They became merchants; and not only did they remain alive, but many prospered and some became very rich. They had a tradition of trade; in the time of Solomon, it had brought great wealth to Israel, and ever since then there had been Jews resident in the Phoenician cities who were bankers and supercargoes to the Phoenician trade.

Now in Babylon, the Jews were in the center of a new world, a world they had never known before. Not only were there the rich Babylonian cities, Erech and Nippur and Sippar and Opis, but there was Babylonian egress to the Persian Gulf and a safe, sight-of-land route to the delta of the Indus

River and thereby to Pattala and the other rich Indian cities. Due east was Elam, and beyond that the vast highlands of Persia. Across the Oxus River was Maracanda, the Samarkand of today, where the Chinese caravans brought to market that precious substance of antiquity, that thing more valuable than gold or jewels, the silk of China. To the north of Babylon were the cities of Assyria, now subject to Babylon, and to the northwest of that, the land of the Lydians, whose wealth was legendary.

In this vast, rich world of antiquity, the Jews became traders, merchants, and bankers. They had brought enough wealth—in gold and jewels—to Babylon to equip caravans and ships, and by the end of the exile, seventy years later, Jewish traders had penetrated deep into India and even to China. Somewhere around that time, they established communities in India, some as far east as Bengal, and I have myself spoken to Jews in those communities who were aware of their extremely ancient beginning. (Interestingly, several of these communities do not celebrate the Feast of the Lights, which commemorates the great agrarian war of the Jews about a century and a half before our era—since they came to India generations before then.)

As these Jews of the Babylonian exile extended their trade routes to city after city, they discovered another curious and valuable situation. In almost every city of Babylon and Assyria there were kinsmen, not Jews, but those of the Joshua tribes of the Beni-Yisrael who had been Yahweh worshippers when they were taken into Assyrian captivity and who had somehow clung to the worship and hazy memory of the distant Yahweh and had resisted the *baalim*, or gods, of Babylon and Assyria. Since they were knit by blood, tribal memory, and language, and since the old hatred of the northern Beni-Yisrael for the Jew was hundreds of years away in a past already hazy, the Jew and the Israelite came together in a reunion of love and mutual compassion. The sad and beautiful songs of Jerusalem that the Jewish trader sang became the common property of the Israelite; suddenly to the exiled Beni-Yisrael Yahweh was alive again.

Not only were these contacts of blood and family and tribal memory; they were also contacts that were invaluable to trade, for here was an opportunity to do business not with strangers in a strange land but with one's own kinsmen—in a mutuality of trust that is almost the indispensable cement for international trade.

Returned to Babylon, the merchants and traders brought news of these kinsmen of long ago—and also troubled stories of how confused, superstitious, and sometimes degraded their Yahweh worship had become. The Jewish traders were aware suddenly that their religion—which also meant their law, their code, and their ethics—was on the threshold of becoming a world religion. Some means had to be found of creating a fabric, a great, imperishable net that would maintain the Jewish community in terms of a single people and a single worship no matter where they were, no matter how they were fragmented.

In response to this need, an editorial committee was formed, probably composed of Levites and the important tribal leaders. (While the ancient southern tribes, the Kenites and the Calebites and the Benjaminites and the Simeonites and all the other clans and gens that had once wandered in the wilderness of Sinai and in the Midianite desert, no longer existed, having been merged into the body of Jewry, as were the Philistines—or what remained of them and of the Jebusites—still the aristocrats traced their bloodline back to original tribe and gen. These were the *nasim*, the nobility; and like almost every Jew, whether of high or low degree, they attached enormous importance to pedigree. So in this editorial committee that was formed, there were not only priests and scholars, but also those considered the most highborn of the Jewish community.)

This editorial committee gathered together the full library of what they had brought out of Jerusalem. It included their very oldest manuscripts, bits of parchment of such antiquity that the date of origin could only be estimated. It included ancient clay tablets with cuneiform inscriptions, scrolls of the books of Moses, the laws of Leviticus and Num-

bers, myths, legends, historical accounts of battles and skirmishes; tales of all the wonderful people who were in the
ancestor-mythology of the Beni-Yisrael—Adam, the first
man, and Eve and Cain, who was the myth-ancestor of the
Kenites and taught them the art of metalworking, and Noah,
who had brought mankind through the flood, and of course
that beloved father of all the Beni-Yisrael, the patriarch,
Abraham, who had made his home once in this same land of
Babylon, in the city of Ur, and who had left his home to
fare forth into the desert—into Yahweh's desert, for was not
Yahweh the God of the wilderness, who had fed the Jews
when they came up out of Egypt?

How large the library of lore and legend and history and
code and religion was, we don't know; but it must have
been an enormous amount of material; and the work of the
editorial committee must have continued for years. The
ancient wars between the Joshua tribes and the Jews were
faithfully recounted, but the old hate was laid to rest. The
editors intended to make a document that would knit all
worshippers of Yahweh together, regardless of the past, and
to do this they brilliantly wove together the legends and history of the Joshua tribes with the legends and history of the
Jews, the Levites, and the Kenites—so brilliantly indeed that
scholars over the next twenty-four hundred years were unable
to wholly unravel the skein that these editors wove. They
gently redirected the worship of other gods—in Hebrew, the
elohim—into Yahweh worship, for now they had come to
believe that every godhood, every worship, every divinity
was in all truth some aspect of this unseen presence that they
called Yahweh.

They were a remarkable group of men, these editors, and it
was a remarkable product that came from their hands—five
books that were named the Books of Moses, or the Law, or in
Hebrew, the Torah. And then a series of additional books
of history, prophecy, ethics, and poetry in praise of Yahweh
—all of it becoming the first gathering together of that literature which would eventually be known as the Bible.

Once the Torah, the five books of Moses, had been put into more or less the form in which we have it today, the Jews in Babylon had created a larger and sounder rock than the great hill of Jerusalem, where the Temple stood. Exodus, Genesis, Leviticus, Numbers, and Deuteronomy were the net, the fabric that would unite Jews the world over for the next twenty-five centuries. It is true that even then in Babylon, the words of the prophets as well as Joshua and Judges and Kings and certain of the Psalms were edited and put into semi-permanent form; but these would be revised and other material would be added. The Torah was set; this was the law.

Five hundred years later, Hillel, the great sage of the Jewish rabbinate, would say: "Love thy neighbor as thyself. That is the whole Law. The rest is commentary."

But even here in Babylon, the Jewish doctrine of peace and love had taken shape. It was in the words of Amos, of Isaiah, of Jeremiah—and finally in the clearest, purest voice of the exile.

This voice adds another mystery to Judaism, for we do not know the name of the man whose voice it was, and it is questionable whether we ever shall know. The voice is sometimes called the Deutero-Isaiah; and again, it is simply called the "voice of the Unknown Prophet."

Howsoever, the songs of the Unknown Prophet were the songs of a man, and there has been endless speculation over what sort of a man he was. Certainly, he was a man who had seen a great deal, witnessed, and suffered—and learned humility and charity. Possibly, he was one of the new breed of Jewish traders, who had taken his caravans into far-off India and beyond and had come in contact with the mystery and beauty of the eastern religions. Or possibly he was one of those intuitive, gifted souls and had come to his understanding there in Babylon during the exile.

From his prophecy came the beginning of one of those enormous changes in Jewish thinking and destiny, in the Jewish concept of God and in the Jewish awareness of themselves. Until now, Yahweh had been above all things a God of justice. The eye for an eye, the tooth for a tooth—this still lingered. Good was rewarded, sin was punished, and the terrible sword of Yahweh, a sword of grim retribution, struck without mercy.

This kind of thinking had led the Jews to an extraordinarily honest examination of their own history and experience; but it had also led them into a reasoning from effect to cause, blaming every misery that occurred on their own iniquity—even when such iniquity was only the process of belonging to the human community.

The Unknown Prophet put forth another idea: Even as the sun's warmth caressed the good and the evil alike, so did the love and compassion of Yahweh permeate the universe. The God Yahweh was not a god of justice in the primitive, tribal sense; he was a god of that justice so plainly evident in the working of the universe, and the Jews had been chosen by him—not for reward, but to carry the core of the burden of man's suffering, to suffer for the gentile and to redeem the gentile; and the essential importance of the Jew was that he bore his torment for the sake of all men and for the redemption of all men:

> Surely he has endured our grief
> and carried our sorrow.
> We judged that he was stricken,
> struck by God and made sick.
> But he was wounded for our transgressions,
> He was bruised for our sins.
> The punishment of peace was put on him,
> And with his lashes we are healed.
> All of us, like sheep, have wandered lost,
> Each of us in his own direction,
> And the Lord Yahweh has laid on him
> The iniquity of all of us.

The Jews looked at themselves differently, newly, nor did all of them agree with this new voice. The prophet Ezekiel probably opposed this line of thinking; others must have— yet those who supported the Unknown Prophet were enough to establish his thinking among the Jews. It was not easy to resist this new voice when it cried out:

Arise, shine! For your light has come,
And the glory of the Lord Yahweh rises upon you,
For, see—darkness shall cover the earth,
And even deeper darkness upon the people.
But the Lord Yahweh shall rise over you,
And His glory shall be seen all over you,
And gentiles shall come to your light,
And Kings will come to this brilliance.

There was a new dimension of mystery and splendor to Yahweh now. The Jews were His chosen people, but it was not for the Jew to question the reason or manner of His choice. Yahweh did not afflict them as some petty judge condemns a criminal or as some king rewards a courtier. Yahweh's purpose was as mysterious as His Being, and it was not for the Jew to either question or interpret His purpose.

Even as the synagogue was to endure over the next twenty-five hundred years, so would the Jew silently and without complaint endure unspeakable horror and suffering in the quiet conviction that somehow he must suffer for all men.

As a part of this, there would arise later among the Jews the strange legend of the *Lamed Vav*. These are two letters in the Hebrew alphabet, which, when used numerically, equal 36. The legend has it that always among the Jews, there exist thirty-six good and saintly men—men who are called, in Hebrew, *nistar* or "saint." They live humbly in obscurity, and they quietly endure the suffering and pain of mankind. When one of them dies, another is appointed by God to take his place, and sometimes the *nistar* himself does not know that God has indicated him. So long as they live and humbly endure, the world will continue; but should no *nistar* be found to replace those who die, then the world will end.

———

Legend has it that Cyrus the Great was an Elamite, and that his ancestor was defeated in battle by the father of all the

Beni-Yisrael, Abraham; but the more probable link between
Cyrus and the Jews was his religion, Zoroastrianism. The
ethical substance of Zoroastrianism, its belief in the pervading
presence of God as light, and its sense of monotheism could
not but appeal to the Jews and indeed was reflected in the
songs of the Unknown Prophet. Cyrus (*Koresh* in Hebrew)
was intimate with many Jews. His nomad vigor appealed to
them, and in turn he respected the enormous knowledge of the
world and its cities that the Jews possessed. He and his Persian
cavalry were creating a new empire, and the Babylonian Jews
helped him plan and carry through the conquest of Babylon.
He came as an enlightened liberator, enthralled by the beauty
and wealth of Babylon, honoring it and respecting it. It became an important part of a great empire that Cyrus and his
descendants carved out and knit together—an empire that was
to last for more than a hundred years.

Those were good years for the Jews, and in the course of
that time, synagogues and Jewish communities appeared in
every city of the Persian Empire.

It was quite natural that Cyrus should allow the Jews to
return to Jerusalem; they had advised him, helped him, provided logistic advice and aid—and in the end had made it
possible for him to enter Babylon peacefully, enlisting pro-
Persian sentiment in the city and opening the gates for him.
He in turn was willing to grant anything they requested
within reason and within his power.

But above all, the Jews welcomed Cyrus and aided him because he appeared as their liberator. No amount of consid-
erate treatment of the Jews by the Babylonians could make
up for the fact that it was Babylon that had ravaged Jerusalem, torn down its walls, and made of it a wasteland. Already at that time, Jerusalem had been endowed with that
mystical quality that it has retained for the Jews since then.

In the year 538 before our era, caravans of Jews began to
cross the desert back to Jerusalem. The Jews had multiplied
greatly during their exile in Babylon, and in the seventy
years their numbers had doubled—in large part through the
adherence of Babylonians to Yahweh worship. Remember

that the Babylonians were of the same race and language, and as always during antiquity, the community of the Jews (for it is better understood as a community than as a religion in our terms) held great attraction for pagans.

(Christianity was the first great proselytizing religion. It was not within the scope of ancient thinking to force or cozen another into your worship. Worship was a contained thing—even in such universal faiths as Judaism or Zoroastrianism or Buddhism. There was no sense of achievement in widening a faith, no drive to conversion, no such concept as the saving of a soul from perdition—indeed no such concept as the Christian hell. Even the Romans never thought in terms of conversion.)

About forty thousand Jews returned to Jerusalem from Babylon, but almost that many remained there, forming the basis of one of the world's great Jewish communities; and for as long as Babylon existed as a city—which would be a thousand years more—that community would survive. Babylon became a center of Jewish culture and wealth, the place where the Talmud was written, a place inseparably associated with Judaism.

Indeed, it was far easier for those who remained in Babylon and in the other cities of the Persian Empire than it was for those who returned to Palestine. Jerusalem was a looted, burnt-out ruin, an empty, desolate city, its walls destroyed, with no population but a handful of Jebusites who hid in underground storerooms and cisterns, living in fear and hiding, much like animals. For seventy years, every wandering band of Bedouins, every band of robbers or desert outlaws, had paused to loot Jerusalem. The Temple that Solomon had built was in ruins, every scrap of metal and polished stone stolen from it. The splendid homes of the Jewish nobility had been stripped of everything of value. Jerusalem was an open city, a ghost city, a whispering ruin of memories.

It was to this that the exiles returned. All that remained of the Jewish state were a few thousand peasants who scraped a grim and hungry living out of the broken terraces and who paid constant tribute to robbers. They lived in the hills around Jerusalem, shunning the ghostly, dead city. The exiles, however, moved into Jerusalem. It was their ancient place, the place of their family palaces, of their Temple—and what was the use of their return if they could not live there? Most of them owned land outside of the city, but where were the men to work the land?

Hunger, anarchy, dissension—a sense of hopelessness and doom and defeat overtook the returned exiles. Each family huddled at night in its own house, barring the doors, while jackals and robbers moved around the city at will. Worship began halfheartedly in the ruined Temple.

The future of the returned exiles appeared so bleak, so hopeless, that word got back to Babylon that the return had failed and that the reestablishment of the Jewish homeland might indeed never succeed.

In this crisis, two extraordinary men appeared upon the scene; and the survival of the Jewish people in Palestine was in no small measure due to them. The first was Nehemiah, a Jewish aristocrat who was cupbearer to the then Persian emperor, Arxerxes. Unable to bear the news from Jerusalem, he begged leave of the king to go there. The king agreed and gave Nehemiah far-reaching power. Nehemiah took a small Jewish military force with him, went to Jerusalem as governor, infused the Jews with hope, turned out the population to rebuild the walls and gates of the city, and organized a militia to patrol the walls. The thieves and bandits were thus dealt with. Then Nehemiah began a campaign to bring Jewish families into Jerusalem, not only from the immediate area but from cities of the Diaspora.

In this he was joined and supported by the second extraordinary man of the time—one Ezra, who is known as "the scribe." Ezra was a *cohen*, that is, a priest by birth, one of that astonishing family that traced itself back to Zadok. Like Nehemiah, he was a man of influence in the Persian court, and again like Nehemiah, he understood the desperate need for support in Jerusalem.

There were scholars who believed that it was Ezra who actually edited the mountain of Jewish and Beni-Yisrael legend and history into the Torah, but of late there is more evidence that the work was done in Babylon before Ezra's time. However, it was Ezra who made the Jews of Jerusalem understand that the Torah was not an exercise in Jewish history, but rather a unifying code of social and religious behavior that must become the core of Jewish life if they were to survive the rigors and privation of the return. They had to be made to understand that they were led out of captivity, like the Levites under Moses, not to live on the fat of the land but to bear witness to the Lord God Yahweh and to His purpose—whatsoever that purpose might be.

Because of this, there has been a tendency among the Jews to class Ezra almost with Moses in stature and importance, but the facts of history hardly bear this out. Ezra was a remarkable man, but we must remember that he had behind him the wealth and support of the Persian court—as well as the protection of Persian arms. Like Nehemiah, he realized that the first need was to provide the city of Jerusalem with a population—so that it could at least put out enough militia to man the long walls and to hold off the wolves that would come flocking at the first word of Jewish industry and wealth arising in the once-deserted city.

With this in mind, Ezra convinced over a thousand Jewish families in Babylon to settle in Jerusalem, where they would be given houses to live in as well as arable land outside of the city. He brought these families to Jerusalem with him, and together with Nehemiah, he set about solving the endless problems of reconstituting life in the abandoned and almost empty land. He also undertook the rebuilding of the Temple—which was planned and carried through by Babylonian-trained Jewish architects.

When Ezra and Nehemiah died, they left behind them a viable Jewish state. True, it was small; it consisted of Jerusalem and perhaps two hundred square miles of the surrounding area, most of this sparsely populated. It had a total population, in all probability, of little more than a hundred thousand, of whom at least three quarters lived in the city. But the city was alive. Its great gates could open and close. Its walls had been rebuilt and were defensible, and in the shining structure of the Temple, a high priest led the worship once again. The Jews had no real army, only a militia, but they had the friendship and protection of mighty Persia. Sometimes this friendship was sorely tried; sometimes there were Persian satraps whose liking for the Jews was less than enthusiastic; but by and large, the Jews lived in peace: growing, joined by many Samaritans from the north—rejecting the desire of Samaria to join to them but accepting individuals—increasing, trading, and communicating with the constantly growing Diaspora, rebuilding the terraces, restoring the fertility of the land, and speaking less and less of Yahweh and more and more of Adonai, the great Lord who was all.

For a hundred years and more, this continued; the exile was dim in the memory of the people; they had joined fully with their ancient land—and then suddenly the power of mighty Persia was over.

The great, sprawling empire which Cyrus the liberator had founded and which was to endure forever went the way of all other empires. Its huge armies were rent asunder, destroyed by the iron phalanx of Macedon and its Greek allies.

A new star appeared on the horizon—Alexander the Great.

PART FIVE

Herod and Hillel

Alexander the Great, whose life spanned the years between 356 and 323 before our era, was one of those extraordinary, power-compelled men who appear almost regularly upon the stage of history and so often change history. Plutarch's account of Alexander's brief thirty-three years of life reads much like a clinical description of paranoia; but indeed no normal man could have sustained the enormous drive for power that Alexander displayed.

The son of Philip II of Macedon, he came to the throne in 336, at the age of twenty. Brilliant—Aristotle was his tutor —dynamic, he immediately put down the restiveness of the more cultured Greek cities of the south. (In sacking Thebes, he symbolically spared the temples and the house of the poet Pindar—which gave him a rather undeserved reputation for both religion and culture.)

Alexander came into the leadership of not only a vital, semibarbarian Greek state, but one that had a unique and revolutionary weapon, the phalanx, a sort of human tank, consisting of row upon row of heavily armored soldiers carrying overlapping rows of long and heavy spears. These phalanxes, supported by thousands of armed men recruited from the southern Greek cities, followed Alexander across the Hellespont into what was then the Persian Empire and which is today's Turkey. He routed the vast, clumsy, and inept conscript army of Darius III, and led his own soldiers to victory after victory, conquering the whole of the Middle East— Egypt, and the area which is today Turkey, Iran, Iraq, Jordan, Syria, Lebanon, Israel, Northern Arabia, and eastward to India.

When he died, this vast area was divided among his generals; but we are interested in perhaps the least military of his conquests, the tiny land of Judea.

Aside from a sort of militia that defended the gates to Jerusalem and perhaps a small force of cavalry in the Persian manner that was able to deal with brigands in the Judean hills, the Jews had given up the habits and practice of war. They had gone through a time of rather ghastly bloodletting and had come to the philosophical conclusion that war solves nothing that God will not solve better in His own good time.

It is true that the Levites—who clung to their clan blood-

line more zealously than any other Jews, perhaps because the
Temple privileges were lucrative—maintained a ceremonial
Temple Guard, a few hundred men armed with spears and
clothed in silver armor; but these were trappings, like the
present-day guard at Buckingham Palace, and hardly anything
to engage an enemy with. The umbrella of protection under
which the Jews lived was the Persian Empire, with a standing
army larger than the entire Jewish population.

When Alexander and his Greeks shattered the Persian
social order and Alexander's armies swept through the Middle
East, the Jews were hardly in any position to resist, even if
they had desired to. They did not. At this point in history,
they were already a very ancient and civilized people. More
than a thousand years had passed since Moses led them into
the hills of Judea, and during that time they had seen many
empires rise and fall, including their own in the time of
Solomon. They made their peace with the Greeks, and about
330 years before the beginning of our era, their tiny land of
Judea became a part of the Greek-Egyptian Empire of the
Ptolemies. The Ptolemies were philosophically receptive to
the Jewish concept of God and the Jewish social structure;
they admired the Jews and found that a relationship with
them could be both pleasant and profitable—for the Jews
were a key to every part of the Middle East. They asked of
the Jews only a modest annual tribute, urged them to establish a center of trade and banking in Egypt, and turned
over to them part of the port city of Alexandria.

For a hundred and fifty years, the Jews and the Egyptian
Greeks lived in peace, in a condition of mutual respect and
benefit.

———•◆•———

Altogether, the Jews, from the time of their return from
exile in Babylon to the end of the protection of the Ptolemies,
experienced a three-hundred-year era of peace—a time during which their religious philosophy matured and their
world outlook became truly international. Yahweh (Jehovah), *the ancient of days,* had lost both His name and His

original character. His name was no longer spoken; he had become God, the Almighty, the pervading presence that was at one with the universe. Even though the old practice of burnt offering in the Temple contu .ed, the Jewish mind rejected it; and Jewish preachers spoke of a God who asked gently why they brought Him burnt offerings when all that lived on earth was His? It was the time of the emergence of the Sabbath as an ethical concept. The world rested on the seventh day, the beasts in the field, the man in his home. The slave was manumitted in the seventh year.

The population of the little Jewish state doubled and doubled again. The land was fruitful and God was good to the Jews. They renewed their contacts with the Phoenicians, and once again Jewish supercargoes and Jewish sailors sailed on the Phoenician ships. Jewish synagogues and colonies were established in the farthest corners of the earth, in Carthage, in Spain, and possibly—as some scholars think— in Cornwall in Britain, already a prime source of the tin that was needed for the manufacture of bronze. The Torah, the code of Jewish law, deepened its hold upon the Jewish people, and after a fashion it became a basis for the network of trade and international banking that the Jews established.

A Jewish merchant, trading, for example, between Tyre and Carthage—waters filled with pirates—doubled his risk if he returned from his voyage with gold. On the other hand, if he could leave the gold with a fellow Jew in Carthage, and receive in exchange a draft on a Jewish banking house in Tyre, he cut his risk in half. But in order for such a system to function there had to be a network of mutual trust and responsibility and a singleness of mind and language that was worldwide. The Torah provided the basis for trust and responsibility, and the vast Diaspora of Jewish social units, built around local synagogues, provided the singleness of mind and language.

During this same peaceful period of three hundred years, the Jewish language shifted from Hebrew to Aramaic. There were northern tribes of the Beni-Yisrael who had never spoken Hebrew but always Aramaic, which was probably the language of the patriarchs, Abraham and Isaac and Jacob. The language is very close to Hebrew, stemming originally from the same source; and the relationship between the two languages as well as the role Aramaic played in Jewish history are so complex and fascinating that they could well be the subject for an entire volume. Aramaic had always been spoken by a far larger group of people than Hebrew—which by the time of the Babylonian exile had become known as the language of the Jews and was more or less restricted to Jewish use. Even though Cyrus, the Persian king, is considered to have been a non-Semite, Aramaic—the pervading Semitic language of that time—soon became the language of the entire Persian Empire. The Phoenicians, who probably spoke the same Hebrew as the Jews, found that Aramaic was a better trade language, and soon it became the Phoenician tongue. The Jews in the Diaspora began to use it, and bit by bit, it replaced Hebrew among the Jews in Judea. During the five hundred years from about 900 B.C.E. to 400 B.C.E. Aramaic had been taught to the Jewish aristocracy, just as French later was taught to the Russian aristocracy—so the switch from Hebrew was both inevitable and easy. However, Hebrew remained the language of the Torah—the *lashon kadosh* or holy tongue. Yet even today, Jews speak a part of their liturgy in Aramaic, as for instance the mourner's Kaddish.

———— · •·• · ————

Superficial studies of Jewish history usually refer to the great agrarian war of the Jews, which was led by Judah (*Yehudah*) Maccabeus, as a revolt against Hellenism; but such studies tend to forget that for a hundred and fifty years before the Maccabees, the Jewish people lived in peace and mutual respect with Hellenism.

Hellenism brought the Jews a step further in their concept of Yahweh; already, out of their intimacy with Babylon and Phoenicia, the Jews knew that the earth was round, that the constellations had seasonal movement, and that the earth itself was vast and mysterious beyond computation; and

now they encountered Greek science and Greek philosophy
—bold enough to compute anything and investigate everything. The Egyptian Greeks, in turn, were fascinated by the
Jewish concept of God, by the ethical rigidity of the Jews, and
by the Jewish humanism which was so far ahead of Greek
humanism, the horror of war and murder that was already a
part of the Jewish world outlook. The Jews drank of the wisdom of Socrates, of the cynical and awful truth of Thucydi-
des, of the indomitability of Xenophon, and of the swirling
wrath and despair and comedy of the Greek playwrights,
and the Greeks in turn recognized the revolutionary view of
the Jews toward slavery, their use of the Sabbath, their
seven-year manumission—and were also awed by the ancient
bloodline of the Jewish family, which had kept so careful a
genealogy for over a thousand years—and often enough one
that probed (mythically) to the creation of man.

In order for this mutual exchange to take place, there had
to be an exchange of language. The Greek learned Aramaic
and the Jew learned Greek. Alexandria moved toward replacing Babylon as the great Jewish center of the Diaspora,
while synagogues were built in almost every large city of
the Greek world. (In fact, the word *synagogue* is a Greek
word meaning "assembly," although the building and the
idea of it originated hundreds of years before the time of
Greek-Jewish culture.)

Greek became—and would continue to be for several hundred years—the second language of the Jews, and the thousands of Jews who settled in Alexandria (including many
converts) made that city a place of wealth and splendor,
whose Jewish district was one of the wonders of the ancient
world.

Legend has it that Ptolemy II, at about the year 240
B.C.E., became so enthralled with Jewish history and culture
that he commissioned the translation of the Bible into the
Greek language. For this, seventy Jewish scholars were chosen
who—each of them—worked separately at separate translations, producing seventy translations whose every word
agreed. Of course, this is legend; but the fact remains that

the Bible was translated into Greek then, and that this translation subsequently became the basis for the Septuagint
(Latin for *seventy*) , or Greek version of the Bible.

This union of Greek and Jewish thought would eventually
produce that rabbinical Judaism that armed the Jews for
the long and terrible experience of living in the Christian
world. It would produce such philosophers as Philo and
Hillel—and to a certain measure it would also produce
Christ.

To the north and east of Palestine lay the kingdom ruled
by the descendants of one of Alexander the Great's generals,
Seleucus Nicator. In the beginning, this kingdom covered
the area of the old Persian empire to the east, but in 198 B.C.E.
a descendant of Seleucus, Antiochus the Great, defeated the
armies of Greek Egypt and occupied Palestine. The long,
serene years of peace—almost three hundred years since
the return from exile—that the tiny, priest-ruled state of the
Jews had enjoyed came to an end. The fine empathy that
had flowered between Jew and Egyptian Greek, the understanding that had enriched both peoples, was over. Both
Antiochus and his son of the same name regarded the land
of the Jews from only one point of view—avarice.

And well they might. For two and a half centuries the Jews
of the entire ancient world had poured their tribute into
the Temple treasury. The Temple in Jerusalem was wealthy
beyond belief—certainly the greatest single repository of
wealth in the ancient world—and the wealth and beauty of
Jerusalem reflected this. The tiny land of Judea—still with
a radius of no more than a man could walk in a day from
the walls of Jerusalem—was like a garden, every foot of the
once-dry badland slopes terraced and irrigated. From the
walls of the city, where once were seen dry hills and sere
valleys, one looked upon orchards of olive trees, vineyards,
and terrace after terrace of wheat and barley and lentils.
Acre for acre, man for man, this was the most valuable spot
on earth.

During these years of peace, Judea (this is the later, Latin name; the Jews of this time probably referred to their land as Eretz-Yisrael, the ancient name for all of Palestine) had been ruled nominally by the current high priest, assisted by a council of aristocrats. The high priesthood, which had ruled Judea for several centuries after the exile, was a hereditary office in the family of the descendants of Zadok. As already noted, this family, which maintained and treasured a most careful genealogy, traced their origin to Aaron, the brother of Moses; something hardly believable but impressive even as a claim. Status-wise, it was the first family of the Jews, even before the bloodline of David himself, and by now there was hardly an aristocratic house in Jerusalem that had not intermarried with the House of Zadok. Thereby, this family considered the Temple treasure—indeed the whole of Judea—as its personal property.

So numerous and powerful were its members that they constituted a party of sorts and were known as the Sadducees, or in Hebrew *Tzedukim,* a word most likely derived from the family name of Zadok. They were the power establishment of the Jews, howsoever much of a power establishment it was.

Opposing the Sadducees, nominally at first and then vigorously, was a group of ancient priestly families (*cohens*) who, though many of them traced their line back as far as Zadok and beyond, were excluded from control of the Temple and the state—and thereby from the vast wealth in the hands of the aristocracy. These excluded priestly families were called Pharisees, *Perushim* in Hebrew, which probably meant "set apart" or "excluded." The Pharisees, who were for the most part small landholders, had their base among the Jewish peasants and in the synagogues of the villages around Jerusalem. Barred from officiating at Temple ceremonies, they tried to set even more rigorous standards in the synagogues than existed in the Temple in Jerusalem and in a sense were more rigidly pious. They were far poorer than the Jerusalem priesthood but also much closer to the people and more beloved of the people.

It is this Pharisaic line of Judaism that was to survive the
destruction of the Second Temple in the first century of our
time and carry the Jews forward into history—and it represented the most humanistic and admirable line of Jewish
thought. This has always been clouded by the incomprehensible paragraphs in the New Testament which have Jesus de-
nouncing the Pharisees; incomprehensible because Jesus
himself could only have been a Pharisee. (However, some
scholars believe that these are later insertions to discredit
the Jews—all of whom, after the fall of the Temple, followed
Pharisaism to one degree or another.)

When Antiochus the Great conquered Palestine (and Judea) in 198 B.C.E., the Jews made no resistance. They had not
had a standing army for almost four hundred years, and the
whole concept of war was alien to them. By 175 B.C.E., even
the militia that once patrolled the walls of Jerusalem had
almost disappeared, so long had the land lived under the
protection of the Ptolemies, and the only organized military
body of Jews was the Levites who served as Temple Guards,
policemen in ceremonial dress. Antiochus IV sent his own
troops to take over Jerusalem—and once this had occurred,
the aristocracy and the priesthood moved heaven and earth
to protect the Temple treasury.

They temporized with the Syrian-Greeks, adjusted to them,
and took pains not to anger them. The Syrians, new to the
Jewish religion, decided to blend it with Zeus-worship, and
to establish a statue of Zeus in the Temple. Or at least, so
Maccabees I and II in the Apocrypha have it, and with Maccabees III, they are all our sources for the causes and beginnings of the Agrarian War. Some of the details of the
abominations supposedly committed by the Syrian-Greeks
are open to question, but in all probability most of the
facts are true.

They took a heavy tribute from the Temple, but since
they were able to come to an accommodation with the establishment in Jerusalem, they laid a heavier hand on the
Jewish farmers outside of the city, taxing, looting, and no
doubt robbing the synagogues without mercy. During the

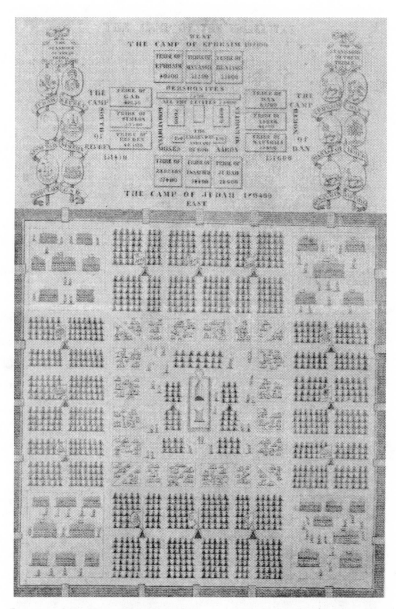

From an old print, a diagrammatic representation of the Tribes of Israel. A careful count will show that when we include the Gershonites and Levites we have 14 tribes rather than 12, 12 being a symbolic number. It should also be noted that in spite of the injunction against graven images, each tribe cherished its standard — in some cases related to the ancient tribal totem / Picture Collection, New York Public Library

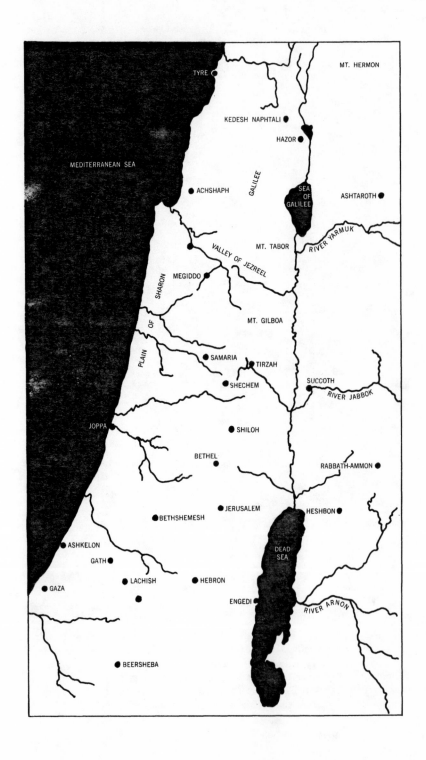

Opposite page: The ancient Land of Canaan

Below: The ancient Near East

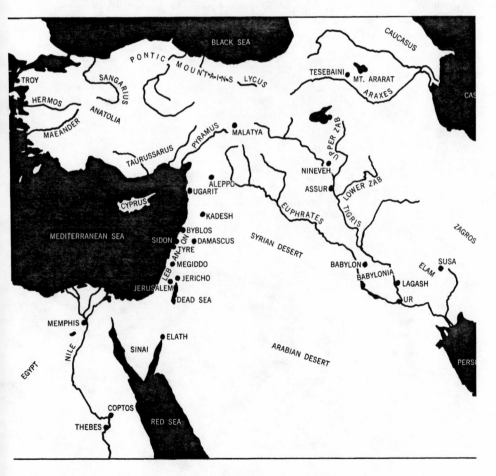

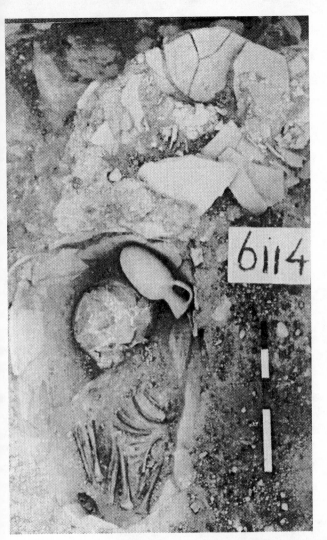

Left: Infant buried in a jar, dates from the Times of the Patriarchs, 18-17th century, B.C.E. / American Friends of the Hebrew University

Opposite page: This orthostat was part of a Canaanite Temple at Hazor, which fell to Joshua's Israelite forces in the 13th century, B.C.E. / American Friends of the Hebrew University

Below: Iron Age vessels, probably dating from the 10th century, B.C.E., found at Tel Arad / American Friends of the Hebrew University

Opposite page: Winged male sphinx, Neo Hittite, 850-830 B.C.E. / The Metropolitan Museum of Art, Rogers Fund, 1943

Right: Small pottery head of Astarte, the Canaanite mother god and fertility symbol / American Friends of the Hebrew University

Below: Sphinx of Hat-shepsut, Egyptian, XVIII Dynasty. The sphinx was probably a very important image to both the Levites and the Tribe of Judah, which took the lion as its symbol and possibly originally as one of its gods. The image of sphinx lion was probably in the First Temple / The Metropolitan Museum of Art, Rogers Fund, 1930

Ramses II, 1292-1225 B.C.E., was most likely the Egyptian god-king in whose long reign the Exodus occurred / The Metropolitan Museum of Art, Rogers Fund, 1934

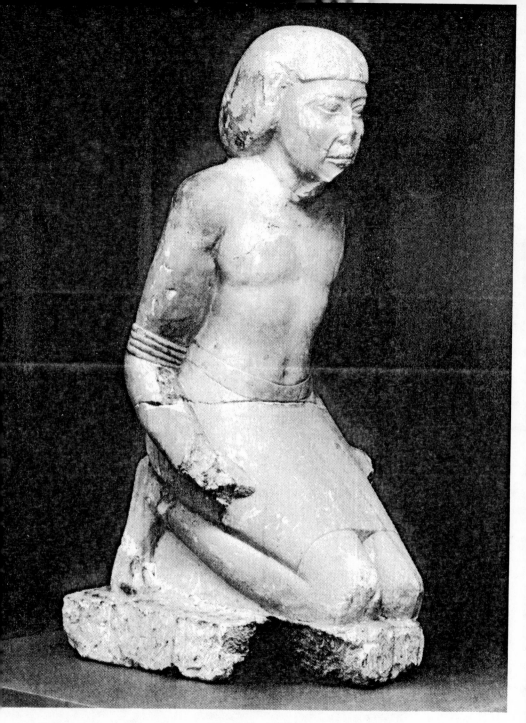

Statue of captive, Egyptian, ca. 2350 B.C.E. / The Metropolitan Museum of Art, Fletcher Fund, 1947

An aerial view of excavations at Hazor, the Canaanite city Joshua captured and burned, which was rebuilt by Solomon centuries later / American Friends of the Hebrew University

Facing page: The great Dome of the Mosque of Omar in Jerusalem, which is built upon the site of Solomon's Temple / Israel Government Tourist Office

Assyrian soldier bringing in captives. Fragment of a wall panel from the Palace of Sennacherib, 705-680, B.C.E. / The Metropolitan Museum of Art, Gift of John D. Rockefeller, Jr., 1932

Assyrian soldiers taking captives across a stream. Also from the Palace of Sennacherib / The Metropolitan Museum of Art, Gift of John D. Rockefeller, Jr., 1932

Three rulers.

Ptolemy II (3rd century, B.C.E), shown here with his wife. One of the heirs to Alexander's Empire, he lived at peace with the Jews in a condition of mutual respect and admiration / The Metropolitan Museum of Art, The Theodore M. Davis Collection, Bequest of Theodore M. Davis, 1915

Antiochos III (222-187 B.C.E.), the Greek-Syrian emperor. His son, Antiochus (Epiphanes) IV, made war against the Maccabees, 168-165 B.C.E. / The Metropolitan Museum of Art, Gift of the American Society for the Excavation of Sardis, 1926

Vespasian, who, as a general, fought in the first part of the last great war of the Jews (1st century C.E.). Josephus saved his life, it is said, by prophesying that he would become the emperor of Rome. It was Vespasian's son Titus who conducted the last great siege of Jerusalem in the year 70 / The Metropolitan Museum of Art, Gift of Louis Levy, 1950

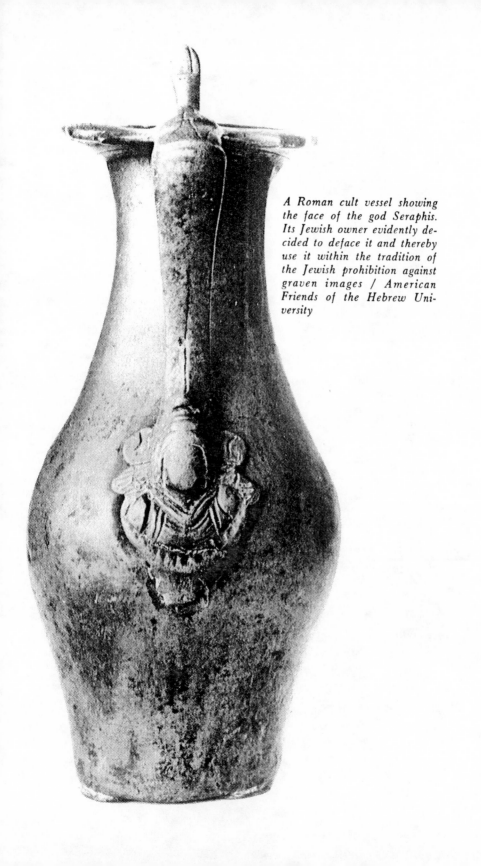

A Roman cult vessel showing
the face of the god Seraphis.
Its Jewish owner evidently decided to deface it and thereby
use it within the tradition of
the Jewish prohibition against
graven images / American
Friends of the Hebrew University

Above — Left: A column from an ancient synagogue excavated at Caesarea, bearing the Greek inscription: "The gift of Theodorus, the son of Olympus, for the salvation of his daughter Matrona" / American Friends of the Hebrew University. Above — Right: Laver once used for the washing of hands, from the synagogue of Kfar Nachum (Capernaum), where it is said that Jesus preached / American Friends of the Hebrew University

Opposite page: Jewish catacombs at Beth Shearim. Note Greek inscription above tomb at top / American Friends of the Hebrew University

An ancient synagogue excavated in Israel / American Friends of the Hebrew University

Opposite page: A bundle of legal documents precisely dated according to both the Roman and local calendars, found by Professor Yigael Yadin in the Judean Desert caves near the Dead Sea / American Friends of the Hebrew University

A Dead Sea Scroll, containing Isaiah I, Chapter 38, v 8 through Chapter 41, v 22 / American Friends of the Hebrew University

Aerial view of Masada / Israel Government Tourist Office

A column found at Masada / American Friends of the Hebrew University

Stone and wood ornaments found with Bar Kochba letters / American Friends of the Hebrew University

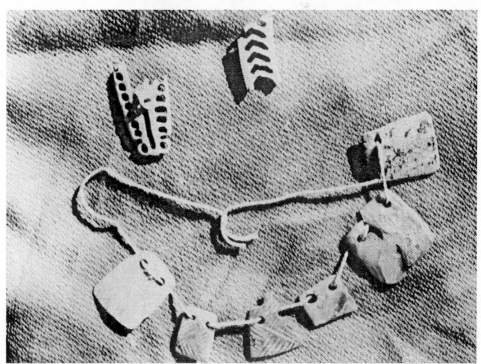

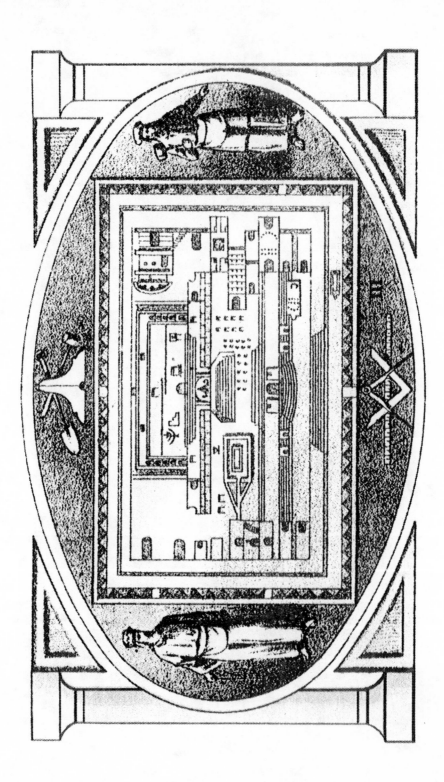

Silver shekel of the First Revolt / The American Numismatic Society, New York

Representation of floor plan of Second Temple / Hebrew Publishing Company

Silver tetradrachm of the Second Revolt. Obverse: Building with four columns showing an arched structure within (sometimes interpreted as the Ark of the Covenant behind the Screen of the Tabernacle). Reverse: Lulab with ethrog / The American Numismatic Society, New York

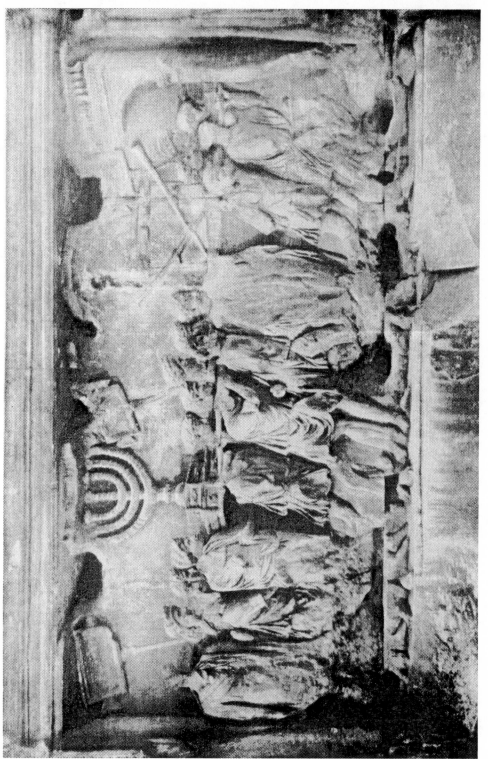

Spoils of the Temple of Jerusalem, depicted on the Arch of Titus / Picture Collection, New York Public Library

Temple period, Jews always resented taxation fiercely. They knew the wealth of Jerusalem, and since they were constantly rendering tithes in both money and kind to the Temple, they saw no reason why they should be taxed in addition. There was a reason, however; the Seleucids were on the path of conquest, and there was no other way for them to function except with mercenary armies. Antiochus IV probably kept a hundred thousand men in the field—at times twice that many, and the core were heavily armed Macedonians. Such troops cost money, a vast amount of money. The Jewish farmers were being squeezed to death; but it took the gestures against their religion to move this people of peace into action.

———————

The village of Modin, a day's walk from Jerusalem, was the home of a priestly family which styled itself *Hashmonai*. In English, this is rendered Hasmoneans, and so far as we know, the Hasmoneans were as valid and ancient a priestly (*cohen*) family as the Zadoks. Since all the population of Judea—certainly well over half a million by now and conceivably as high as a million—were descended from the handful who had picked up the pieces after the exile, the Hasmoneans probably had relatives and family connections all over the country, as well as in the Diaspora. But they were one of the excluded families of *cohens,* excluded from the inner circle of patronage in the city and from the Temple function as well. Naturally, this would give rise to jealousy, and naturally the excluded *cohens* would question every action of the Temple group.

When Syrian-Greek tax collectors came to Modin and blasphemed the name of God and affronted the religious beliefs of the villagers, it was the last in a series of acts that the village Jews had found increasingly intolerable. An old *cohen,* probably the head of the Hasmonean clan, whose name was Mattathias, killed one of the Syrian-Greeks, and with the aid of his five sons and the villagers, drove the rest of the Syrians away. Thereby started the revolt that became the Great

Agrarian War—and which led finally to the reconstitution
of Palestine as a Jewish land.

The five sons of the old priest were named Judah (often
rendered Judas), Jonathan, Simon, John, and Eleazar. They
must have been an extraordinary family, for not only did they
create an army out of a tiny guerilla movement, but under
their leadership the Jews endured years of privation and suffering.

The struggle against Antiochus and the Syrian-Greek kingdom was carried on at first by Mattathias, his five sons, and a
handful of the Modin villagers. They had no arms, no
armor, and no experience in war; they had no tradition of
war. But their courage, their ferocity in battle, and their
willingness to attack, regardless of the odds against them,
soon attracted the attention of the entire ancient world—
and Rome in particular. The rebels gathered their men
from the villages, for in Jerusalem the Jewish establishment
would have nothing to do with them, giving them neither financial aid nor comfort.

Judah Maccabeus, one of the five brothers, took command
of the revolt and proved himself one of the rare military
geniuses of history. He armed his band with weapons taken
from dead mercenaries; he attacked again and again against
impossible odds, using his intimate knowledge of the defiles
and hills around Jerusalem. The name *Maccabee* (a name
whose derivation and precise meaning are unknown) became
and remained a symbol of courage and nobility. It would
seem that all five of the Hasmonean brothers were unusual
men, gentle, self-effacing, intelligent, and courageous—this
perhaps the best tribute to the old *cohen*, Mattathias, their
father.

The old man died, and the sons carried on. They made
great advances, built their little force into an army, and
under Judah they fought their way into Jerusalem, took the
Temple, and cleansed and rededicated it. The Syrians and
the city establishment of Jews held part of the city, but the
rest belonged to the rebels.

Judah and his brothers now decided to break the Syrian

power throughout the whole of Eretz-Yisrael. Actually, during the years since the exile, Jews had spread out through Palestine, so that there was no part of the land without at least a minority Jewish population. The Hasmonean force moved from victory to victory, but was finally halted by an elephant column that Antiochus sent against them. Here, Eleazar was killed. Later, Judah led a band of eight hundred men against a vast mercenary force, in an effort to rout them by the sheer power of his name and reputation. He was killed, and his force was practically wiped out. Exhausted, what was left of the Jewish resistance forces moved across the Jordan. John, another brother, was killed during this time.

There is evidence that at this moment of low ebb, a column of Macedonian mercenaries came over to the Jewish side, in part because Antiochus was running out of funds with which to pay his soldiers and in part out of admiration for the Jewish courage and tenacity. In any case, Jonathan, one of the two remaining Hasmonean brothers, was able to regroup his forces, make a sort of peace with the Syrians, and reenter Jerusalem. He secured the city, and forced the exhausted and nearly bankrupt Syrian-Greeks to give the Jews at least semi-independence.

Jonathan was slain, and the last of the Hasmonean brothers, Simon, the eldest, took over the struggle. Simon completed the liberation of the land and the city. He was installed as high priest and *ethnarch* (Greek for "governor"), and under his rule, the land was free and in peace. This was in 142 B.C.E. Simon the Hasmonean ruled the Jews for seven years. In 135 B.C.E., he was murdered. So ended the strange and noble moment of the five Hasmonean brothers upon the stage of history.

———•——•——

John Hyrcanus, the son of Simon the Hasmonean, took over the leadership of the Jewish state when his father was murdered. (Why he adopted the surname Hyrcanus we do not know, and explanations offered are confused and unsatisfactory. Hyrcanus was an Alexandrian-Greek name, and be-

fore John's time, we find several important Jews bearing it.)
The Syrians had raised an excellent mercenary army, and
they advanced against Jerusalem. John Hyrcanus tried to stop
them and was badly beaten—after which the Syrians once
again took and occupied Jerusalem.

However, the main enemy of the Syrians was Parthia—
the people of the heartland of the old Persian empire. Their
nobility was to a large extent Jewish—by conversion—and
their attack on the Seleucids of Syria was calculated to help
the hard-pressed Jews under John Hyrcanus. While the
Parthian cavalry occupied more and more Syrian mercenaries, John regrouped his Jewish soldiers, and brought in
Macedonian arms and armor as well as Macedonian drill-
masters. Almost overnight, this iron-willed and ambitious
man turned his defeated soldiers into a disciplined military
force. He then struck smashing blows at the Syrians, who
were caught between the fury of the Parthians and the Jews
—and who thereupon crumpled and began their retreat
into obscurity.

Still unsatisfied, John Hyrcanus turned his phalanxes
against Idumea to the south of Judea and Samaria to the
north. He conquered both areas, tripling the area of the Jewish state. He retook Jerusalem and refurbished the Temple.
He instituted himself as high priest and turned over the
vast wealth and the worship of the Temple to his own family, the Hasmoneans. The Hasmoneans and their relatives
and associated families had become the new ruling class;
they took over the great palaces and homes in Jerusalem and
they disassociated themselves from the village Jews.

The Pharisees, whose base was in the villages and who
looked to the rabbis for leadership, were horrified at the actions of Hyrcanus, whose father had been one of the beloved
Hasmonean brothers. They saw their land becoming a garrison state, and they pleaded with John to abandon a policy
of warfare and conquest.

His reply was to break once and for all with the Pharisees. His family, the Hasmoneans, had made their peace with
the House of Zadok, had intermarried with them, and had

forgiven those of the old aristocrats who survived. The Hasmoneans were now rich and powerful—so why look down upon the Sadducees? Instead, they joined them, and became the core of the Sadducee movement.

John Hyrcanus died in 105 B.C.E., and his son Judah, who succeeded him, lasted only a few months. John had another son, Alexander Yannai, whom both he and Judah hated and feared—and with good reason, for this Yannai was a sort of monster. Judah imprisoned Alexander Yannai, and some believe that Yannai had him done away with by intrigue from prison itself. Released after the death of his brother Judah, Yannai, second son of John Hyrcanus and grandson of Simon Maccabeus, made himself king.

It is almost impossible to write objectively of Yannai, and even a matter-of-fact description of him is difficult to believe. He proved again the maxim that power corrupts. When he took power and made himself king and high priest, he murdered every opponent he could lay hands on. Apparently, he killed with pleasure. He used the Temple treasury to buy a huge army of mercenaries, and with it, he conquered all of Palestine up to the north of Galilee. He conquered the Greek cities of Palestine where Jews were a minority and he laid up a great store of hatred. Years later, during the time of the Roman procurators, the people of these cities took bitter revenge upon the Jewish minorities. His time was the only instance in history of Jewish proselytizing on a mass scale. He gave certain populations, including the Idumeans in the south, the choice between Judaism and death.

These and other actions so horrified the Pharisees that they forswore their hatred of war and organized a revolt against Yannai. This war, between the mass of the Jewish people and Yannai's mercenaries, cost the lives of fifty thousand Jews. In one case, Yannai allowed the Jews to come to Jerusalem to worship in the Temple. When the Temple court was filled with thousands of defenseless people, Yannai turned his mercenaries upon them and slaughtered them. In another case, he took eight hundred Pharisee prisoners who had fought against him—Jewish farmers—and cruci-

fied them. While they hung from their crosses, he murdered
their wives and children before their eyes. He destroyed
entire Jewish villages, wiping out men, women, children,
killing even the fowl and the livestock. Yannai was insane
with power, and an itemization of his cruelties can only
sicken. Thousands of Jews left Palestine during his reign and
made their home in the Diaspora.

When he died, his widow, Salome Alexandra, reigned as
queen. She welcomed the Pharisees to the court, and somehow, out of their agony, they became once again the major
force in the Jewish state. With Salome's death, her sons attempted to prove themselves worthy heirs of Yannai, but
their charade of hate and death was short-lived. Their great-
uncle, Judah Maccabeus, had made a pact of mutual assistance with the Romans. Now the Romans moved to put an
end to the bloody madness of the Hasmoneans, and they installed as governor of a severely reduced Judea the Idumean
named Antipater. He was then succeeded by his son, Herod,
whom history remembers as Herod the Great.

———·•·——

The bloody rule of the Hasmoneans over Israel had lasted
seventy-two years, from the death of Simon Maccabeus in 135
B.C.E. to the ascension of Antipater to the throne of Judea in
63 B.C.E. During that time, thousands of Pharisaic Jews had
left Judea for Galilee, Alexandria, Babylonia, Tyre, Rome,
and many other cities in Greece, Spain, and Italy. Judea
as a garrison state was distasteful to them, and they found
the taking of human life an intolerable notion. Their synagogues arose everywhere in the ancient world, and to civilized
and thoughtful pagans who were witnessing the disintegration
of their native religions under the blows of conquering
Rome, the Jewish centers in the cities were havens of culture,
decency, and civilization. To many others, of course, these
Jewish settlements were objects of hatred and envy. Anti-
Semitism is as old as the Diaspora itself.

The Greek civilization, which had conquered so much of
the ancient world by arms and by culture, was experiencing

what was aptly termed "a failure of nerve," and perhaps the
Jewish civilization was experiencing something of the same;
although the Jews had reservoirs of strength the Greeks
lacked, a serenity of belief and a solidarity of family that
would last for centuries to come. Like the Greeks, the Jews
had watched old institutions crumble, had witnessed unspeakable cruelties—acts of mass murder and destruction
which would have been unthinkable under the Persians, the
Babylonians—even the Assyrians. As Greek fought Greek,
so did Jew fight Jew. Both survived, but thousands of Greeks
turned to the Jews, endured the rite of circumcision, and
became part of the Jewish community.

Part of the reason for this was the mystical trend among
both Jews and Greeks—a steady influence of eastern thought.
When Greek cities crumbled under the hammering of new
powers, when Greek gods died in their own futility, a man
called Zeno led a new current in Greek thought—a current
called Stoicism, taking its name from the *stoa,* or "porch,"
where Zeno held sway. Zeno taught that man's salvation
is within himself, in his acts, in his personal virtue, integrity, and dignity. He taught the Buddhist doctrine that
man's soul is part of the universal soul, that God is all, and
that images and altars and burnt offerings are childish nonsense. To a degree, his teaching paralleled the development
of Jewish thought—to a degree it did not; for the Jews believed in their own role as a people chosen by God to carry
the burden of all mankind. Yet so close were Jew and Greek
during the years after the death of Zeno that there had to be a
syncretism of Jewish thought and Greek thought. Philo, the
Alexandrian-Jewish philosopher, reflects something of this
syncretism—as did other Jews and Greeks.

Educated, cultured Greeks found no barriers to Judaism.
The island of dignity and stability that the Jewish family
presented, wherever they were, their gentleness, their serenity of existence, their abstinence from liquor, both attracted
and repelled. Greeks became Jews; other Greeks murdered
Jews. The Jews were loved and they were hated—as the
stranger who remains strange is always hated. Their refusal

to become part of the pagan *urb* in which they dwelled, their wealth—not always, but very often the case—their aloofness which many saw as arrogance, their refusal to bear arms and their willingness to hire others when armed service was necessary—all these contributed to the rise of a particular kind of hatred, a specific hatred that was to remain around the Jew for all time to come, the hatred which the world knows as anti-Semitism. As long ago as two hundred years B.C.E., this hatred began to erupt into frightful mob action against Jews in the Diaspora, lynchings and massacres. In time, it increased.

———•——•——•———

During the two generations which followed the period of the Hasmoneans, two men put their mark upon the Jewish scene. The first was a gentle philosopher and teacher named Hillel—whom many Jews even today regard as their father in wisdom; and the second was a king named Herod.

Hillel is regarded as the first among the fathers, those wise and tolerant rabbis, most of them Pharisees, whose teaching is gathered together in the *Pirke Abot,* in English "The Wisdom of the Fathers," and whose thinking was to a large extent responsible for Rabbinical Judaism. Some of the *Pirke Abot* dates back to Babylon just after the exile, but most of it is the thinking of rabbis who followed Hillel and were to one extent or another guided by him. Many of these rabbis lived in cities outside of Judea. Indeed, Hillel himself was born in Babylon, and he came to Galilee in his fortieth year. There, he established the "House of Hillel," a phrase covering a home, a school, a movement, and a philosophy.

His origins are obscure; his childhood background one of great poverty, and in all probability he was by birth neither a *cohen* nor an aristocrat. We are not aware of his ancestry, nor did it appear to be an important factor in his life. Like most important rabbis, he acted at times as a judge in the inner Jewish court of law, but very few of his legal decisions survive. (At that time and through history to the twentieth century, Jewish settlements and communities judged their own legal disputes. The rabbi sat as a judge, and he used the law according to his interpretation of the Torah and according to precedent, which included previous legal decisions.)

Other rabbis, some of them Hillel's contemporaries, left more important legal decisions; Hillel's fame, however, rests upon his ethical concepts and his interpretation of Judaism. It was he who, clearly and simply, first enunciated the Golden Rule, so called, and gave it a proper place in the Jewish religion. A pagan came to Hillel and told the rabbi that he was determined to become a Jew but despaired of his ability to comprehend and use the five books of Moses, the Torah, and all the other Jewish writings that by now were included under the general term *law*. Hillel replied, "To love thy neighbor as thyself. That is the whole Law, and all the rest is commentary."

Often, Hillel's teaching was in direct opposition to the teaching of other rabbis of the time, particularly the famous Shammai, who taught a narrower, more rigid Judaism; but so great was his authority and prestige that no attack against him could prevail. Hillel believed in the pervading presence of God and felt that the only way man could serve God was through his actions. He taught a mystical union of man and God, and within the framework of his teaching, the ancient Yahweh, the angry and terrible God of the wilderness, disappeared. There was no place for meaningless ritual or formalism in Hillel's teaching, and he put forward the view that man is directly responsible to God for his actions.

At the same time, Hillel taught self-esteem, regard for oneself as a human being; a way of life somewhat comparable to Zeno's teaching but antithetical to the self-hatred and sense of sin that was so much a part of Christianity. The most famous saying of Hillel is directly to this point: "If I am not for myself, who will be for me? And if I am only for myself, what am I? And if not now, when?"

Hillel has God address the Jews thus: "To the place in which I delight my feet bring me. If thou comest to my house I come to thine. If thou comest not to mine, I come not to thine."

And even more to the point of the universal union of man
and God: "If I [God] am here everyone is here. If I am not
here nobody is here."

Hillel taught life as opposed to death. War was total evil,
and if man countenanced war, he countenanced all other
evil. Life was sacred and good, and the living of life was the
will of God and also part of God.

———•••·———

Herod's name has come down to us through history, cou-
pled with horror, while the name of Alexander Yannai—
so much more awful a man—is more or less forgotten. Part
of the reason is the birth of Jesus so soon after the death of
Herod; thus Herod figures in Christian as well as Jewish folk
memory; but a more important reason lies in the fact that one
prefers one's own monster to a foreign monster. Actually,
Herod was much less of a monster than Yannai, but he happened not to be Jewish. At least in the eyes of the Jews, Herod
was not Jewish. By his own definition he was.

There was a sort of historical justice in the ascension of
Herod, for only a few short decades before, Alexander Yannai had forced Judaism upon the Idumeans. The Idumeans
were more or less the descendants of the ancient Edomites;
more or less, because identification in a modern sense is impossible. The Idumeans spoke the same language as the Jews
and were also of the Beni-Yisrael. They had been Jews of a
sort even before Yannai forced his will upon them, and in
the first century, during Titus' siege of Jerusalem, what was
left of able-bodied Idumeans went to the aid of the most
fanatical defenders of Jerusalem, helped them to murder
the last of the Pharisees in Jerusalem, and were in turn destroyed by the Romans. Their strut across history as a nation
was thus short-lived, but while it existed they occupied the
territory south and east of Jerusalem, and in a loose, Bedouin
sense, much of the Negeb.

They are best remembered because they produced the
Herodian dynasty, the first of this dynasty in Judea being one
Antipater, who, as we have noted, was installed by Rome as

governor of Judea. He was the son of an Idumean favorite of
Alexander Yannai, and being both clever and strong-willed,
he placed himself and several thousand Jewish and Idumean
fighting men at the disposal of Julius Caesar. In return for
this support, he was made the first Roman governor or procurator of Judea. As was not unusual among rulers of that
time, he was murdered with poison, and his position among
the Jews was assumed by his son, Herod.

Herod had already displayed talents in the direction of
kingship. Appointed governor of Galilee by his father, he
put down incipient dissatisfaction by crucifying every Pharisee who openly stated his dislike of the House of Antipater.
Some Galilean farmers then refused to pay taxes. They
were poverty-stricken, but Herod promptly crucified them
and put a summary end to tax dodging. For these crimes, he
was summoned to Jerusalem to be tried by the Great Sanhedrin. The Sanhedrin would have sentenced him to death had
not the Romans intervened, and made Herod king of Judea.
Being of long memory, Herod, once he was crowned king,
had the members of the Sanhedrin who had sat in judgment
on him put to death.

When the gates of Jerusalem were barred to Herod by
order of the Sanhedrin, he then, with the help of Roman
legions, took Jerusalem and put the leaders of the defense
to death. He was an energetic man, and he alertly murdered
every opponent, including his brother-in-law, Aristobulus
III, who was the last Hasmonean high priest. Suspecting his
wife Mariamne of plotting against him, he had her murdered,
and then becoming suspicious of his two sons by Mariamne,
he had them murdered too. He subsequently murdered his
own firstborn son, Antipater, whom he suspected of plotting
against him.

Indeed the catalogue of Herod's infamy is both tedious
and terrible. He appeared to live like most rulers of men,
frightened, suspicious, deluded by visions of persecution
and murder—a terrifying object of fear and hatred. Like
so many paranoid rulers, he created public works with fero-
cious compulsion: roads, baths, theaters, gymnasiums, race-

tracks—piling stone upon stone, terrified of his own approaching death and frantically trying to create immortality for himself.

Under him, Palestine was a Roman province, and its enormous wealth poured into Rome, as did the wealth of so many other lands. Rome parceled out the land to tax farmers, rewarding them thus for military and other forms of service.

In spite of this, the land prospered enormously. The center of Jewish population, since the Hasmoneans had made Jerusalem an uneasy place to live in, had shifted to Galilee, where Hillel had founded his Academy and where a new city was being built on the warm, pleasant shores of the Sea of Galilee. In Galilee and in Babylon, Jewish sages and scholars discussed Jewish law and literature, debated point after point, taking part in the process of creating that enormous storehouse of ancient Jewish culture, the Talmud. But the prosperity was not limited to Galilee; given a few years of peace, Jewish energy was fast converting Palestine as a whole into the most prosperous land on earth.

Herod grew old. He was a dropsical old man, whining in his pain and watching with frightened eyes as death approached. He complained to his courtiers that he would have no mourners, that in all the world there was no one who would shed a tear over the death of Herod the Great.

Legend has it that one of the courtiers suggested that at the moment of Herod's death, Hillel be slain—and then the whole world would weep.

But even at death's door, Herod had no stomach for this. Hillel, the gentle, saintly teacher in Galilee, was a force Herod could not comprehend or defeat.

So Herod died, unmourned, in the fourth year before the birth of Jesus, and fourteen years later, Hillel was dead. It is said that in all the time of the ancient world, there was no mourning like that for Hillel. A whole world wept, not only Jews, but thousands and thousands of pagans who crowded into the synagogues to share the sorrow at the passing of a saint.

It was the end of an era, the end of the Jew's first passage through history. Yet like a whisper through time, Hillel's curious, negative, yet holy injunction echoed and re-echoed:

"Do not unto others as you would not have them do unto you."

PART SIX

Jesus
and Christianity

There is a tendency to regard the capture and destruction of Jerusalem in the year 70 as the end of the Jewish state in Palestine and even as the end of the Jewish presence in Palestine. Neither conclusion is true, for one can carefully trace a continuing Jewish presence in Palestine without a real break from the time of Herod until today. It is true that at times this Jewish presence in its ancient homeland narrowed to a very small community indeed, but it never disappeared.

In the first two centuries of our time, the Jewish population in the Diaspora increased while the population in Palestine decreased, and in the third and fourth centuries this process was accelerated—not by the Romans and their legions but by other historical forces. During the first hundred years after the death of Christ, great wealth and growth occurred in Jewish Palestine, and if not for the tragic series of events in Jerusalem and the Judean hills, Palestine might have outshone Italy. However, we are interested in history as it was and not as it might have been.

Three or four or five years after the death of Herod, a Jewish child was born in Palestine who would be remembered by the Western world as Jesus Christ. We are sure of neither the exact date nor the exact place of his birth, and our knowledge of his life is sketchy at best. We suspect that he may have been a leader of one of the many rebellions against the Roman control of Jewish Palestine; we have some of his sermons and teachings, and we have the details of his tragic death. He comes upon the stage of history less in himself than in the work of one Paul of Tarsus, but in order to comprehend the impact of Jesus and Paul upon the ancient world, we must bring the history of the Jews forward past the birth of Jesus, to the time of Paul's preaching; and perhaps a little beyond that, since there are no straight lines in history.

———————

The Roman procurators were of the *equites* class, which meant that they were moneymen riding hard on the road to riches. Among the equites—or knights—of ancient Rome, the lust for money and the drive for wealth were unlike any-

thing the ancient world had ever seen. And the greatest
plum that one could have, as a knight, was a procuratorship
—or the right to bleed a nation or city to death. In Roman
society, money had become an enormous force, and the kind
of bleeding the procurators did was a new phenomenon in
history.

Aware of this and also aware of the type of man who drove
to the point of procuratorship, the Roman emperors usually
awarded these plums in territories that posed a threat to
Rome—or in territories that the Romans were not courting.
Judea was such a territory.

Judea, at the beginning of our era, was paired by the
Romans with Samaria [which was what remained of the ancient kingdom of the Beni-Yisreal]. Through the centuries,
Samaria had arrived at a sort of Yahweh worship which did
not exclude certain ancient Canaanite deities; and while the
Temple priests despised this worship, the Samaritans considered themselves Jews of a sort, and when they moved into
cities of the Diaspora, as they were constantly doing, they
would settle in the Jewish communities, where they were
received with a warmth lacking in Palestine. Since they preserved the rite of circumcision, there was no barrier to their
joining the synagogues, and it is quite likely that there is
Samaritan lineage in millions of Jews alive today.

In every war of the Jews since their return from exile—
and most particularly during the Great Agrarian War—the
Samaritans had thrown in their lot with the Jews. They were
fierce fighters, intractable, with an unbroken military tradition that dated back to David. They were philosophically untouched by Pharisaism and they still worshipped the ancient
war god, the angry and truculent Yahweh.

Because of this and the danger they presented to Rome,
their territory was joined to the procuratorship of Judea,
and indeed whoever the procurator happened to be, he governed from the Roman city of Caesarea, a seacoast city on the
edge of Samaria. Actually, the procurator of Judea tax-
farmed an area from Beersheba in the south to Megiddo in
the north, from the Mediterranean Sea to the Jordan River,

an area not only enormously rich and fertile as farmland, every acre cultivated the way the fertile areas of Japan are cultivated today, but an area of many rich cities, particularly Jerusalem and the untold wealth in its Temple compound. To have this procuratorship was to become rich indeed; and also to face a good many thorny problems that did not exist in other places.

Even in Palestine, a minority of Jews resided in Judea, the great area of Palestinian Jewry being in Galilee—a place even richer than Judea, but outside of the procurator's command. The Jews of Galilee—and of the Diaspora as well—had a very different relationship to Rome than existed in Judea (by which we mean the whole area of the procuratorship including Samaria); the Temple and the holy city of Jerusalem were both under the procurator.

Excluding the governorship of Antipater, the father of Herod, there were fourteen procurators between the beginning of our era and the year 70, when the Temple and Jerusalem were destroyed. Except for Pontius Pilate, who was procurator when Jesus was crucified, the names of the others are meaningless. They were men distinguished only by avarice; they were hated by the Jews, whom they in turn hated. They had the power of life and death over non-Roman citizens, and they used it. They taxed the Jewish farmers into poverty and landlessness; looted the aristocracy—the alternative to payment was death—and periodically exacted their toll from the Temple treasure.

As a result of this, they sowed perennial seeds of revolt. There was a revolt in the first decade; military action against the Samaritans, and several revolts under Pilate—in all likelihood Jesus led one of these—and then a constant succession of revolts and petty wars under Marcellus, Marullus, Caspius Fadus, Tiberius Alexander, Antonius Felix, Festus, Albinus, and Florus—Pilate's successors. The final revolts and the indignities which had provoked them led to the tragic war with Rome and the destruction of Jerusalem.

The procurators applied a force which the Jews despised and reacted to. For reasons we shall go into, the Jews re-

sented taxation more bitterly than other people; they also
resented the primitive vulgarity of the Roman emperor worship—just as they resented the—to them—primitive and
mindless professional soldier who was the Roman legionary.

Force created a counterforce, and a new, strange grouping
arose among the Jews.

————•••••————

No one knows exactly how many Jews lived in Palestine
at this time, nor can the population be computed in terms
of Jewish wealth. Crassus, the Roman general who destroyed Spartacus and put down the great servile revolt, was
reckoned as the richest private individual in the world. It is
estimated that he looted the Temple of precious metal worth
twenty billion dollars; but this is obviously an enormous ex-
aggeration. Howsoever, his fortune was built on Jewish
wealth. More exactly, we do know that Gabinius, a Roman
governor with the right to put his itching hand into Galilee,
extracted twenty million dollars, mostly from the Jews of
northern Palestine, without making any great raid on the
Temple treasury. What the fourteen procurators of Judea
took out of the land defies the imagination; but it must be
remembered that Jewish wealth stored in the Temple had
been accumulating for five hundred years.

Yet wealth can be used as a sort of guide, and it is conjec-
tured that Palestine and the Phoenician and Syrian cities
immediately north and east probably had a total population
of some ten millions, of whom at least five million were Jewish and another million the Samaritan Beni-Yisrael. It is also
estimated that at least five million additional Jews lived in
the Diaspora. But these are only estimates, educated guesses
and deductions; the actual numbers can never be known. We
do know, however, from Josephus, the Jewish historian of
that time, that villages were on the average less than a mile
apart, that every inch of land was terraced and fertilized on
the hillsides, not to mention the valleys. The normal
population of Jerusalem must have been close to a million,
far over a million on Passover. In both manpower and wealth,

the power of the Jews was greater than Rome; but the Jews were fragmentized and essentially antiwar; the Romans were organized, and the prime purpose of Roman existence was to make war. Jew and Roman were as far apart in manner and outlook as Jew and gentile would be a thousand years later.

To the greatest extent, it was the greed and senseless cruelty of Rome, the use of crucifixion as a daily punishment, that fragmentized and regrouped the Jews. We have already seen that the masses of Jewry the world over had accepted the leadership of the gentle Hillel and the general philosophy of Pharisaism. However, at the same time a large group of the Jews, but a minority, moved away from the dedicated pacifism of Hillel toward a philosophy of war and resistance. This new minority party among the Jews was called the Zealots, or in Hebrew *Kannaim*.

The period of the Zealot—between the death of Herod and the destruction of Jerusalem in the year 70—was short-lived, and is generally misunderstood. The Zealot is pictured, for the most part, as a religious fanatic on the one hand and as a sort of priest of rebellion and abstract freedom on the other. He was a little of each, but mainly he was a farmer dispossessed of his land. It is worth remembering here that the Anglo-Saxon word *freedom* was in its original form *free-doom, doom* being a landholding. In ancient agricultural society, freedom apart from freehold of land was hardly conceivable. The Jews were not an agricultural people when they entered Palestine, but by the time of Roman procurator rule, they had been in the land for almost thirteen hundred years. There were many non-Jews in Palestine then, but over 80 percent of the arable land was owned and farmed by Jews and Samaritans. Palestine then can only be properly described as a Jewish garden, every inch of soil holy and beloved. In a few acres of land, the Jewish farmer had his olive grove, the trees as old as time, his fruit trees, his tiny vineyard, his wheat field, and his garden. He had chickens, perhaps a few stock animals. The little farm, with its multiple crops and the wizardry of fruit and vine culture that the Jew practiced, not only supported his family in a sort of affluence that was the envy of the world but supported the Temple as well. The uncountable treasures of the Temple did not come from war and looting. They came from the Jewish farmer and the Jewish merchant-trader—not as taxes but as voluntary religious gift offerings.

It was on this farmer that the Roman procurator laid his deadly burden of taxation; and he accomplished what no enemy since the exile had been able to accomplish: he destroyed this farmer and uprooted him from the land. Not all Jewish farmers broke under the burden of tax-farming, but thousands and thousands did. Thus was created the Zealot and his hard core, the Sicarii, which means daggermen or assassins, the name originating from the *sica,* the dagger that the Zealot always carried and which was his weapon of terror.

The uprooting of a Jewish farmer often meant the sale of his family—himself included—into slavery to pay back taxes. The Jew knew this, and most often he managed to escape. How was he to live? How were his children to live? Within the confines of Palestine, there was no existence for him. Perhaps he could find some relative or friend to care for his children; if so, he went alone into the badlands of the south and southwest. He became a dry, hard bundle of hate. Often enough, he was from Galilee, and he could remember the fertile green valleys that he had traded for the desert.

In the beginning, in the first years of the Christian era, there were only a few hundred of these Zealots or Sicarii. They were hard men, and to survive they preyed upon the caravan routes. Their robber bands controlled the roads, and at first they robbed only Roman or Greek caravans. But as their numbers and their bitterness increased, they preyed upon the Jewish caravans as well, reasoning that only through collaboration with the Romans could Jewish merchants survive.

Soon, their hundreds became thousands. In the desert, they changed gradually from small robber bands to small armies, with whom the Romans fought an endless battle. They gained adherents in the cities; they moved in and out of Jerusalem

at will. If there was rumor of a Jewish farm or a Jewish aristocrat's estate that was friendly to the Romans, they moved in
and killed every living thing. They kept a list of people who
were marked for murder, Jew and gentile, and they carried
out their assassinations daily.

They built their murder creed out of a fanatical hate-nur-
tured piety, rationalizing, as religious fanatics do in every
time and place, that they were the hand of God, doing God's
will. By the year 70, they were the ultimate opposite not
only of the Pharisees and the mass of the Palestine Jews, but
of Jews the world over.

At that time, the ancient custom of political decision by
democratic assembly still existed in some places. In Jerusalem, when the Great Sanhedrin (a sort of Jewish parliament
with very limited powers) wished to have some legal or
political matter approved, they would call an assembly (in
Hebrew *Keneset Yisrael*) and perhaps fifteen or twenty
thousand people would gather in one of the great plazas of
Jerusalem. By the fourth decade, the Sicarii had begun to in-
filtrate the assembly. They would mark for death not only
the collaborators—by their judgment—but also those who
might vote against their decision. Their daggers would be
under their cloaks, and when the assembly was over, the
bodies of the murdered would lie on the plaza.

The Sicarii, numbering perhaps fifty thousand, were the
hard core of the Zealots. There were perhaps another hundred thousand who were not outlaws but who supported the
Sicarii for reasons ranging from fear to piety. There were
also perhaps twenty thousand Idumeans (Arabs or Edomites
living south of the Dead Sea who practiced a sort of primitive
Judaism, having been, as noted earlier, forcibly converted
to Judaism by the infamous Yannai; Antipater, the father of
Herod, was of their nation), who at one time or another
joined the Sicarii in their raids, and who lived with a murderous hatred of the Pharisaic Jews with their cities, their
fertile farms, their caravans and ships, and their synagogue
communities all over the Diaspora.

I go into this in such detail because without it there is no

understanding what happened in Palestine in the years leading up to 70. Jewish Palestine was more populous than Rome,
wealthier and more powerful. Jerusalem, with the kind of
organized defense the Jews could have put on its walls, was
impregnable, and, attacked, the city could have held out for a
decade. But there was no organized defense; the Zealots destroyed the store of millions of pounds of wheat and barley;
and in the end, the Zealots destroyed each other.

———————

By the year 70, a series of cruelties and indignities that
stretched over five decades finally produced a situation where
a majority of the Jews were willing to support the Zealots
and to make war with the Romans. From Galilee to Judea,
from Beersheba to Kedesh, from the Jordan to the sea, Palestine broke into flames. The entire land exploded in violence.
In the Greek-Roman cities of the coastal plain, where the
Jews were a minority, anti-Semitism erupted in the murder
of thousands of Jews. Where the Jews were in the majority,
they won the inner-city war, only to have the cities reduced
later by the Romans or surrendered to the Romans.

Many Jews joined the rebellion reluctantly; the House of
Hillel opposed it, and the Pharisees would have prevented
it had the Zealots not held the upper hand. Pharisaic aristocrats, like the historian Josephus (Yusef ben Mattityahu ha
Cohen, his Hebrew name, explains much of his background
and position, and we should add the opening lines of his
short biographical sketch, in which he states: "The family
from which I am derived is not an ignoble one, but has descended all along from the priests; and as nobility among
several people is of a different origin, so with us to be of the
sacerdotal dignity, is an indication of the splendor of the
family"), accepted commands but remained antiwar. (It
should be noted that in the first stages of the war against
Rome, these Pharisees were sought out by the Zealots for
leadership. Although they accepted this leadership most
reluctantly, there were only one or two cases of their be-
traying even by ineptitude the men they led. By and large,

they were murdered by the Sicarii during the last years of the war.)

In the first engagements, the Jews won great victories. This was the period of unity between all parts of the Zealot party, and the entrapment and destruction of the first Roman army dispatched against Jerusalem—six thousand Roman dead—raised wild hopes among the Jews. But Vespasian, the Roman general who bore the responsibility for conducting the war, was both patient and able. He regrouped his forces, trained auxiliaries, had his son Titus bring up a legion from Egypt, and then proceeded methodically to destroy resistance in Galilee and the northern cities.

This was the time when Josephus, the historian and aristocrat, decided that the struggle was hopeless, and went over to the Romans. Whether or not this act of surrender by Josephus was treason has been debated by generations of Jews. The remaining soldiers of Josephus made a death pact and slew each other, leaving him for last—whereupon he decided to live and join the Romans. The actions of Josephus must be seen in the whole context of the war. In his magnificent histories, Josephus never impugned either the courage or the dignity of the Jews. He wrote of the Jews with passionate pride and love, as his own people, and he defended them well in his answer to the anti-Semitic slanders of Apion, a Greek writer and orator. Nothing in his writing indicates the mind or guilt of a traitor.

Having subdued the north without too much trouble, Vespasian then turned south to Jerusalem. The defeated Zealots meanwhile had converged on the city. Allowed entry by its defenders—the Pharisee-led militia and the Temple Guard of Levites—they proceeded to take over. They murdered all the Pharisees they could lay hands on, and then turned on the militia, who were no match for them. Those of the Jewish city militia who did not surrender they killed without mercy.

Then the Sicarii, excluded so long from the Temple worship, scaled the Temple walls and attacked the ceremonial Levite guards. The Levites were no match for them and were slain mercilessly, so that not one Levite remained alive in the Temple area. In the end, however, it was the Romans who destroyed the Temple itself. In their lunatic fury, the Sicarii set the vast food reserves on fire, and Jerusalem's hope in a long siege went up in flames. During these events, those inhabitants of Jerusalem who could escape fled, not from the Romans but from the insanity of the Sicarii. Thousands of Jews left Jerusalem, but thousands more were trapped there, held hostage by the Sicarii, who by now realized that Jewish horror at their role had reached such proportions that the Jews might well join with the Romans to exterminate them.

Now the moderate Zealots, sickened by the slaughter in the Temple and by the senseless murder of thousands of innocent Jews by the Sicarii, turned against them. Samaritans had entered the city to support the Jews, and since most of them went over to the moderates, the Sicarii in turn admitted thousands of Idumeans. Jerusalem was turned into a charnel house.

Called back to Rome by the death of Vitellius, the Emperor, Vespasian turned over the Jerusalem campaign to his son Titus. An excellent commander and a rather cautious man, Titus did not make the mistake of storming Jerusalem immediately. He knew what was going on in the city from those who escaped, and he knew that he could only gain by waiting. Whereupon, he proceeded to build a wooden wall around the city. For this purpose, every tree within twenty miles of Jerusalem was cut down—fruit trees and olive trees a thousand years old, as well as the magnificent stands of cedar that the Jews had planted and nursed so lovingly through the centuries.

The Romans burned or destroyed every village in Judea. They broke the terraces, so that with the rain the soil washed away and the hills were denuded. They took every single head of stock and poultry, until the once lovely country —described by travelers as "the brightest jewel" on earth— became a sere, forbidding scene of desolation, in the midst of which the ruined city smoked in its slow burning.

Still Titus did not make the mistake of attacking.

The war of Jew against Jew in Jerusalem went on. There was no place to bury the dead, and the awful smell that came from the city was almost more than men could bear. Inside, Jerusalem was a scene of indescribable horror. What was left of the peaceful Jewish population was dying of starvation, for neither the Zealots nor the Sicarii would provide food. The Sicarii had holed up in the Temple area, and the less fanatical Zealots could not dislodge them.

Finally, Titus moved his legions in. The dying, burning city of death and horror could put up little resistance, and Titus took it with minimum effort and small loss of life. But Eleazar, the leader of the Sicarii, escaped with a band of his assassins and managed to occupy Herod's castle, Masada. There, he and his men held out for almost three years. When the Romans took Masada, the Sicarii committed suicide rather than face crucifixion.

It must be said of Titus, possibly because he was in love with Berenice, the last princess of the line of Herod and the Maccabees, that he showed mercy toward the Jewish population that had survived the months of horror. Or perhaps Titus had had his fill of death. In any case, there was no slaughter of the innocent. He fed the starving prisoners, and only the Sicarii leaders whom he captured were marked for the Triumph in Rome and for execution. By a heroic effort of the world Jewish community and the Jews of Galilee, enough money was raised to buy the rest of the Jewish captives from Titus (being a Roman, he sensibly preferred money to revenge) and to settle them in Jewish communities in a dozen cities.

So passed from the Jewish scene that dreadful manifestation of religious fanaticism, hate, and horror, the Sicarii. The movement perished utterly in Jerusalem and Masada, and the subsequent revolt against Rome, led by Bar Kochba sixty-five years later, from 132 to 135 of the Christian era, and equally tragic in its final conclusions, wiped out even the memory of the assassins. In effect, the result of the downfall of Jerusalem, the most important result, was the Jewish realization that war was senseless, evil, and tragic in its conclusion, regardless of cause and circumstances. Whereupon the Jews gave up war, even as a means of survival, and for the next eighteen hundred years survived without it—the longest nonmilitary period of any people on earth.

———•◆•·———

The Jewish state ceased to be. A state can be thought of as a company of people who speak the same language, live in and rule contiguous areas, and in turn are ruled and controlled by whatever force or establishment governs them. The Jews no longer lived in contiguous areas, they were ruled by local authorities wherever they were, they no longer spoke the same language—Hebrew was simply liturgical and Aramaic was spoken only by the Middle Eastern Jews—and they ruled nowhere. Even in Persia, where they were admired and cherished, they did not govern themselves, and in Palestine, with the death of Berenice's brother Agrippa, even the poor shadow of an independent principality ceased to exist. Galilee was wealthier than ever, perhaps more populous during the years after the fall of Jerusalem than ever before, but history was moving to the west and since the Temple was gone, more and more Jews would move with it. The Judean hills were desolate and lifeless, and Samaria would never recover from the destruction wreaked upon her by the Romans, in return for her joining the Jewish rebellion.

With the Temple in ashes and the great wealth of the Temple gone forever, the Pharisee rabbis took over, not only in Palestine but throughout the world. The synagogue became the central focus of each Jewish community, and the rabbi governed by consent within the gentile governmental apparatus; and in turn Jews brought their disputes to the rabbis. During a time when the ancient world was in a process of enormous dislocation and disintegration, with infanticide and murder endemic in the Mediterranean area, the Jewish communities were quiet areas of refuge and decency. During this time, in the interval of comparative peace between the end of Jerusalem and the triumph of Christianity, thousands

of pagans flocked into the Jewish community, accepted circumcision, and became Jews. It is quite possible that if it had
not been for the role Christianity played, Judaism would
have become the religion of the West.

Also, during the two centuries following the end of the
Temple, two great Jewish academies arose, one in Galilee
and the other in Babylon. The Jewish social order had
changed; the Jerusalem aristocracy had been fragmentized
or had perished; the great landed estates of Judea were gone;
and the *cohens* no longer had the inexhaustible wealth of the
Temple to support their princely way of life and their splendid Jerusalem mansions. Though they clung fiercely to their
title *ha-cohen*, "the priest," shortened later simply to *cohen*,
they found that they had to intermarry with the families of
ordinary Jews to survive. Their priestly function became
vestigial; they were valued in Jewish communities for their
ritual intercession with God during the redemption of the
firstborn and for their necessary presence on certain high
holy days, but this was a small charade which Jews indulged
as a memory of ancient times. To this day, in fact, the priests
have cherished their bloodline.

Replacing the *cohens* and the related aristocrats, a new
rabbinical aristocracy of scholarship arose among the Jews.
In Galilee and in Babylon, there was a succession of rabbis
who bore the title *Nasi*, "prince," but their domain was only
in the minds of their people. They led the work that would
gather together that marvel of human scholarship, the Talmud, created in part in Palestine and in part in Babylon—
over three million words of Jewish history, legal code, folk-
lore, mythology, medicine, astrology, astronomy, poetry,
prophecy, and practically everything else that these astonishing scholars thought worthy of inclusion.

This body of material was, for hundreds of years, the national substitute by the Jews for place and homeland. They
were "the people of the book" not only in terms of the Torah,
the written law, but also the Talmud, which was called the
Oral Law, that is, the unwritten law.

It is most likely that this unwritten law began as rabbinical

commentary on the Torah as long ago as the Babylonian exile
—indeed at a time before the rabbi as such had made his
place in the Jewish scene secure. Over hundreds of years,
these commentaries, memorized and handed down by teachers from generation to generation, became the clothing, so
to speak, of Pharisaism. This material was finally compiled in
the second century of our time as the Mishna, a section of the
Talmud. Then another great set of commentaries became
the second section of the Talmud. Within this existed the law,
legend, and life of the Jewish people—as much as such a
thing can exist within the covers of books.

They—these rabbinical scholars and jurists who compiled
the Talmud—set the tone for a people who refused to die
with their ancient land, but instead increased in numbers
and wealth, and who, in a murderous and barbaric world,
put away their weapons and lived in a tight family structure
of love, scholarship, and compassion.

Of course, it must be remembered that the early Christians were a part of these same Jews, and perhaps the time
that they were a part of the Jewish community was the time
they lived best according to the teachings of Jesus.

———·••·———

There is an irreverent rhyme that reads: "Roses are red,
violets are bluish. If it weren't for Jesus, we'd all be Jewish."
"If it weren't for Paul" would be more to the point, for only
Jews knew and followed Jesus. His life covered the first three
decades of the procuratorship just described—that is, the
rule of Coponius, Ambibulus, Rufus, Gratus, and, of course,
Pontius Pilate—the first five procurators of Judea. So he
knew very well the implacable hand of Rome and the oppression of his own people. We know the words of Jesus better
than the man, and his sermons and parables are all Pharisaic.
His rage at the Pharisees could only have been a later interpolation directed against Pharisaic Judaism. Thousands of
Jews who opposed Rome were crucified as Jesus was—and
always by the Romans. The malignant charge, set down in
the Gospel and used through the centuries, that the Jews

killed Jesus is as puerile and sick as any other part of the anti-Semitic philosophy. Nor is there any basis in the attempt to link Jesus with the Essenes, who were most likely Zealots.

The indication is that Jesus came from Galilee. He fell under the influence of John the Baptist, who was one of the latter-day Jewish prophets, and who believed in the symbolic washing of the soul and rebirth in purification. Gentiles and Jews alike are for the most part ignorant of the fact that baptism is one of the most ancient of Jewish rites and that anointment is a part of Jewish baptism—current not only among the Jews but among most tribes of the Beni-Yisrael. To this day, Orthodox Jews use the *mikvah* (a Hebrew colloquialism, literally meaning "collection," but applied to a pool of water) for the rite of baptism, mostly for the symbolic purification of a woman after her period, but often enough for men too.

In John's time, baptism had taken on mystic overtones and was connected with the Hellenic-mystery concept of death and rebirth. This doctrine, a part of the whole history of mysticism and possibly stemming from Buddhism and Zoroastrianism as well as from Pharisaic Judaism, is misunderstood today and more often than not confused with the far more ancient primitive magic fertility ritual that involves the death and rebirth of the king. So cloudy is our understanding of ancient religion today and so unwilling are we to allow for progress in antiquity that we constantly confuse and lump together movements hundreds of years apart in time, as if antiquity were timeless.

So we look for tricks, drugs, and miracles in the death and rebirth of Jesus—failing to comprehend that this death and rebirth was central to the mystic concept of the time, central to what John the Baptist preached. It is neither my purpose nor my task in this brief book to enter any of the numerous arguments concerning the historical fact of Jesus; the plain truth is that we have only the Gospels for that; but in the sermons of Jesus, we have much that was current in all Jewish thinking at the time. To a large extent, he preached what Rabbi Hillel preached. His parables were on the lips of the Pharisaic rabbis everywhere, and when he died, it is understandable that Jews remembered him with love and compassion for the awful manner of his death. These followers of Jesus were not Christians, because they were Jews. It is as simple as that. They could not have blamed the Jews for anything, because they were the Jews. No one, not Jesus, not his disciples, tried to convert them to Christianity because there was no Christianity, and they hated Pontius Pilate as Jews under the procurators must perforce have hated him.

I doubt that any contemporary (Jew) of Jesus's time ever used the word *Christ*. Why should he? The Hebrew word is *mashiah*, which means "anointed one" or more frequently "messiah." If his followers truly believed that he was the "anointed one," they might have referred to him as *Yehoshua Hamashiah*, a term of love and respect, not the brittle Greek translation, Jesus Christ.

Jesus died, and he was remembered and loved—as were many Jewish martyrs. Perhaps as with the death of Hillel, the death of Jesus was noted and mourned by Jewish communities the world over; but if so, the reaction has been lost in the endless crucifixion of the Jewish people which followed upon the coming of Christianity.

But this was not the doing of Jesus, but of one Paul, a Greek-Jewish tentmaker.

———————

Whatever is said of Paul of Tarsus (his original name was Saul) by Jew or Christian, it must be admitted that this was one of the remarkable men of history. As much as any single human being—and more so than Jesus if we do not accept the divinity of Jesus—he was the creator of Christianity and the Christian Church. He was called "apostle to the gentile [or pagan]"; he never saw Jesus in the flesh—yet of all the apostles he was the most decisive.

Interestingly, we have a physical description of him—a very rare thing at that time of history. He was rather short, legs crooked—probably from childhood disease—a long nose, heavy brows over bright blue eyes, vertical lines where the brows so frequently frowned, yet so electric a personality that he was described as appearing at times like a man and at times like an angel. He is easy to visualize, so many Jews of today seem to fit the description. He was subject to constant physical pain and torment and probably suffered from epilepsy; but he was possessed of enormous energy and an indomitable will.

It is held that he boasted a genealogical descent out of the tribe of Benjamin and some apparent kinship to King Saul, but this is trimming after the fact. By Paul's time, such genealogies had been abandoned, nor had tribal records of Benjamin and Simeon been kept for hundreds of years. It has also been claimed that he was a leading Pharisee and had studied with famous Pharisaic rabbis, but his preaching is almost devoid of the tenets of Pharisaism. He was a man of extraordinary brilliance and inventiveness, and much of what he taught and what became basic tenets of Christianity was the result of his own syncretism or his own invention. Most likely, he was highly pragmatic, and like most great teachers he constantly adapted his views to conform to the objective situation.

Underlying most of his thinking was a concept very like the ancient dualism of the Persians, the endless struggle between light and darkness, right and wrong, good and evil— a view which Judaism had abandoned centuries before.

It was said that Paul played a part—at least as an unmoved observer—in the stoning of Stephen, one of the followers of Jesus, and that he carried out other acts against the disciples of Jesus; but this is probably a colorful invention after the fact; the fact being that before his conversion, Paul disliked or despised both Jesus and his followers. Certainly this dislike or aversion to the cult of Jesus played a role in the mystical experience that brought him to Jesus—or to his mind's conception of Jesus. In a vision, he saw Jesus and was fired and dedicated to his own missionary role. Thereafter, enduring great privation and physical pain, Paul preached all over the Greek-Roman world during a period variously estimated between fifteen and twenty years. He was martyred in Rome, but when he died he left behind an already unshakable structure.

There is great uncertainty as to the dates of Paul's writing and preaching—even as there is to his life. It is accepted that he was killed some time during the seventh decade of the Christian era, in one of the anti-Christian persecutions carried out under Nero, but no one can even properly estimate the date of his birth. Since he was an adult at the time of the death of Jesus, Paul was probably over fifty, perhaps over sixty when he died. The bulk of his writing and preaching was done during the last twenty years of his life.

Before we examine the geographical and political framework in which Paul labored, it is worth examining precisely what he taught and how it differed from Judaism.

Judaism (in some measure as we know it today) had taken shape both mystically and philosophically among the great Pharisaic rabbis. Its mystical content—as opposed to the complex metaphysical polytheism of most pagan faiths—consisted of its rejection of dualism. The God of Hillel and the rabbis was not one; He was all. The struggle for monotheism over a thousand years had been accomplished, and Jewish thought had passed beyond simple monotheism to a sense of God as being a total presence in the universe. Every Jew had a direct relationship with the Almighty, as did every human being; the Jew differed only in that his responsibility was greater, his burden heavier. He had been chosen, not for reward, but for the mysterious purpose of God, which purpose could be neither questioned nor explained. In order to fulfill this purpose, the Jew must live within an ethical and ritualistic framework. This framework was not exclusive. Any human being could enter it, but once he entered he must take on the *berit*—the contract between the Jew and his God. And he must assume this *berit* in the sense of its utter directness and simplicity; since the Jewish concept of God was direct enough to be defined in two words, *reason* and *love*. Man and God, life and God could not be separated. The Jew believed that man was good, life was good, God was good —a faith that permeated the Jewish existence and was able

to survive all the grief, misery, and persecution that life provided. This combined with a sense of the sacredness and
holiness of all life and particularly of human life. The Jew
had become, out of the logic of his religion, a pacifist; and the
followers of Jesus were filled with love and pacifism, not because they were Christians, but because they were still
Jews.

Paul preached a very different religion indeed. Whereas
Rabbi Hillel believed that the basic and true worship of God
was to "love thy neighbor as thyself," Paul preached that only
acceptance of Jesus, blindly or otherwise, could bring man
to salvation (salvation being a concept nonexistent in Judaism).

Paul defined man as basically evil (via the original sin of
Adam and Eve). Paul preached that the natural, healthy
impulses of the flesh were evil, filthy, controlled by Satan
and dedicated to sin.

Paul preached immortality as the reward for the acceptance of the divinity of Jesus—heaven for Christians, hell for
all others. Man was not to be judged by his actions but by his
pronouncements.

Paul substituted the concept of grace (Christian faith) for
the ethical code by which a Jew measured all his acts.

Paul condemned the pursuit of reason (the *logos* of Philo)
as "folly" and embraced a world outlook that was committed
to metaphysics and superstition.

Paul defined the Jews as "vessels of wrath, fit for destruction" and thereby embarked the Christian religion upon its
ultimate obsession—the hatred and destruction of the Jew—
a program of mass murder and hate under the guise of religion that had never appeared before on earth, that was to last
for almost two thousand years, that is still with us, that has
provoked the murder of untold millions of human lives in a
manner so fierce, so senseless, so malignantly cruel that it will
brand mankind with shame so long as he exists on earth.

Paul began the destruction of the Pharisaic concept of
total toleration, as expressed in Hillel's gentle dictum: "Do
not unto others as you would not have them do unto you."

This dictum, the outgrowth of the very ancient Jewish reverence for the stranger or foreigner and the laws Jews made for the comfort and protection of foreigners—this dictum was turned on its head by Paulinism to read: "Do unto others as thou would have them do unto thee," which became the Christian apology for righteousness and proselytism.

───────•─•─•─•───────

After his vision of Jesus, Paul's guilt at his earlier persecution of the followers of Jesus—or his dislike for them—must have played a role in his developing hatred for his own people. Yet at the beginning of his mission, it was to the Jews that he turned. Only when he had failed with the Jews did he become apostle to the gentiles.

He failed because he never truly comprehended the nature of Judaism. He was too full of his own vision and purpose, and there was good reason for that vision and purpose. The social and religious framework of the ancient world was crumbling under the power and greed of Rome. The Romans took over thousands and thousands of small family holdings, turning them into great latifundia, or plantations. The Romans wanted cash, and to get cash they had to produce cash crops.

This drive on the part of Imperial Rome to set up slave plantations and produce cash crops was accomplished in a number of ways: through taxing the small holder out of existence—as in Palestine; through drafting the small holder into the army; through expropriation and through conquest and punishment. Thus lands formerly producing wheat and vegetables could be turned to the production of wine and olive oil and particularly sheep products, wool and mutton.

Pagan religion in the Mediterranean world was basically a household and family matter, the household gods and crypt being basic to worship. As the small holder vanished, so did his possibility for worship—and the morale of society began to disintegrate. Not only the peasant-turned-slave, but also the Roman-citizen-peasant who remained free but landless and became a part of the urban mass, faced a future of hopelessness and moral disintegration. And the slaveowner, the Roman citizen of standing or wealth, he too was enmeshed in the tragic moral collapse of ancient society. The household gods perished; the ancient city gods succumbed to Roman imperial edict and the elevation of emperor to god. Ancient man could not exist without religion, and in the empty desolation of his life, he looked about him and saw in his world those curious islands of calm and security and profound belief—the Jewish communities clustered around their imageless synagogues.

During the first few hundred years of our era, the breakdown of ancient society was paralleled by man's desperate need for worship and belief. In that time, the best, the most thoughtful and sensitive elements of society—the householders, the scholars, philosophers, professional men, and small nobility—turned toward Judaism.

Judaism was not then a proselytizing faith, not then nor afterwards. The Jewish mission has never been to convert; if Jews see themselves philosophically as "chosen," they are chosen only in terms of their own ethical behavior. They bear witness to a religious belief; they do not presume to know or carry out the will of God.

Yet they do not close their doors. Those pagans who desired to become Jewish were welcomed into the Jewish community, and thousands entered it. The pagan women were instructed in the Torah, the first five books of the Bible, and they were "baptized" in the *mikvah*. The men and boys had to undergo the rite of circumcision—which is far less painful to an adult than might be imagined—as well as the Biblical instruction. The Jews—and many other Middle Eastern people—were highly skilled in the surgery of circumcision; they practiced excellent prophylactic methods, using strong, clear wine as an antiseptic, and as far as we know, cases of infection even in adults were extremely rare.

Nevertheless, in the Greek and Latin cities, there was a great fear of circumcision and a superstitious belief that it was a form of castration. In so unstable a society, impotence in men—along with every other form of psychosomatic illness,

as witness the examples cited in the Gospels—was quite
common, and the fear of circumcision contributed to the
impotence of some of the circumcised men. Not only was
this grist for the mill of anti-Semitism, but it kept thousands
of pagans who desperately wanted to be Jewish from taking
the final step. It did not matter that there was absolutely no
relationship between circumcision and impotence; fear alone
can create impotence.

Thus while thousands of pagans became Jewish, many
times this number found the step into Judaism too frighten-
ing in terms of their sexual superstitions. These people became what might be called *observer-Jews,* or *semi-Jews.*
They adopted many of the Jewish rituals; they worshipped
the unseen presence that Jews called God; they studied the
Greek version of the Bible if they were literate; they kept
the Passover feast and the Feast of the Lights; and in many
communities they were allowed to worship in the synagogue
when there was room for them. In many other Jewish communities they were urged to build synagogues of their own.
They had a relationship toward the Day of Atonement that
was comforting, but this, like their other religious practices,
never passed the transitional stage. These people were in
motion; the Jews neither included nor excluded them; each
presented to the other a new stage in religious history and
practice, an enormous problem that might have been solved
in time.

It was never solved, however, because one man of enormous energy entered the scene. That man was Paul of Tarsus.

––––––––– · ✦ ✦ · –––––––––

Nothing in the teaching of Jesus had changed or appreciably altered the situation described above. Those who followed Jesus were a small group, and their direction was toward Jews. Their manner was apocalyptic, not missionary,
and they preached the immediate second coming of the Messiah.

Paul was a missionary, and like all men of destiny, he sensed
truly the need and manner of his time. He not only lived in

a disintegrating society; he was aware of its nature—and he recognized the enormous hunger for belief. His first direction, quite naturally, was toward the Jews, and the Jews rejected him. They instinctively feared and disliked the system of belief that he was already structuring, the substitution of belief for acts, of faith for ethics, and his enormous promise of salvation and immortality. The Jews did not require immortality. The Jew was part of a continuum; the presence of God permeated his world and his being; his religious existence could be summed up in the words of the Twenty-third Psalm: "Yea, though I walk through the valley of the shadow of death, I will fear no evil: for you are with me." The preaching of Paul repelled them, especially his insistence that Judaism should give up the rite of circumcision and abandon its dependence upon the Torah as the rock of its being. Jewish thought was Pharisaic thought, and of Pharisaic thought Paul appeared to know nothing. Instead, his brilliant, nimble, creative mind was putting together a new religion of Judaism and paganism combined.

With his projection of Jesus as the literal son of God, Paul shattered the rabbinical monotheistic concept of God as the all-pervading presence of the universe. After the Jews had won their thousand-year-old battle against anthropomorphism and relegated such things to mythology, he revived not only God the physical father but God the physical son. It is understandable that the rabbis turned against him with contempt and anger.

And so, at a point, Paul realized that he had created not a religion for the Jew but a religion for the pagan—which perhaps had been his deeper purpose from the beginning—and with the pagan he was enormously successful, not only with the gentile but ultimately with the semi-Jew as well.

Paul offered a means of existence in a world that had made existence difficult indeed. To those pagans who suffered poverty, hunger, disease, and often enough slavery beyond hope, he offered a shining hereafter. "Only believe in Christ risen and the Kingdom of Heaven is yours." If life had become unbearable, Paul made death delightful, and instead of the onerous ethical demands of the Jew, he made a single, nonethical demand—belief. He explained away evil with original sin, and in a society where, among the very poor— which was most of society—infanticide had become a way of life, Paul preached the evil of sexual intercourse and the virtue of celibacy. In the deeply distressed world that he knew, Paul had something for everyone—except for the Jew.

He could offer the Jew nothing, for in a strange way, the Jew was not truly a part of this world to which Paul preached. The Jew was what Ludwig Lewisohn so aptly termed "an island within" and the Jew would continue as such an island. The Jewish world could no more disintegrate than God or the universe could disintegrate, and if life appeared to be utterly chaotic and purposeless, the Jew was content in the certain conviction that God was aware of purpose and that God saw meaning in the chaos.

Little wonder that this calm and dignity and certainty of the Jew should anger Paul. It angered any number of Roman writers of the times who found the quiet withdrawal of the Jew from the lunacy around him, the establishment of his own family fortress, intolerable. They felt in the Jew an attitude of controlled superiority, and while Suetonius found it admirable, Juvenal and most other Latin writers mocked at it. In fact, it would seem to me that Shakespeare took some of his information about Jews not from the literature of his time but from Latin writing of the first and second century.

Paul was enormously successful—indeed the most successful preacher and missionary of all time, for out of his own brilliant mind and enormous creativity and energy, Christianity was born. He took the hundreds of thousands of men and women who had looked upon Judaism with hope and admiration, and he gave them what he called a new Judaism, an easy, quick path to everything they dreamed of. And because their need was so great, they seized what he offered them.

And with all the rest he gave to the pagans, Paul gave them a curious concomitant—which was indeed an innovation. For the first time in man's history, a religion was created with a built-in hate, a holy incitement to murder and destroy, namely anti-Semitism. Paul did not invent anti-Semitism. It was as old as the Jews, and basic to it was envy and resentment, resentment of what was seen as Jewish superiority, envy of the fact that the Jews constituted a brotherhood beyond tribe or nation, an island, a walled region that closed off the world, a way of life that was always different. But this anti-Semitism was without an ideology; it was a reaction of human envy and resentment, and the Jews had learned how to live with it. Pauline anti-Semitism was something else entirely; it was ideological and religious; it was woven into the whole metaphysical fabric that Paul created.

Paul did not preach the fanciful accusation that the Jews had killed Jesus, murdered God. He lived during the awful years of the Roman procuratorship in Judea, and people knew only too well who had killed not only Jesus but all the thousands who were crucified during that time; but he did preach hatred of the Jews, and he did connect that hatred with the intrinsic practice of Christianity. He laid a foundation that would condemn his own people and the people of Jesus as well to a continuing nightmare of almost two thousand years, a nightmare of endless murder and persecution.

Of course, Paul did not know this. He only knew that those he loved best and valued most had rejected him, and because they rejected him, he in turn rejected and hated them.

————•—•—•————

The exact date of Paul's death is uncertain, given by various authorities as somewhere between the year 60 and the year 68. During that period, the Sicarii revolt had already broken out, and if Paul was involved, even to the extent of preaching the gospel of a leader of a former insurrection, it might have led to the actions taken against him by the Roman authorities. Paul left behind him a monument and achievement that few men in history have equaled—namely, the Christian Church.

Until the death of Paul—and in certain places, as in Palestine, long afterwards—Christians did not distinguish themselves from Jews; they were simply a sect of the Jews who believed apocalyptically in the second coming of Jesus and the immediacy of the Judgment Day. The nature of apocalyptic thinking is to believe in the immediacy of the Kingdom of God—and from the time of Alexander Yannai onward, conditions were intermittently so awful that many of the poorer Jews engaged in one sort of apocalyptic thinking or another. There was a plethora of minor apocalyptic prophecy —so much so that nothing in the preaching of Jesus could have been strange or untenable to a Jewish audience. (That is, if we remember that all of the four gospels postdate the fall of Jerusalem, and that the earliest, Mark, is probably closest to what Jesus actually preached.) That a group of Jews in Palestine believed that their leader was the Messiah and would return could not have been offensive, since this desperate hope would arise again and again among the Jews.

Even outside of Palestine, the early Christians called themselves Jews and thought of themselves as Jews. Paul drove the first wedge between Christian and Jew, but so long as the early Christian was persecuted by Imperial Rome, the Christian did not turn upon the Jew. He needed the Jew too desperately. It was only when Christianity became the official state religion of the Roman Empire that the separation of Jew and Christian was complete, and anti-Semitism became one of the foundation stones of the new religion.

There is apparently no foundation for the claims by some Christian writers that the Jews mistreated or rejected these early Christians—quite to the contrary, the Christians depended upon the Jews during their years of persecution. Already, by the end of the first century of our era, the Jewish Diaspora consisted of an international brotherhood with roots in every city of the Mediterranean and Middle Eastern world. This was a unique world brotherhood of warmth and embracing love. Jews taken captive were bought out of slavery by this brotherhood of Jewish communities; Jews were sheltered, housed, fed—often passed on from city to city to whatever place might be best for them; and this brotherhood did not exclude the Christians. Again and again, Christians were saved from death by Jewish bribes; and thousands of Christians were bought out of slavery by Jews—just as Jewish influence and Jewish money were used to prevent the destruction of the Christian synagogues (or churches as they came to be called). During these early years, Christians were regarded as Jews by Jews—a condition that lasted into the fourth century in some cities of Asia Minor.

Through the years, by diplomacy and payment, the Jewish communities had won unique privileges in the Roman Empire. Jews were exempt from military service and they had many other privileges, such as freedom from the obligation of emperor worship. (Many of the Latin writers of the time note this with scorn.) The early Christians shared the Jewish hatred of war and looked upon idolatry with the same horror —if anything, with more horror—for they were converts and intensely apocalyptic in their thinking; but unlike the Jews, they had no specific exemptions. In their necessity they turned to the Jews, nor were they rebuffed. They were hidden in Jewish homes, taken to safety on Jewish ships, fed and sheltered by Jews—not in singular instances but over a time of three hundred years by the hundreds of thousands.

It is of no credit to the Christian Church that it erased these years, so that the murderous attitude of so many Christians toward Jews, in the centuries that followed Rome's acceptance of Christianity, might not be softened by any memory of Jewish mercy and loving kindness toward Christians. Even during the long years of persecution of Christians, the Christian Church nursed anti-Semitism, took from the Jews with one hand and taught hatred of Jews with the other. The early Church fathers, Origen and Jerome, for example, were torn between their respect for Jewish virtue and their anger at the intransigence of the Jews in regard to Pauline teaching.

So as the years after the death of Paul passed, Christians grew in strength and numbers and increasingly dedicated themselves to the dissemination of hatred of that people from whom not only their Savior had sprung, but all the other initial founders and leaders of their church. This anti-Semitism was restrained and tailored to a form that would not cut off Jewish help, and thereby it was held in check.

By the end of the second hundred years of our era, the persecution of Christians by the Roman establishment had lessened very considerably. In many cities, Christians, by virtue of their industry and interdependence, had become the ruling force, and in such places pagans submitted willingly to baptism. Early Christianity was charitable toward converts; they still followed the Jewish practice of feeding the hungry; and they were elastic in their missionary zeal. The condition of the pagan world only worsened, and in their increasing misery and hopelessness, people turned ever more readily to Christianity.

By the time of the Emperor Constantine, Christianity had won the tacit approval if not the total commitment of the most viable and thoughtful section of the Roman Empire's population. The need for Jewish help had been lessening over the third hundred years of our era; now it ceased.

———————

The Emperor Constantine's full name was Flavius Valerius Aurelius Constantinus. To Jew and Christian alike, he was the most important Roman emperor. He was born in the year 274 and he died in the year 337. He was proclaimed emperor in the year 306, and he won his first campaign against his rival, Maxentius, in the year 312—by virtue of the fact that Christians sided with him, that Christian regiments fought for him, and that Christian centurions led his legions. He went into battle against Maxentius with crosses on many of his legions' standards, and on his battle flags, here and there, was the anchor and the fish, symbols of Christianity. Needless to say, Maxentius lacked similar support.

Constantine set aside all persecution of Christians and admitted them to his court at the very beginning of his reign. When he defeated the Eastern Roman Emperor Licinius, he established full equality for Christians, and shortly thereafter he began a cautious and politic repression of paganism. By the nineteenth year of his reign (325), he called together the first ecumenical council at Nicaea. Four years after this, he began a series of legal actions which expressed his hatred for the Jews.

In the year 329, Jews were forbidden to perform the act of circumcision on slaves who wished to embrace Judaism. They were also forbidden to own Christian slaves, although Christians were permitted to own both Christian and Jewish slaves.

A year later, all people in the Roman Empire were forbidden to convert to Judaism. For any who did convert, the death penalty was prescribed.

The death penalty was specified for all Jews who taught the Torah to gentiles or encouraged gentiles to embrace Judaism.

Jewish converts to Christianity were promised certain privileges and rewards.

The death penalty was prescribed for any Jew who married a gentile. All intermarriage was forbidden, unless the Jew converted to Christianity. The Jewish woman as well as the Jewish man would suffer death for intermarriage.

Judaism was referred to in imperial pronouncements as the *secta nefaria* or the *secta feralis,* namely the "unspeakable religion" and the "bestial religion." And Christianity was installed as the official religion of the Roman Empire.

As a final touch, Constantine reinstituted the ancient command of the Emperor Hadrian, issued after the Jewish uprising of Bar Kochba, which forbade any Jew to set foot in Jerusalem.

So it was done, and Christianity was established in the Western world in the holy hatred of Judaism—a hatred that would exact from the Jew suffering beyond description, untold millions of lives, and a river of blood.

PART SEVEN

the Diaspora

Jesus said to the Jews: "You are the salt of the earth, and if the salt should lose its taste, with what can it be salted?" There was a double meaning here; not only did Jesus see the Jews as a measure for the purpose of mankind, but his simile referred also to the Diaspora (Greek for "dispersion") of the Jews, already half a millennium old in the time of Jesus. Subjectively, Jews used the Hebrew word *gola,* which means "exile"; for in the Jewish mind the Diaspora was only tentative, a brief interval interrupting the Jewish continuity in Palestine, a momentary but necessary departure. Even to Jews born in the Diaspora, with ten or twenty generations of Diaspora Jews behind them, the interval was momentary. Even after two thousand five hundred years of the Diaspora, it was still temporary; and the peculiar, undying hatred for the Jews of the Christians, which drove the Jews so fiercely from place to place, from city to city, from country to country, increased this feeling of intermittency. And from time to time through the centuries, the Moslems joined in—lest the Jew assume an attitude of complacency in Moslem lands.

In fact, if we assume that Jewish history—apart from myth and legend—begins with Moses about thirty-three or thirty-four hundred years ago, then the period of the Diaspora is almost three times as long as the period without the Diaspora —accepting the condition that prevailed so long of double existence, a large Jewish population in the Diaspora and in Palestine as well.

This makes the writing of Jewish history complex. It cannot be told chronologically; it must be something woven out of time and space, backward and forward. For example, even a brief outline of the Diaspora, as follows, can only be an introduction to the pattern of life—totally unique—which the Jews alone evolved:

The Diaspora properly begins in the sixth century before our era, although before then there was probably a small Jewish community in Babylon. Most of the Jews carried into the Babylonian exile did not return to Palestine. Over the next hundred years, they were scattered among all of the Persian Empire's 127 provinces. During the same period, the Jewish colony in Egypt came into being and grew furiously.

Meanwhile, there is every evidence that Judaism was strong in the Phoenician ruling class, and there were probably Jewish synagogues in most of the Phoenician cities, Carthage, and cities in Spain as well—even possibly in Cornwall in England.

During the time of Greek hegemony, Jewish communities arose in practically every Greek city of consequence—in Syria as well as in the Mediterranean area. Roman relations with Judea brought the Jews into the Latin cities; in both Greek and Latin cities, there were great numbers of converts. During the Imperial period, synagogues arose in Gaul, in France, and in parts of Germany, again with a constant flow of converts.

Through the Middle Ages, Jews pushed north and their communities were established in England, the Low Countries, and throughout Germany. Persecution drove the Jews up the Baltic coast and into Poland and the Ukraine.

Meanwhile, Spain had become one of the great Jewish centers of the world, until persecution drove the Spanish Jews out of a land they had lived in far longer than the Christians who expelled them. Most of the Spanish Jews went eastward to Greece, Turkey, and North Africa. Some of them came to the New World.

In the nineteenth century intolerable conditions in Eastern Europe started a great mass exodus of Jews to the United States—where there had been an earlier flow of Spanish and German Jews. This exodus also turned to Canada, South Africa, and Australia.

And finally, the madness of Nazism drove a new immigration of Jews into their ancient homeland in Palestine.

This, above, is the most cursory outline of the Diaspora over a period of two and a half thousand years. I present it only in order that the reader may have a sort of map to refer to as he reads what follows.

———•••———

There is no parallel in all of human history to the Diaspora of the Jews. Here a people scattered across the face of the earth maintained itself for two thousand years without either a homeland or a common language. They maintained their religion, their identity, their separateness, and above all, their communal brotherhood—so that a Jew from one community might enter another community in another nation two thousand miles away, yet be immediately accepted and among his own.

This meant a unique type of social organization. It is not possible to comprehend either the Jews or the Diaspora without seeing this community organization in detail. By and large, it retained its social and organizational form from Roman times to the nineteenth century. Certain minor adaptations were always necessary, for it is not conceivable that precisely the same social organization could exist in North Africa and in England, for example. But the differences are far less than one might imagine, while the uniformity is remarkable. Space permits only a single, general description— yet from that description the reader will have a view of the whole.

Firstly, the Jewish community in the Diaspora established its own standard of citizenship. As befitting a people so mobile, full citizenship in the community was granted to anyone who had lived there for more than a year. Half-citizenship was granted to those who had lived in the community less than a year but more than thirty days. Transients (with specific rights) were those who remained in the community for twenty days or less.

The community was ruled by the consent of those governed —the governing board being a committee, usually of seven or twelve members. This committee conducted all matters pertaining to the broad life of the community. It supervised the collection and distribution of funds for charity (considered the most important function in every Jewish community), imposed taxes according to Jewish custom, and passed on all sale or purchase of community property. It issued police regulations and had a sort of watch to enforce them. It supervised all general functions, commercially and socially, specified wages, fixed prices, and checked on true weight and measure, and usually appointed *shohets,* men trained in the ritual slaughter of all meat used in the community.

If the community was in an area or state where Jews acknowledged a *nasi* (the old Hebrew word for "prince," but now come to mean a rabbi of wisdom and distinction) this *nasi* would appoint a *dayyan* (Hebrew for "judge"), who was in himself a sort of supreme court, empowered to make final judgment in all financial disputes, even to overruling the committee.

All criminal cases, political disputes, religious disputes, contractual disputes were tried before a court of three rabbis, who were usually appointed for life. Such was the honor of this office that no wage was paid to the rabbis. If the rabbi on this court had no other means of support, his minimum necessities were provided.

In addition, there was the *habar,* a distinguished citizen, associated with the court. He would act where arbitration was necessary.

Minyan is the Hebrew word for "number," and it refers to the number 10 and specifically to the ten Jewish males over the age of thirteen needed for communal prayer. Jews in the Diaspora could not consider themselves a community unless they had ten males of *minyan* age. But if they had these ten males, then communal status was imposed upon them by Jewish law, and they were obligated to build a synagogue, the affairs of which were then placed in the hands of the *rosh ha-keneset,* Hebrew for "head of the congregation." He might be assisted by one or several men who were called *shammash,* Hebrew for "one who serves." The liturgical and ritual part of the synagogue was under the supervision of the *hazzan* (this was the title of one of the ancient Temple functionaries in Jerusalem), who conducted the service, often together with a rabbi and a member of the congregation called a reader. In later times, the *hazzan* sang the liturgical chants, frequently assisted by a choir of young male voices.

In every case, the synagogue was the social heart of the Diaspora community. Where the community was large and rich, the synagogue might be a magnificent building, rivaling the Christian churches in splendor, but such cases were rare. In most instances the synagogue was a modest, inconspicuous building—sometimes a hut, a shed, a place of hiding, sometimes a secret place built underground with a secret entrance.

So important was the role of the synagogue as a school that in Yiddish-speaking areas the common term for synagogue was *shule*, the Yiddish word for "school." Education was primary in the Jewish community, regarded as a holy injunction placed upon the Jewish people, for surely they were the "people of the Book," the Torah and the Neviim and the Ketuvim—namely the Pentateuch, Prophets, and Hagiographa—as well as the Talmud; their very relationship to their God depended upon their literacy. Throughout the two thousand years of the later Diaspora, it is estimated that never were less than 90 percent of the Jews literate and often enough well over 90 percent—a record matched by no other country or people; and one must consider that during most of those two thousand years, by and large, literacy in Christian countries was limited to the clergy and a handful of others.

School attendance was compulsory in the Jewish community. Most often, the synagogue was the school; but sometimes an attached building was used. The teacher, a person of dignity and respected in the community, had to be married and over forty. He was permitted to teach no more than forty children; after that, a second teacher had to be added—and a third when the number of children reached fifty.

Charity was a prime and built-in function of the community. Without the Jewish community's absolute dedication to charity the Jews could not have survived the Diaspora. Two types of charity were performed in every community—first, a fund for the resident poor, who were always fed and sheltered, and second, a fund for transients; for the Jew was very much a wandering Jew during this period, and every community considered that a sacred, religious injunction had been placed upon it to feed and shelter every Jew who came to the community or passed through it. (In the bleak periods of the Middle Ages, thousands of Christian poor, serfs, and peasants, facing starvation or death from the cold, went to the Jewish ghetto for food and shelter. The Jewish commitment to charity was not on a basis of race or religion; everyone who begged had to be fed, and rarely were the Christians turned away.)

There were other funds, funds for the care of orphans, funds for holidays, like Purim, clothing funds, burial funds, and funds for publication.

As the community matured, it possessed itself of social material necessary to Jewish life: scrolls of the Torah and the rest of the Bible; libraries to house the books of the Talmud; funeral facilities; *mikvahs*, that is, ritual baths; slaughterhouses; special lodging houses for travelers; courtrooms; community centers for marriage and for *bar mitzvah*. (This custom—the bringing into the community of the thirteen-year-old male—may not have existed before the thirteenth century, but there seems to be some evidence for dating it back to Roman times.)

Such, in rough outline, was the Jewish community of the Diaspora. Naturally it varied, for it existed under a host of different conditions; and once a condition of freedom prevailed, as in various places from the eighteenth century onward—earlier in a few places—the Jewish community merged into the non-Jewish community to some extent.

———·◆·◆·◆·———

With the Jew forbidden by the Catholic Church either to own farmland or to engage in the basic industry of the time, agriculture, he had to turn to commerce and finance. It is true that the ghetto or closed Jewish community provided all the services necessary; there were Jewish butchers and shoemakers and coopers and carpenters and weavers and tailors and goldsmiths and coppersmiths and woodcutters and anything else that went to service a viable community; but Jew served Jew by and large (goldsmiths, jewelers, and physicians were an exception to this), and the raw materials, whether food or iron or wool or cotton, had to be bought outside of the community and brought into it. (It is also true that the Jew had far more freedom and latitude of choice in Moslem lands, but more and more through the centuries did the balance of Jewish population swing toward the Christian world.)

Anti-Semites would have us believe that the Jews survived through moneylending, but this is hardly the case. The Jews lent money, but Catholics lent far more.

The one indispensable service the Jews performed—and which made it possible for them to survive the early Diaspora —was to keep open the routes of trade. Trade and commerce have been called the bloodstream of civilization, and again and again, in those parts of the world cut off from trade with other nations civilization ceased to progress and turned in upon itself in a process of decay.

I have already described how Jewish supercargoes on Phoenician ships and a network of Jewish synagogues maintained trade routes all over the ancient world. The position of the Jews in Babylon made them a pivot in the trade between the Near East and India and China. When Mohammed, in the early part of the seventh century, put into motion that gigantic Arabian sweep called Islam, he cut the world in half and interposed the Moslem power between the Christian West and the Moslem and Buddhist and Hindu and Zoroastrian East. While there were moments in history when the Moslems turned upon the Jews, there was never the built-in hatred characteristic of Christian anti-Semitism, and by and large relations between Jew and Moslem were on an almost compatible basis. But the Moslems had an implacable hatred of the Christian—the uncircumcised infidel—and the Christians hated Moslem power and regarded it as their first enemy.

In this situation, East-West trade could not be conducted by either Christian or Moslem, and the main currents of it fell to the Jews. There is an interesting historic mention of Charlemagne watching a ship sailing into Narbonne, deciding at first that it was a Jewish ship and then changing his mind and guessing that it was a Norman ship. The Jews moved their ships and caravans everywhere, and like the Swiss of today, they survived because the other nations needed them. They were the only people of the West, for example, who could bring goods in and out of Rhaga, which was near Teheran in Persia, and which was the great commercial and caravan center for Armenia, Chorasan, and Chazaria.

A fascinating note about Chazaria, a great stretch of land to the southeast of Kiev in Russia; the Chazars were a virile and wealthy nomad people, great sheepherders who produced wool and furs that were probably the equivalent of today's Russian broadtail and Persian lamb. Only through Jewish caravans could this fur reach the markets of the Low Countries and Germany, where it was so urgently needed. Through their intercourse with the Jewish merchants, the entire ruling class of the Chazars turned Jewish and submitted to circumcision. Eventually, the Chazars were defeated by the Ukrainians. How many of them survived in the Jewish communities of old Russia, we do not know.

By the middle of the ninth century, the Jews had almost monopolized the trade between Asia and Europe; and while this monopoly was not to prevail very long, it was an enormous source of Jewish wealth while it lasted. Consider this interesting passage, translated from an Arab book by Ibn Khordadhbeh, which was written in the first part of the ninth century:

They [the Jews] take ship in the land of the Franks, on the Western Sea, and steer for Farama. There they load their goods on the backs of camels and go by land to Kolzum [Suez], which is five days' journey over a distance of twenty-five farsakhs. They embark in the Red Sea and sail from Kolzum to Eltar [the port of Medina] and Jeddah [the port of Mecca]. Then they go to Sind, India and China. On their return, they carry back musk, aloes, camphor, cinnamon, and other products of the Eastern countries to Kolzum, and bring them to Farama, where they again embark on the Western Sea. Some make sail for Constantinople, where they sell their goods to the Romans. Others go to the palace of the King of the Franks to place their goods.

Sometimes these Jew merchants, when embarking in the land of the Franks [probably Marseilles] in the Western Sea [probably the Mediterranean], make for Antioch. Thence they go by land to Al-Jabia and Al-Hanyya [on the bank of the Euphrates River]

where they arrive after three days' journey. Then they take
sail on the Euphrates for Baghdad. Then they sail down the
Tigris to Al-Obolla. From Al-Obolla [where they put their goods
on shipboard] they sail for Oman, Sind, Hind and China.

These different journeys are also made by land. The [Jewish]
merchants that start from Spain or from France go to Sous
Al-Akca [Morocco], and then to Tangiers, whence they march
to Kairowan and the capital of Egypt. Thence they go to
Ar-Ramla, visit Damascus, Al-Koufa, Baghdad and Bassora. They
cross Ahwaz, Persia, Kirman, Sind, Hind and arrive at China.
Sometimes they take the route behind Rome [Constantinople],
and passing through the country of the Slavs, arrive at Khamlij,
the capital of the Chazars. They embark on the Orjan Sea [the
Black Sea], arrive at Balkh [this is in Afghanistan, so an enormous
overland journey is involved], betake themselves from there across
the Oxus, and then continue their journey toward Yourt, Toghoz-
ghor, and from there to China.

What a picture this evokes!—Marco Polo's journey, taken
via several routes not once but a thousand times through a
thousand years by Jewish merchants who considered these
vast distances a matter of course. This book of Ibn Khordadhbeh was titled *A Book of Roads* and it served as a road map
and traveler's guide in his time. It is the most explicit early
record we have of Jewish caravan and shipping routes, and
the curious boldness with which these Jewish merchants
traveled where none else dared to evokes a moment almost
a thousand years later, in the early history of the United
States.

Then, in the immediate post-Revolutionary period, there
were established communities of Sephardic Spanish and Portuguese Jews in New York City and Philadelphia. Just a tiny
trickle of Polish Jews into America had begun, and these
uncouth, bearded, Orthodox Jews rather embarrassed the
Sephardic Jews, who had been in the country for several hundred years and who were both wealthy and elegant. The
Spanish Jews fulfilled their obligation toward their Polish
brethren by providing them with a pack animal and a store
of peddler's goods—and then sending them westward to
trade with the Indians. The Polish Jews carried no firearms

and they were forbidden by religion to eat game—yet they went boldly among the Indians, traded for furs, penetrated beyond the Canadian border, beyond the Mississippi, and to many places where no white man had ever been before.

———•—•—•———

The wool and fur (black lamb) of the Chazars were valued highly in all the Scandinavian countries, and thus by the twelfth century the Jews had set up terminal trading posts on the Baltic among the Lithuanian heathens, who welcomed their presence. The Vikings, considerable merchants in their own right, would put in with their ships, buying the wool and fur eagerly, and in turn selling the Jews precious ambergris, on which they had a sort of monopoly, salted fish, which not only the Jewish communities but all of Middle Europe valued highly, and gold ornaments that they had looted. (The ambergris was important to the perfume industry, which at times during this long period of the Diaspora was a Jewish monopoly.) So large was this trade with the Vikings that during the twelfth and thirteenth centuries, more Arabic than native coins were used in the Scandinavian countries. The importance of this trade was increased by the Crusaders' violent destruction of Jewish trade centers in southern Europe.

Up to the time of the Crusades, the spice trade between East and West was practically a Jewish monopoly; but with the coming of the Crusades, the Venetians—who hated the Jews bitterly as business rivals—broke the Jewish monopoly and then carried on a systematic campaign of destruction against Jewish traders. Jewish-owned ships were pirated and sunk, and port after port in Italy, France, and England and the Low Countries closed its docks to the Jews and refused to handle Jewish merchandise. A few large Jewish traders managed to carry on in the port of Marseilles—and even own ships—until the fifteenth century; but long before then the enormous bulk period of Jewish trade was over.

Jewish trade, however, was by no means over. Instead of being able to command ships and caravans, the Jewish merchant was limited to what he could carry upon his person. (An exception to this was the silk trade. Since the Jews had the best connections with China, Christians frequently made agreements for the use of their shipping—which would change flags on approaching Moslem territory. This went on until the beginning of the eighteenth century.)

As to what the Jew could carry on his person that had enormous value—there were two items, jewels and the essence of perfume. Then, as today, fine essence came from the East, and in a time of poor plumbing and few baths (Europe during the Middle Ages and the early Reformation was probably the most unwashed place of all time) good perfume was of great value. An ounce of essence would bring enough to keep a family in food for a year. Pearls were also highly valued, and the Jews had access to the pearl regions of the East.

And of course there was moneylending. From the time of Constantine to the time of the French Revolution (and afterwards in Germany and Russia) the Jews lived in fear—persecuted as no other people in man's history. They had no way of defending themselves except by their wits. They were nowhere powerful enough to engage in armed combat—nor did they have any desire to engage in combat. Their aversion to war and violence became a central peg in Christian hatred, for during the period of the Diaspora all standards of nobility and worth were measured by skill in violence.

Therefore, money and the use of money became a central means of survival. But all the legends of Jewish usury, gobbled up and dispensed by an army of writers more credulous than informed, failed to take into consideration one thing, namely—if the Jews were such usurers, why did the Christian come to them for money? The answer is shockingly obvious—because the Christian moneylender asked ten to twenty times as much interest as the Jew.

It is worth dwelling a moment on this question of usury and the Catholic Church. Historians seem to take it for granted that because the Church frowned on usury no Catholic practiced moneylending. But the Church frowned far more strongly upon adultery, murder, incest, and a number of other practices that were far less profitable than money-lending, yet were nevertheless carried on relatively widely.

Unlike adultery and the rest, moneylending was not a serious sin, if indeed it was regarded as a sinful practice at all by the Church. Church historians tend to be rather confusing upon this matter. We know that the First Council of Carthage in the year 345 declared that the practice of usury was "reprehensible," yet neither "venial" nor "mortal." Various Church pronouncements during the twelfth and thirteenth centuries were harsher in their condemnation of usury—but the very fact that they dwelt upon it is an indication of how widespread the practice was. Actually, the Catholic Church was less troubled by moneylending than it was by the common Christian practice of exacting from the borrower 200 percent interest, and 300 percent, and in many cases, 400 and 500 percent. Often enough, the interest was endless—until total ruination of the debtor took place. In fact, the Christian practice of lending money to destroy the borrower had become so widespread—especially in Italy—that the Catholic Church was caught in a very troublesome dilemma. The Church realized that no economy, even the most simple, could remain viable if moneylending ceased, and the Church also knew that no one in Europe (not even the Holy See) would or could lend money without some rate of interest. Thus the Church tried to be more severe toward large usury and less severe toward minor usury. In the eighteenth century, the Church formalized its position by declaring for a reasonable rate of interest as a nonsinful practice.

Within the above framework, from the fourth to the nineteenth century, Christians in need of funds turned to Jews. As bitter and strange as it is to write this, they turned to Jews for the following reason: Jewish moneylenders were ethical; Christian moneylenders were not. The Bible speaks of usury (specifically, an excess of interest) as follows: "He has lent on usury; he has taken interest; he shall surely not live, having done these abominations." (The quote is from

Ezekiel 18.) It also should be noted that the Hebrew word for "usury" is *neshek*, meaning literally "a bite," but used more often as a bitter term of contempt.

If a duke or a prince or some pettier nobleman turned to a Jew for money, he recorded it in terms of hatred and resentment. As always, it was not what the Jew did but the fact that a Jew did it. Of course, it must be understood that the legal rate of interest in the Middle Ages and early reformation period was quite different from today. France in the fourteenth and fifteenth centuries permitted a legal rate of interest varying from 40 to 50 percent per annum. King John of England, in 1360, allowed legal interest to 80 percent. In most parts of Spain 25 percent was legal and in Portugal the legal maximum was one-third of the loan, or 33⅓ percent. In Italy, the legal limit varied from 30 to 70 percent. In Germany and the Low Countries, the variation was anywhere from 20 to 80 percent per annum, each small state fixing its own rate of interest.

A German ruler of one of the many petty German states, in need of funds, could go either to a fellow princeling, who would charge 300 or 400 percent, or to Florence or Venice, where he would pay anywhere up to 200 percent, to Holland, where he would pay a round 100 percent, or to the Jews, who would charge anywhere between 10 percent and 50 percent. So with less lordly borrowers. Sometimes the Jew was repaid, sometimes not. For him, moneylending was a dangerous game, but once the roads of commerce were closed to him, he had no other choice. How ironic that Shakespeare should have chosen Venice for his drama of Shylock; for Venice was the heart of Renaissance usury. The great Venetian bankers, known throughout Europe for their great wealth and cold hearts, rarely charged less than 100 percent interest. Jews —because the Venetians regarded them as such dangerous commercial rivals—had not been permitted to live in Venice as a community before the German conquest of 1509; and when Shakespeare wrote his play, their role as bankers was utterly insignificant.

The Jew was forced into the role of moneylender, but his

role was a minor one. However, he created a curious atmosphere of trust and decency in a field that was essentially without either. For this reason, toward the closing years of the Diaspora, Jews were able to establish international banking houses of great importance.

Even as they had once used a common ethic as a means of international banking during their great commercial period, so as moneylenders they began the use of international financial paper; and through mutual trust, they were able to draw upon each other over great distances and thus avoid the transfer of funds in generally troubled times.

———————

There was another social and economic service that the Jew performed in the Diaspora. The Jew was physician to the Christian and Moslem world.

Jewish medicine is very ancient, and because so much of Jewish medical knowledge was incorporated into the Talmud, Jewish medical knowledge has a peculiar continuity. In a world where literacy was almost confined to the clergy, Jews could read and write; and among a very large proportion of the Jews, perhaps well over 50 percent, Aramaic as well as Hebrew and local tongues were readable if not conversational. There has never been among Jews, as among Christians, an absolute prohibition against the dissection of the human body, although autopsy was frowned upon. The practice on every male child of circumcision, minor operation though it is, gave the Jews a beginning for operative techniques. In Biblical times, they had already mastered many operations, particularly those arising from war. They knew the use of wine as an antiseptic, and they had drugs (unfortunately forgotten) which they used to induce unconsciousness during operations. In Talmudic times (the beginning of our era) they performed Cesarean sections and numerous other operations (possibly appendectomies), wrote books on techniques of surgery, made excellent surgical instruments, observed heart disease and tried vainly to save perforated hearts through surgery.

In ancient times, all meat killed for use by Jews had been considered as a sacrifice to Yahweh. Part was for God, part was allowable as food; and the religious nature of such slaughter made it mandatory that only animals in perfect health be used. Considering that there were always poor Jews and hungry Jews, to condemn an animal as unusable because of disease was no light matter, and the slaughterer (*shohet* in Hebrew) had to be a trained and frequently well-educated person. However, so many fights arose between prudent housewives and *shohets* that every rabbi began to have experience with diseased animals. By and by, these diseases of animals were catalogued and described in great detail, as a guide to *shohets* and consulting rabbis; and since so often dissection followed diagnosis, the Jewish rabbis advanced, for the first time in history, what afterwards became the basis for all internal medicine: namely, the theory that surface symptoms were the result of internal tissue changes and degeneration—and that by careful cataloguing, a specific symptom could always be related to the same internal set of conditions.

Not even Hippocrates—whom Jewish doctors studied diligently—had ever advanced a theory so revolutionary.

The art of suture was highly advanced among the ancient Jews and they appear to have been able to deal with such complex problems as severed veins and arteries. So far as I know, no complete, thoughtful study of forensic medicine among the Jews has ever been made, but even a cursory glance at Talmudic material is fascinating and rewarding. We find that the rabbis discuss vegetable growth on the lungs (*zemahim* in Hebrew)—related to adhesion of the lungs to the thorax. A Rabbi Jacob, two thousand years ago, discusses injury to the spinal cord. A nameless editor of the Mishnah (Talmud) disagrees with his findings. A long, detailed discussion in another part of the Talmud on pathological changes in the lungs. A discussion of pus, its color, meaning, function—remarkably correct. A scholarly discussion of the liver, its diseases, its function, degenerative and pathological changes. Deformities, malfunction of limbs,

causes of retarded growth, brain disease, head shapes related
to brain malfunction—all this in the Talmud—not superstitious prattling but precise, scientific observation, catalogued
cases, conclusions drawn on the basis of dozens of cases of
recurring symptoms. In the Mishnah—the curious wedding of
religion and medicine—we have a catalogue of 140 pathological conditions which, in accordance with the Torah,
make a man unfit to perform any religious services in the
temple.

Venesection, bleeding by leeches, cupping, extirpation
of the spleen, reduction of diseased testicles, intubation of
the larynx, removal of dead flesh in suturing of wounds,
reposition of organs where abdominal viscera protrude
through a wound, removal of nasal polyps, plus a whole
science of treatment of sword and spear wounds—all this
was a part of Jewish medical practice as long ago as the time of
Jesus.

I could go on and on, detailing the areas and curiosities of
Jewish medical practice, but there is space only to emphasize
the point that for almost two thousand years the Jew was
physician to the Christian and Moslem world. Not only did
this occupation of the Jew play a part in his life during the
Diaspora; to some measure, it was a basic reason for his survival. The physician is a neutral. You do not kill a physician,
for in doing so you may take your own life. Regardless of
belief, the physician is respected today. During the Middle
Ages he was almost worshipped.

The Jew was not the only physician, but by and large
during those long middle years of the Diaspora, he was the
only physician with real skill, knowledge, and scientific
method. He was this because he had several things the gentile
physician lacked. He had linguistic access to the Talmud and
to specific Jewish medical books written in Aramaic. He was
literate. And he was apprenticed to Jewish doctors who had
been apprenticed to other Jewish doctors. In a time where
the sexual-religious attitude of Christianity made any serious
investigation of the human body and its functions impossible,
there were no medical colleges or training places worthy of

the name. The average Christian physician was a barber-
undertaker, unwashed, superstitious, and deplorably ignorant.
Understandably, the gentile physician sneered at Jews and
avoided them; and the Jews were hardly eager to disseminate
their knowledge—even if it had been possible to do so. It
was not specifically Jewish knowledge. The writings of Hippocrates were an integral part of Jewish medical knowledge.
His books had been translated into Arabic, but an amazing
number of Jews were literate in Greek and Latin as well as in
their local tongue and in Hebrew and Aramaic and Arabic—
and later in Yiddish and Ladino. The very fact of the enormous illiteracy of the Christian world—apart from the clergy
—made the training of Christian physicians almost impossible.

A word must be said concerning a translation of Hippocrates, which was done by the Jews. Up to the fifteenth century, there were three great medical authorities; firstly, Hippocrates, who is considered the father of modern medicine.
He was a brilliant Greek who lived during the tragic Pel-
oponnesian War—the time when the Jews, returned from the
Babylonian exile, were attempting to rebuild Jerusalem.
Whether there was any intercourse between him and the
Jews we do not know. Secondly, there was Galen, another
brilliant Greek, who practiced and wrote during the third
century. And thirdly, there was the Arab Avicenna, who
practiced during the eleventh century and who wrote the
famous *Medical Canon*.

By the twelfth century, however, classical Greek was almost unknown in Europe, since the Church language was
Latin, and Greece itself was eastward oriented and strangely
isolated from Europe. Hippocrates and Galen were practically unknown in Europe to anyone but Jews. Greek-language
copies of their books were very rare. However, the Arabs had
translated Hippocrates and Galen into Arabic, and Avicenna
wrote originally in Arabic. The long Jewish presence in Arabic Spain and North Africa, as well as in Palestine, had made
Arabic a familiar language to Jews. It was linguistically related to Aramaic and Hebrew, and Jewish doctors spoke and

read Arabic even as American physicians spoke and read German in the nineteen-twenties—to have access to medical
knowledge. Not only were the three major works in Arabic,
but at least twenty Spanish and African Jews had written au-
thoritative medical books in that language.

Even earlier than the twelfth century, Jews began a systematic program of translation of medical books from the
Arabic into Latin and Hebrew, beginning with Hippocrates
—who was presented to Europe not in classical Greek but in
Latin, via Jewish translators. Galen and Avicenna and numerous other medical works were also translated into Latin by
Jews—and thus Europe was given at least a basis for medical
training. But meanwhile, the Jew was physician to Christian
Europe.

———————•◆•◆•◆•———————

In Baghdad and other Moslem centers, from the eighth to
the twelfth century, the Jewish physician was an honored
equal with his Arab colleague. Since educated Arabs were
able to read Aramaic, Jew and Arab used the Talmud as a
source. In Baghdad, there were fine hospitals and medical
institutions, colleges and research centers, where Jew and
Arab worked and taught together. Indeed, the first medical
college and hospital as such was founded by the famous
Harun al-Rashid. In Spain, during the same period, there
were hundreds of Jewish physicians, many of them famous
throughout the Moslem world. One of these, Abu Merwan,
wrote his own medical treatise, going far beyond Hippocrates
and developing the Talmudic method of checking surface
symptoms against postmortem pathology. We have the names
and dates of almost one hundred Jewish physicians in Moslem
Spain who made important contributions to the practice of
medicine.

When the Jews were expelled from Spain in 1492, the
Jewish physicians went to a number of places—Italy, Africa,
Greece, Turkey, Portugal, Germany, Holland, and the New
World. We have some evidence that Jewish physicians
sailed with Columbus, and the Portuguese royal house and

nobility would hardly cough without a Jewish physician in attendance.

In Italy, we have an almost uninterrupted procession of Jewish physicians from Roman times to modern times. Jews played a central part in the establishment and conduct of the medical school at Salerno, and from the ninth to the thirteenth century Jewish physicians were in attendance in every city in Italy. Not without opposition. Gentile physicians fought an unremitting campaign of hate and slander against their Jewish colleagues. Jewish physicians were murdered, killed by mobs, burned at the stake on occasion. But most often, with the use of his wits and skill, the Jewish physician of the time survived and did well for himself.

In France, the Church and Christian physicians managed to have all sorts of laws and restrictions passed against the Jewish physician; but the French nobility, engaging for hundreds of years in chopping, spearing, hacking, and varied types of mutual mayhem, preferred to ignore the laws and be repaired, operated on, and sutured by Jews rather than by gentiles. Their will to survive was so much greater than their anti-Semitism that the Jew endured. Even when he was expelled by dictum, the nobility managed to maintain him by hook or crook. In France and England and Germany, the nobility circumvented the mass expulsions of Jews by having mock baptisms, by lying about their Jewish doctors, hiding them, and disguising them. Many a Jewish community was saved by the need for its physicians.

Plague was the great danger to the Jewish physician. Europe of the Middle Ages was periodically swept by plagues and contagion, bubonic plague, varieties of influenza, cholera, smallpox, and so on, and when one of these struck, the Jewish doctor was always accused of poisoning the wells and starting the plague. In fact, medieval Europe developed a psychosis on the subject of Jews poisoning wells. In 1348, in Vienna, a Jewish physician was executed for starting a plague. This was an occupational hazard.

Thousands of Jewish physicians worked in Germany. From the first historic mention of Jews in German lands, we have

records of physicians and their work. Jewish physicians introduced the art of medicine into France, Germany, England,
and the Low Countries. In Belgium and Holland, Jewish
physicians were treasured, and of course among the Polish
and Lithuanian heathen they were regarded as saints, workers of miracles. Even in Christian Poland and Lithuania,
Jewish physicians were respected and given many special
privileges.

Two other things contributed to the special position of the
Diaspora Jews in medicine. First, right up to the fifteenth
century, the Jews had a sort of monopoly of the drug trade
with the eastern countries; and second, they were the pharmacists of Europe, with unique knowledge in the art of preparation of medicine, particularly for the relief of pain.

PART EIGHT

the Wandering Jew

China was not the first land of the Diaspora, since the first synagogue was built there somewhere between the year 60 and the year 70; but it is certainly the most romantic and intriguing. How long ago China became known to the Jews is a matter of dispute, but there is reason to believe that Jewish merchants either made their way to China or bartered for silk at an exchange point at the time of the Babylonian exile, that is, about five hundred and fifty years before our era, over twenty-five hundred years ago. We have reason to think that the Hebrew place-name *Sinim* refers to China.

Two Moslem travelers, in *An Account of a Journey Through India* (translation published in London in 1733), remark that "the Jews have been settled in the Empire of China from time immemorial." A number of early writers connect these Chinese Jews with the "Ten Lost Tribes," but since these are more or less a myth, the supposition is quite specious—as are all of the thousand and one tales of the so-called Lost Tribes of Israel. A Catholic missionary, Father Brotier, interviewing Jews at the famous synagogue of Kai-Fung-Foo in the nineteenth century, quotes the Jews as stating that their ancestors had settled in China at the time of the Emperor Han Ming-ti, which would place that date of settlement between the year 58 and the year 76. Sulaiman, a romantic Jewish traveler of the ninth century, is in accord with this and gives the date as the year 65. Jews have a dogged cultural faithfulness to historic dates, and I feel that the above dates can be believed.

Graetz, the great Jewish historian, chooses the year 231—but his sources on this subject are limited. That these people came by sea from India is more or less acknowledged, and we know that very early in their history, perhaps as early as the fifth century, the Jews were known everywhere in China by a common name—*Tiao Kiu Kiaou,* which meant "those who practice venesection," from the Jewish custom of removing certain veins from meat before it was eaten. The Jews were highly esteemed by the Chinese, and China was one of the few areas on earth where the Jews were never persecuted.

Marco Polo refers to the powerful "commercial and political influence of the Jews in China," but by his time they had been large factors in the silk and jade trade for over a thousand years. Indeed, in dealing with Cabala and mysticism in the Jewish religion, it is tempting to speculate upon the contribution of the philosophy of Taoism. Later in this book, we will attempt to clarify the question of Cabala and its role in Judaism, but Taoism is in a sense the historic if not the geographical companion to it. Taoism derives in part from Lao-tse's book, *Tao Tê Ching*—or so legend has it. Lao-tse lived during the sixth century before our time. It is more than a coincidence that his life dates appear to parallel the life dates of the Buddha and the Unknown Prophet; and since we cannot absolutely date any of the three, we must perforce wonder at the fact that a century encompassed all of them. Each was in a sense the stimulating force of a great world religion, and the three tendencies are remarkably related to each other; all of them partake of pantheism, which regards the entire universe as one with man, and all of them are gentle, reflective, and eminently civilized. I am not for a moment indicating that the Unknown Prophet (Deutero-Isaiah) founded any clear new method of Judaism, yet he infused it with the gigantic mystery of man and the universe and laid the basis for the mystical direction that much of Judaism would take. In time, he was separated by two thousand years from the *Baal Shem-Tov*, the founder of Hasidism—whom we will discuss later—but in thought he was a logical father, as were Lao-tse and Buddha. There is not space here to go into the entire background to this, but a curious reader will find it a fascinating page in the history of man's thought if he cares to pursue it.

The Jewish merchants who traded for so many hundreds of years between China and medieval Europe were understandably secretive about both their routes to China and the Jewish presence in China; so it was not until the seventeenth century that Catholic missionaries brought back to Europe stories about the extraordinary and beautiful synagogue in Kai-Fung-Foo, the capital of Honan Province. This synagogue has since been destroyed by fire, but let me quote from the translation of a marble inscription in the Chinese language, found at the synagogue before it was destroyed:

Seventy families came from the Western lands offering tribute of cotton cloth [Indian cotton] to the Emperor, who allowed them to settle at Peen-lang [Kai-Fung-Foo]. In 1163, the synagogue was erected by a certain Yen-too-la; and in 1279 it was rebuilt on a larger scale. In 1390, the Jews were granted land and additional privileges by Tai-tsou, the founder of the Ming dynasty. In 1421, permission was given by the Emperor to Yen-tcheng, a physician greatly honored by him, to repair the synagogue, incense for use therein being presented by the Emperor. In 1461, the synagogue was destroyed by flood, but was restored by a prominent Jew. New copies of the Law were procured; and the table of offerings, the bronze vase, the flower vases, the candlesticks, the Ark, the triumphal arch, the balustrades, and other furniture were presented to the synagogue by prominent members of the Jewish community.

Another inscription, set up in 1512 by a Chinese mandarin, reads in translation in part:

Those who practice this religion [the Jews] are found in other places than Peen [Kai-Fung-Foo]; but, wherever they are met with, they all, without exception, honor the sacred writings and venerate Eternal Reason in the same manner as the Chinese, shunning superstitious practices and image worship. These sacred books [the Bible] are studied by all men, kings and subjects, parents and children, old and young. Differing little from our [the Chinese] laws, they are summed up in the worship of Heaven [God], the honor of parents, and the veneration of ancestors.

Again, the inscription adds of the Jews that they "are highly esteemed for integrity, fidelity, and a strict observance of their religion."

The above is fascinating. "Eternal Reason" is possibly a translation of the Chinese word *Tao*, bringing back thoughts of the "Logos" of Philo, the "ethical all" of Hillel, and the "wind from God" in the Torah in the first paragraph of Genesis.

Philo was an Alexandrian Jew whose life span paralleled

that of both Hillel and Jesus. A profound thinker and an interesting historian, his writings are most important for their literate and sensible reflection of the main currents of Jewish thought of the time, that is, such Jewish thought as was dominant in the Diaspora. His theory of the Logos is related not only to Taoism and Buddhism but to Cabala as well, and this, of course, is understandable.

Philo taught that God created the world (and the universe) from matter that has no beginning or end, the matter of eternity, and that God does not directly move, change, or influence the earth. He proposed a *force*—the "ray of creation" in some systems, the "wind from God" in the Torah, the "Holy Ghost" of the early Christians—which he called the Logos, which mediated between God and man, and he taught that little-understood injunction of Jesus, "the Kingdom of God is within you," namely, peace through meditation and thereby the "enlightenment" of Buddhism or the *satori* of Zen. He taught that Judaism was the most perfect vehicle for enlightenment, and that the Torah opened the way for this personal union between man and God, being an allegorical path for man to salvation.

However, the impact of the West upon China touched the ancient Chinese Jews as well as the Chinese people and culture. By 1900, the old Jewish community of Kai-Fung-Foo numbered only 140 people. There was no social community, no synagogue, no leaders. The synagogue had burned in 1870, and this evidently struck a death blow to the community. (The burning was accidental.) In a similar manner other ancient Chinese Jewish communities were disintegrating. Today, although we know of some recent settlement of Jews in China in the post-Hitler era, the old colonies have disappeared.

————•◦•————

India was one of the first lands of the Diaspora, but hardly ever a very important one. Jewish intercourse with India goes back almost as far as Jewish history, and there is no question but that the Phoenician-Jewish ships that King Solomon sent out of the port of Elath traded regularly with India. Certainly, the religious influence of India was important not only to Judaism but to all the Mediterranean world. However, India is unique in the continuity of Jewish settlement there; as I mentioned earlier, I have myself spoken to Jews in Bengal whose ancestors came there before the Maccabean war, or well over twenty-one hundred years ago. Curiously, India has (or had until recently) two kinds of Jewish communities: the white communities, which are European in origin, and the black (or native Indian) communities, whose origin is lost in antiquity.

The Cochin Jews do not claim so early an origin as the Bengal Jews, their tradition holding that they came from Judea after the destruction of Jerusalem by the Romans. They purchased a large piece of land, remained apparently independent and undisturbed for many years, and then in 1524 were attacked by the Moslems, their synagogue and property burned, their numbers decimated.

Most of what we know directly about early Jewish presence in India comes from the journals of one Benjamin of Tudela, a Jew born in Tudela in the north of Spain. Benjamin set out in 1165 on a remarkable eight-year journey, going just about everywhere that a man of that time could go. In his journal, he speaks of the Jews of India as people indistinguishable from the native population in appearance. He describes them as good Jews and honest people, honoring the Ten Commandments and the word of the Torah. He states that they study Talmud and observe ritual and high holidays with devotion.

———•◆•◆•———

Persia was indeed the first land of the Diaspora, but in a broader sense the Beni-Yisrael had their beginning in what would be the Persian Empire, which as an area included ancient Babylon and the great desert of Mesopotamia where the Beni-Yisrael wandered as nomads. As long ago as the time of King Solomon, there was active trade between the Jews and the cities of the Tigris-Euphrates bottom, particularly the

seaports in the neighborhood of ancient Ur. Although the
site of Ur is now miles from the sea, in Solomon's time the
alluvial silt deposit was probably a hundred miles north of
where the Persian Gulf shoreline is today. The Jews traded
with the cities of Babylonia both by sea and by land; but in
those days (the seventh, eighth, and ninth centuries before
our era) synagogue Judaism had not yet been born, and it is
doubtful that any permanent community of Jews existed.
Since Jew and Babylonian spoke almost the same language,
it is probable that there were always Jewish merchants in
residence there.

With the Babylonian exile, Jews became an institution in
Babylon, and the Jewish community established there existed for hundreds of years. With the end of the exile, Cyrus and his Persian horsemen conquered the whole great
area that was once Babylonia and Assyria and a dozen lesser
countries, and ushered in the long period of Jewish peace
under the Persian rule. This was the time when the synagogue began to take shape, and when synagogue Judaism
(or Rabbinical Judaism as it is better called) matured under
the guidance of the Pharisees.

The Book of Esther speaks of 127 provinces of the Persian
Empire where Jewish communities of one size or another
existed. The Jews in Persia at that time were respected,
wealthy, educated, and not without power. They were engineers, road builders, guides—the international authorities
in a vast international empire. They had a large community
in Susa, the capital, and they had influence at the court.

When the Parthians, the fierce, wild horsemen of the
northern highlands of Persia, overthrew Greek rule in so
much of the old Persian empire (in the third century before
our era), it was almost as if they had already a relationship
of time and knowledge with the Jews. (Or perhaps there
was something in nomad people that knit them to Jews, as
witness the Chazars.) In any case, thousands of Parthians
became Jewish. Their war chiefs became Jewish, and unlike
the Chazars, thousands of their common people also became
Jewish. The Roman hatred of the Judean Jew was not un-

connected with the fact that Parthia was the one nation Rome could not defeat, that legion after legion, for over three hundred years, was wiped out of existence by the Parthian horsemen, and that Parthia was so much Jewish.

It was in its union with Parthia that Jewish life flourished most highly in Babylon, that the Babylonian Talmud was put together into its final form, that the overland routes to China and India were opened, that Jewish synagogues were built all over Persia—and that a sort of golden age of Diaspora Jewry, not unlike a later age in Spain, came into being.

But like the horsemen of Chazaria, the horsemen of Parthia could not prevail. When the Persians regained power, the hold of the Parthians was broken, and with the defeat of the Parthian cavalry came the defeat of the Jews. From the downfall of Parthia until the Arab conquest of Persia in the years 641 and 642, the history of the Jews in Persia is vague, fragmentary, definite only in the fact that at times the Jews were severely persecuted.

The basis for this persecution, curiously enough, was the similarity rather than the difference in the two religions. There is even some speculation that primitive Zoroastrianism merged with Judaism, and that out of this syncretism historical Zoroastrianism emerged. Like Judaism, the Persian religion was highly ethical, with strong monotheistic elements, but unlike Judaism it was dualistic, whch caused the Jews to turn against it.

It is important here, I think, to say a few words about dualism in its religious sense, the more so since the absolute rejection of dualism is an element which distinguishes Judaism from Christianity as well as from Zoroastrianism. Dualism is that element in religion which sees the universe, and the world, as a dueling ground for the forces of good and evil, God against Satan, the angels against the devils, the forces of light against the forces of darkness, the lurking devil, the lurking temptation, the sinfulness of sexual acts, etc. All of this is firmly rejected by Judaism, which has always regarded dualism as childish nonsense. Two and a half thousand years ago, the Unknown Prophet put it simply and magnificently—Isaiah 45:7—"I form the light and create darkness; I make peace and create evil; I am the Lord that doeth all these things."

In this case, it was not the Christians but the Zoroastrians who persecuted the Jews, holding that Judaism was a mockery of Zoroastrianism.

Those Jews who survived supported the Moslems, and with the coming into being of the Eastern Caliphate at Baghdad, a new life in Persia began for the Jews.

Then, in the seventh and eighth centuries in Persia, the various communities of Jews were centrally governed by an exilearchy (*Resh Galuta* in the Aramaic that was the common tongue of the Jews of Persia), a form that had come into being during the Babylonian exile and was to a degree hereditary. Also important in the unity of these Persian communities was the *Gaon,* a sort of princely rabbi, unique to this area and lasting into the eleventh century.

Up to the twelfth century, the Persian Diaspora was unique. It was most closely and directly connected with the Jewish past, tracing its existence to the year 538 before the beginning of our era, when the first caravan of exiles from Jerusalem reached Babylon. Unlike all other regions of the Diaspora, the Persian communities of Jews had an absolute continuity of language: the ancient Aramaic, the language of Palestine, the language of Babylon, the language of Jesus continuing as its own language in most Persian communities up to the fifteenth century and in a handful of communities up to our own time.

But like other parts of the Eastern Diaspora, the communities of Persia lacked the viability of the Mediterranean and European communities. Perhaps this was because the Moslem persecution that began in the sixteenth century was so cruel; perhaps because the whole area of Persia was in a sort of stasis and decay, or perhaps the great mercantile gifts of the Jews were no longer needful in Persia as they were needful in the West, where a new, vigorous, and burgeoning era of mercantilism had begun. The Jewish nation, which numbered perhaps a million, perhaps twice that in the eleventh century, has shrunk to about eighty-five thousand at the most recent count. Almost fifty-seven thousand Persian Jews have gone to Israel since the State of Israel came into being. Those who remain in Persia (the Iran of today) are for the most part quite poor and depressed.

Egypt is as old as Persia in Jewish history, and if the Beni-Yisrael came out of Persian grasslands, the Levites came out of Egypt and possibly were Egyptian in origin. The gigantic figure of Moses, who put his stamp so indelibly upon the Jews as a people, is intimately connected with Egypt and even bears at least part of a royal Egyptian name.

The Egyptians were a Semitic people—by language definition—and since their land bordered upon the land of the Jews, commercial and military relations were constant. There must have been Jewish trading centers in Egypt at the time of Solomon; but there, as in Persia, the conditions necessary for Diaspora Jewry had not yet arisen.

Yet with the Persian conquest of Egypt a Jewish colony arose there shortly after the Babylonian exile began; and there may well have been some military Jewish colonies before then. From the time of the Persian conquest in 525 before our era to the defeat of the Persians by Alexander the Great and his conquest of Egypt in 333, various Jewish colonies and trading centers were established, none of very great importance. However, in these two hundred years, the synagogue concept of Judaism matured, and by the time of Alexander there were a number of synagogues in Egypt.

(It is worth noting again that the development of synagogue Judaism, as opposed to centralized Temple-worship in Jerusalem, was an integral part of the Diaspora. It might be argued that other people, such as the Greeks, had their own diasporas; but not in similar religious circumstances, that is, monotheistically with a single sacred city, a single Temple, and a single God of a high place. Each Greek city had its own deity and its own temple or temples; denied this, Jewish philosophy moved toward the omnipresent deity, whose place and house were everywhere and anywhere—thus the synagogue, which was not a temple but simply a community building used for prayer as well as for other communal matters.)

Under the Ptolemies, a great flowering of Jewish life and culture arose in Egypt—particularly in the city of Alexandria. In their enchantment with all things Greek and in their warm and mutually affectionate relationship with the Ptolemies, the Jews poured into Egypt, making their center of population in that Greek seaport city. During this period many thousands of Greeks were converted to Judaism—willingly and without any proselytizing pressure—and Alexandria became, to a very large degree, a Jewish city. Not again until the Jewish immigration into New York City in the twentieth century would there be such a population of Jews in any one city—close to a million at the height of Jewish-Alexandrian wealth and culture. (This figure is disputed by some, but it is generally agreed that the population was over four hundred thousand.)

The language and culture of these Egyptian Jews were Greek—but Greek in terms of their Judaism. There they produced the Septuagint. There the Jewish books of the Wisdom of Solomon, the Sibylline Oracles, parts of Maccabees were composed—also, as far as we know, the first lay literature of the Jews, plays, epics, secular poetry, comedy, and anecdotal material. Philo, the Jewish philosopher, was part of this culture.

The Jews of Alexandria became wealthy and powerful. In its beauty, in the richness of its buildings and the majesty of its synagogues, the Jewish quarter of Alexandria became one of the wonders of the ancient world.

Just prior to the Maccabean war, a high priest who had been driven out of Jerusalem by the Seleucids, Onias by name, convinced Egyptian Jews that it would be right and proper to give up the Temple in Jerusalem and to build a rival "true" Temple at Heliopolis in Egypt. The Egyptian Jews put up the money and the Temple was built—and con-

Nuno Gonçalves, from The St. Vincent Altarpiece / 15th-century Jew holding the Torah / Picture Collection, New York Public Library

Ambur Hiken, photographer / 14th-century Spanish Haggadah (Passover service) / Library of the Jewish Theological Seminary of America

Chappel / Deputation of Jews before Ferdinand and Isabella of Spain / Picture Collection, New York Public Library

Title page of the account of an Auto da Fe, which ironically means act of faith — the euphemism for the sufferings of the Spanish Marrano Jews who were burned to death for back-sliding. Eleven died in this one in Lima, Peru, 1639 / Picture Collection, New York Public Library

Disputation between Jewish and Christian doctors of the law, Germany, 1483. Such disputations of theology were quite common during the Middle Ages. Note the conical hat worn by the Jews (right) in accordance with the decree of the Lateran Council of 1215. By the 15th century, however, it is less likely that the wearing of the hat was enforced than that the Jews wore it out of their own choice and desire for separateness / Picture Collection, New York Public Library

After the recognition of the doctrine of Transubstantiation by the Lateran Council of 1215, the Jews were accused of defiling the sacred elements of the Catholic ceremony of the Mass in order to renew the agonies of Christ. Time and again, over hundreds of years, this charge led to the persecution and murder of Jews. This 1477 series of woodcuts from Passau, Germany, shows Jews in the act of desecrating the Host and then their arrest and execution by Christians / Picture Collection, New York Public Library

1614 massacre of the Frankfurt Jews. The attack on the ghetto was led by Vincenz Fettmilch, who called himself the "New Hamaan of the Jews" / Picture Collection, New York Public Library

Memorial Book of the Frankfurt Ghetto; its entries date from 1626 through 1900 / American Friends of the Hebrew University

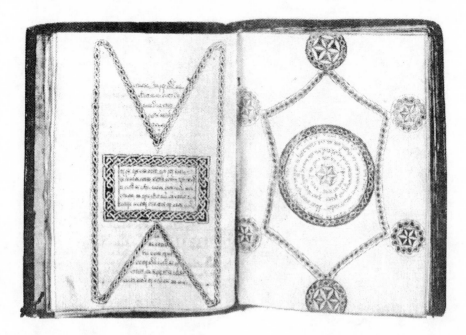

Ambur Hiken, photographer / Astronomical tables of Jacob Bonet (ben David, ben Yom-Tob Poel), Perpignan, 14th century / Library of the Jewish Theological Seminary of America

Ambur Hiken, photographer / Siddur Tsafarat with commentary, France, 14-15th century. In the center of the page is the Prayer Book according to the old French rite, with 14th-century commentary. In the margins is a 13th-century code of ritual law / Library of the Jewish Theological Seminary of America

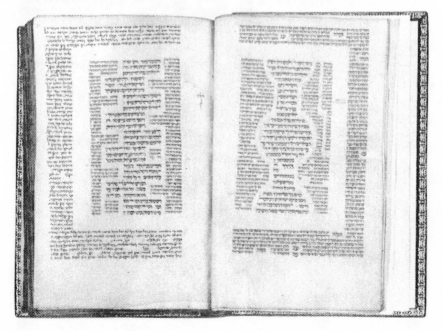

Rembrandt's paintings and etchings of Jews are particularly interesting because in almost every case he used Jewish models, that is, Jews resident in Holland at that time. He depicted these people with both fidelity and love. Above: "The Synagogue," 1648; below: "The Great Jewish Bride," 1653 / The Jewish Museum

Above: 17th-century sketch of a Jew (the man in a fur hat and robe) conversing with two gentiles in a Polish marketplace. The picture has been executed with surprising objectivity / Picture Collection, New York Public Library. Right: Portrait of Tobias Cohn, a Polish physician, 1652-1729, taken from the frontispiece of his Ma'aseh Tobiyah, published in 1707. Tobias was born in Metz, Germany, where his father, also a physician, had fled from Poland to escape persecution during the Cossack Revolution of 1648. In 1673, Tobias returned to Poland to receive his education at Cracow. Subsequently, he attended the University of Frankfurt-on-the-Oder (at the expense of the elector of Brandenburg) and the University of Padua. He practiced medicine for some time in Poland and then went to Adrianople, where he was physician to five successive sultans. For the last five years of his life, he lived in Jerusalem / Picture Collection, New York Public Library

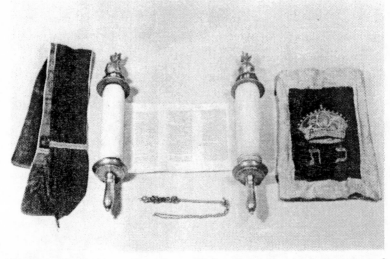

18th-century Torah scroll on silver rollers, with pointer, velvet wrapper, and velvet-and-brocade mantle / The Jewish Museum

Pair of Sabbath Candlesticks, German, 1752 / The Jewish Museum

German Kiddush cup, ca. 1680 / The Jewish Museum

19th-century cabalistic amulet made of tortoise shell / The Jewish Museum

Mohel knife used in circumcision, ca. 1720 / The Jewish Museum

In 1811 Napoleon emancipated the Jews of his newly created Confederation of the Rhine, making them full citizens. This German cartoon of the period mocks Napoleon's decree. Note the banner (carried by the Jewish soldier in the three-cornered hat) which depicts Christians pulling a plow for a Jewish farmer. The Tables of the Law on the end of the bayonet are an interesting example of the German imagination / Picture Collection, New York Public Library

Gottinean in Erlangen, photographer / 1860 portrait of Felix Mendelssohn-Bartholdy, the outstanding Jewish musical talent of the 19th century. The grandson of the great German Jewish philosopher, Moses Mendelssohn, Felix Mendelssohn ironically became a convert to Christianity — as did many German Jewish intellectuals of the time / The Jewish Museum

Portrait of Alfred Dreyfus by an unknown artist. The Dreyfus Affair of the 1890's had far-reaching consequences for the Jews. On the one hand, it stirred up virulent anti-Semitism; on the other, it forged Jewish solidarity / The Jewish Museum

Right: Julius Meyer, a Jewish Indian trader of the 1870's, with some of his friends and customers / Picture Collection, New York Public Library

Left: Letter from George Washington addressed to the Hebrew Congregations of Philadelphia, New York, Charleston, and Richmond / Picture Collection, New York Public Library

Left: Title page of The Jew, *the first Jewish periodical in the United States, published in 1824 / Picture Collection, New York Public Library*

Right: This handbill dates from the 1880's, when an unsuccessful attempt was made to establish a Jewish agricultural colony in the Dakota Territory / Picture Collection, New York Public Library

THE JEW;

BEING

A DEFENCE OF JUDAISM

Against all Adversaries,

AND

PARTICULARLY AGAINST THE INSIDIOUS ATTACKS

OF

ISRAEL'S ADVOCATE.

עֵת לַעֲשׂוֹת לַה' הֵפֵרוּ תּוֹרָתֶךָ
וְאֶעֱנֶה חֹרְפִי דָּבָר כִּי בָטַחְתִּי בִדְבָרֶךָ

It is time to work for the Lord; they make void thy law.
And I will answer the Blasphemer at thy word, for I repose I on thy words.
Psalm cix.

EDITED BY S. H. JACKSON.

NEW-YORK:

PRINTED BY JOHNSTONE & VAN NORDEN,
No. 1334, bowery-street.

רוז וומסץ ש׳ ײדישע פֿאַרמער קאָלאָ וועקסליער אין באָרלעא קאָאָנט אין אַמעריקא

RUSSIAN JEWISH FARMER SETTLEMENT WECHSLER
BURLEIGH COUNTY DAKOTA TERRITORY.

Portraits of four Jews who visibly affected and changed the course of human existence

Above — Left: Karl Marx. It should be noted that Karl Marx's father turned Christian. Marx himself departed from reason and rationality in his fulminations against the Jews / Wide World Photos

Below — Left: Leon Trotsky / Wide World Photos

Above: Sigmund Freud / Wide World Photos

Right: Alice Gutman, watercolor, 1953 / Portrait of Albert Einstein / The Jewish Museum

Left: A. Portnoff, bust, 1916 / Sholem Aleichem — the literary father of the Yiddish language and perhaps the most beloved Jewish author of modern times / The Jewish Museum

Right — Top: Frederic Remington / Jewish recruits in Russia, 1894. Many young Jews fled from Russia to avoid conscription / Picture Collection, New York Public Library

Right—Bottom: Jews bewailing the destruction of their synagogue, Sochaczew, Poland, 1890's / The Bettman Archive, Inc.

Below: A Jewish shtetel (village) in Russia near Zhitomir, very like the setting of many of Sholem Aleichem's tales / Picture Collection, New York Public Library

An old Jewish couple in Russia with a young boy who might be their grandson. Taken somewhere in the Jewish Pale of Settlement half a century or more ago, the picture evokes a time and way of life now gone forever / YIVO Institute for Jewish Research

A Russian cheder /
*YIVO Institute for
Jewish Research*

*Young Hasidic Jew in
doorway of bakery,
Warsaw / YIVO Insti-
tute for Jewish Research*

Jewish merchants in Czenstochau, Poland / The Bettman Archive, Inc.

A Jewish marketplace in Poland / YIVO Institute for Jewish Research

tinued to function until the Romans destroyed it in the year 71—when the Temple at Jerusalem was destroyed.

However, the Jewish Diaspora in Egypt was too large for the time and place. The half-Hellenized Egyptians resented the Jews, envied their wealth and power, hated their separateness and, if the truth be told, their arrogance. When the Ptolemies were overthrown by the power of Rome, a century of warfare between the Jews of Alexandria and the Egyptian-Greeks began. The Jews were rich, powerful, and they had their own armed forces, raised out of their own community. Their power and numbers shrank, but they managed to hold their own until the time of Christianity—when formal anti-Semitism replaced the intermittent anti-Semitism that they had combatted for so long.

Yet they maintained themselves as an important community until the year 415, when Bishop Cyril instigated a brutal mob movement against them. Thousands of Jews were slaughtered by the Christian mobs, and thousands more were given the choice of baptism or death, watching their wives and children blinded. Some chose death, but many more gave in and accepted baptism. Subsequently, most of those who had been baptized fled from Egypt to begin life again as Jews in another land.

When the Arab Moslems invaded and conquered Egypt in the year 640, the Jewish communities had shrunk to a few thousand people, poor for the most part and of no importance in the political life of the land.

Under the Arab rule, however, the Jews shook off the past, increased in numbers and wealth, and established a great Karaite center in Egypt. At this point, a word must be said of the Karaites.

Karaitism arose in Persia in the eighth century, a movement in Judaism that accepted the Torah, the first five books of the Bible, but rejected the Oral Law. In this, the Karaites were like the Sadducees of the Temple era. The Oral Law was a Pharisaic method of interpreting the Torah and carrying out specifically the broad commands; it was declared oral but meticulously learned and taught as a commitment of memory over several hundred years. Finally, it was written down as the Mishnah and incorporated into the Talmud.

The Karaites were never in the mainstream of Jewry, but always on the edge, yet they gained numbers and adherents in Persia and in Egypt after the Moslem conquest. Strains of Karaitism moved with the Jewish emigration north to the Baltic countries and to Russia. Denounced by many Jewish leaders, it was never actually specified as a heresy. The Karaites have many customs other Jews do not follow, and they reject many other Jewish customs, such as the *mezzuzot* (a bit of paper in a container on a Jew's doorpost, which says, "You shall love the Lord your God with all your heart and all your mind and all your might") and the *tephillin* (tiny boxes and leather bands, containing the same words as the *mezzuzot*, which an Orthodox Jew binds across his brow and upon his arms while at morning prayer).

Today, possibly three or four thousand Karaites survive in Israel.

The great Moses ben Maimon (better known as Maimonides) halted the spread of the Karaites in Egypt. Maimonides was born in Córdova in Spain in 1135, at the time of the Almohade conquest. The Almohades were fanatical Moslems who gave the people they ruled a simple choice between conversion or death. They destroyed most of the Jewish settlements in Moslem Spain, killing thousands of Jews and driving those who survived out of the country—ironically, into Christian Spain.

Maimonides' father fled with the family to Palestine—but it was the time of the Crusades, and Palestine had become impossible for Jews. When the Crusaders had captured Jerusalem in 1099, every Jew and Karaite in the city had been hunted down and murdered, often in a manner that beggars description. Western civilization has thrown up some odd specimens at times, but for sheer insane bloodlust and cruelty, the Crusaders are hard to match.

Some of the Christian prelates were understandably upset at this display of Christian love and charity, and they persuaded the leaders of the Crusade to extend toleration to the Jews who still survived outside of Jerusalem, reminding the Crusaders that this was once a Jewish city and that Jesus himself was Jewish. This "toleration" was trumpeted around Europe as an example of the "mercy of the Church," and it persuaded Maimonides' father to seek refuge in their ancient homeland after a long period of miserable wandering in North Africa. Moses was thirty years old when the family reached Palestine, and only a few weeks of watching the run-of-the-mill persecutions of the Crusaders convinced them that there was no hope for Jews in Palestine while the Crusaders remained. The family went on to Egypt, where they settled permanently.

By this time, Maimonides had already established himself as one of the most brilliant minds of his time. Fluent in Spanish, Arabic, Aramaic, Hebrew, Greek, Latin, and various dialects of North Africa, he was one of the prominent linguists of his era. He had read every medical book available, been tutored by some of the great rabbinical physicians, worked with Arab physicians and surgeons, and had already become, by the time of the family's arrival in Egypt, one of the famous physicians of that time—writing authoritatively on various branches of medicine as well as pharmaceutics.

The Egyptian Jewish community welcomed him both as a physician and as a rabbi. Within three years after their arrival in Egypt, Maimonides had become the spiritual leader of the Cairo Jewish community. He was thus a rabbi, a scholar, a famous physician, and a world authority on jewels, which he traded as the simplest and quickest means of supporting the family. By 1170, he was personal physician to the Viceroy of Egypt, but not exclusively so. His practice was large. He wrote many books, some on medicine, most on religion. His *Guide to the Perplexed* is perhaps the most famous of his works—and he had many opponents as well as supporters. He was one of the most remarkable men of his time, perhaps of any time. He was a man of great energy, personal beauty, and rare dignity. His struggle against the Karaites was in defense of Jewish unity, and by the force of his personality as well as his arguments, he broke their hold on any important section of Judaism. He died in his sixty-ninth year.

Many Jews have fondly referred to the two Moses, he who led the Jews out of Egypt and Moses ben Maimon, as two of the brightest jewels in the history of the people. In any case, the time of Maimonides was the moment—perhaps the final moment—of glory in the Diaspora of Egypt. From the twelfth to the nineteenth century, the Jews in Egypt lived perhaps more quietly than elsewhere in the world. For many years, the descendants of Maimonides exerted a sort of leadership. But the community dwindled, and revived in vigor only in the nineteenth century, when European influence in Egypt brought an immediate response from the Egyptian Jews—who took quickly to European ways and methods of trade and manufacture.

Understandably, considering their geographical location, Zionism was never welcomed by them. In spite of that, more than thirty-seven thousand Egyptian Jews have emigrated to the State of Israel. Thousands of others have gone to Europe and the United States. In 1947, the Jewish population of Egypt was almost one hundred thousand. Today, less than twenty thousand remain.

———•◦•———

Greece is best placed with the eastern Diaspora and can hardly be treated apart from Turkey, for Greek and Hellenized cities were scattered all over the Turkish peninsula and Greek islands lined the Turkish coast. Crete and Rhodes and Cyprus come into that grouping, and on the peninsula itself, Bithynia and Mysia and Lycia and Galatia and Pamphylia and Cilicia were some of the ancient areas. After the Moslem conquest, the separation between Greece and Turkey was more specific.

Between these two areas of Greece and Turkey, directly on the Hellespont that separated them, was ancient Byzantium, which became Constantinople and remained the eastern capital of the Roman Empire until its capture by the Turks in 1453. Constantinople must be treated as a separate entity, for it was a unique area of alternating hatred and re-spect for Jews—and of misery visited upon the Jews. But this was between Jew and Christian. Between Jew and Greek was something else entirely.

More than with any other ancient people, the Jews had a rapport with the Greeks. They revered the Greeks, admired the Greeks, copied the Greeks, produced such classic writers in the Greek language and culture as, for example, Philo, Aristobulus, and Ezekiel (not the prophet but the playwright). I have mentioned the Jewish-Greek relationship previously and only underline it here.

In his epistles, Paul of Tarsus mentions the many Jewish communities in the Greek cities. There was hardly a Greek city of size and importance without such a community, and for the most part, especially in European Greece and on the Greek islands, Jew and Greek lived together amicably. The two peoples shared very ancient memories and experience, and Josephus backs up the apocryphal Book of Maccabees in the claim that there was a mutual assistance and blood-brotherhood bond between the Spartans and the Jews since Jonathan Maccabeus. Scholars today are making interesting discoveries in linguistic connections between Jew and Greek, between Crete and ancient Judah, between Crete and main-land Greece; and some of these we have touched on.

One thing, however, seems clear—that ethnically Jew and Greek were apparently inseparable. (I have avoided the en-tire question of race, firstly because mankind is as mixed as an old fruit pudding, and secondly because racial designa-tion is less a science than a tool of bigotry. But even in this shady realm of ethnic specification, certain generalizations can be made about the Jews. They are—again with many exceptions—a Mediterranean people, which means simply that for the first twenty-five hundred years of their existence they mixed and intermarried with the various peoples of the Mediterranean world. The largest amount of this mingling has been with Greeks; and, from the time of Alexander the Great to the time of the Emperor Constantine, Greek was the second language of Mediterranean Jews, Aramaic being the first. Because of the religious injunction against idolatry, Jews in the old times were forbidden tó paint or carve the human face, and because of this we can only surmise what they looked like. However—as a matter of amusement—one can go to a museum and compare the Greek portrait sculptures with the Jews of today. Some exhibit a remarkable resemblance; others do not. The living people of the Mediterranean today are not distinguishable physically from the Jews among them, and that was likely the case in ancient times.)

There were no ghettos in Greece. The Jews in residence there were not driven and hounded. (This is the Greek peninsula, not Constantinople.) This, of course, was the case after the reign of the Emperor Constantine. By the ninth century, the Jews of Greece were famous for their cultivation of the silkworm, which they had brought from China. They were prosperous and they lived in peace. Pethahiah of Regensburg, an indefatigable German-Jewish traveler who kept an excellent journal of his travels in the Middle East, reports that there was a very large Jewish population in Greece in the twelfth century, possibly some hundreds of thousands. Benjamin of Tudela also was intrigued by Greece at about the same time, and he found large, stable Jewish communities in Corinth, Patras, Crisa, and Thebes. The Jewish community of over two thousand in Thebes was considered to have the best dyers and weavers of silk in Greece. The Greek historian Nicetas reports that the Byzantine emperors sent their buyers to Athens and Thebes and Corinth to buy Jewish silk, as did the German and French and Italian princes and barons.

In Greece as in many other places of the Diaspora, our information concerning the Jewish presence is spotty at best. But lives that are quiet, fulfilled, and prosperous do not invite special recording. That is reserved for the nightmarish interventions.

When the Spanish Jews were driven out of Christian Spain in 1492, Greece welcomed thousands of them. They added to the prosperity of the country and appear to have lived quietly and well. Then the question must be raised: What happened to the Greek Jews? By 1900, their numbers had shrunk to no more than fifty thousand. This increased somewhat during the twentieth century, but in World War II the Germans killed all but a few thousand of the remaining Greek Jews. Possibly, part of the great population of Greek Jews was absorbed into Christian Greece.

———— •••• ————

Constantinople, the Roman Empire in the East, was something else entirely, and if it proved anything, it proved that Jews can endure a great deal indeed. While a most important part of the Diaspora, Constantinople meanwhile—until the coming of the Arabs under Mohammed—ruled Palestine; and as we saw earlier, the Jewish presence in Palestine dwindled but never ceased. As has been previously mentioned, during the time of the Emperor Hadrian—the year 132—a Jewish leader in Palestine, Simeon Bar Kochba by name, raised up a hopeless revolt against Rome. It was put down savagely, and for the following two hundred years, the Jews of Palestine licked their wounds, put war and resistance away, and simply attempted to survive.

They might have survived, had not Constantine (his capital was no longer Rome but Constantinople) declared his Christian war of attrition against the Jews. While Constantine remembered that the Christian attitude toward Jews was largely of his promulgation, his sons received it as the will of God. There was a very large Jewish population in Constantinople—possibly several hundred thousand; we have no way of knowing exactly—and Constantine's son Constantius bled them unmercifully. Against the Jewish population of Palestine, he was even more cruel—and he pushed them to the edge of total despair.

This led to the final war of the Jews in Palestine, a strange, pathetic, heartbreaking struggle of which we know very little. Unlike the Zealot revolt of the year 64 or the Bar Kochba revolt of the year 132, it was not a response to an affront of religious dignity. It was a war of survival, a war against the intolerable persecution by the Christian Romans of Constantinople. We are not even certain who led the revolt. The Romans respected him and called him "Patrick" or "Patricius," and in Jewish records he is referred to as "Natrona." But the Jewish references are obscure—for what reason we do not know. Most of our information comes from Roman sources, for Patrick or Natrona was a tough, hard enemy. With his few thousand men, he fought the Romans for months, and in the course of the war, two Jewish cities in Galilee, Sepphoris and Tiberias on the Sea of Galilee, were completely destroyed.

There is reason to believe that the massacre of the Jews who took part in the revolt was so complete that no one survived to hand on a detailed account of what had happened. Constantius barred all Jews from entering Jerusalem after the war, and all over Palestine Jews were hunted by Roman slave dealers, who worked hand in hand with the tax farmers, picked up men, women, and children, and sold them into slavery.

So the light of the Jew in his ancient homeland flickered low; indeed, it almost perished. Here and there, in the more obscure wadies of Judea—already turning into bleak badlands—Jews hid and managed to survive. In Galilee, a handful lived on in the ruins of Tiberias, building rude shelters from the broken remains of the city of Hillel; and in the other cities of Palestine, there were tiny, frightened Jewish communities, many with their synagogues hidden underground—all of them fair game for any robber band.

In Constantinople, the Jewish community was more populous than the entire Jewish population of Palestine. They had wealth, prestige, and knowledge; they owned fleets of ships, and their camel caravans roamed the Eastern world. All of this, Constantius, the son of Constantine, proceeded to change. He confiscated ships and wealth; he taxed the Jews enormously; he permitted every insult and indignity to be practiced against them; he encouraged the constant assault on and murder of Jews—which became a daily occurrence. There was a short breathing space for the Jews of Constantinople when Julian the Apostate became emperor, but after his death conditions worsened—until the Emperor Theodosius, in the year 430, forced the Jews of the city into a ghetto. This was located on the opposite side of the Golden Horn in a district called Stenum, which now came to be called Juderia.

In 480, the Party of the Green, one of the two divisions in the lunatic chariot-racing-civil-war madness that overtook Constantinople, turned from their endless squabbling with their rivals and decided to burn a Jewish synagogue. Once it was on fire, they conceived the notion of throwing living Jews into the flames. Hundreds of Jews, men, women, and children, were thrown into the pyre. When word came to the Emperor Zeno, he growled that it was a pity they had not burned the lot of the Jews and ended the problem then and there.

But in all truth, he did not want the problem ended then and there. The most important merchants in Constantinople were Jews and Samaritans, and they brought great wealth into the city. (In the Diaspora the Samaritans—the descendants of the Beni-Yisrael—tended to merge with the Jews, to intermarry, and eventually to disappear as a separate entity. By the tenth century, we hear no more of the Samaritans in the Diaspora. They have become Jews or Christians.)

For the next five hundred years, there was a seesaw of killing and counterkilling of Jew and Christian in Constantinople. Apparently, it was the only place in the Christian world where the Jewish community continued to fight back; and in various parts of the shrunken Eastern Roman Empire, Samaritans still fought, although the Jews had relapsed into a kind of exhaustion. Here and there were small Greek cities that had never become totally Christianized; their inhabitants were Jews of a sort and Christians of a sort. They bypassed circumcision but read the Torah in Hebrew and kept the high holy days, admitting Christ only as another prophet. In Phrygia, there were sects of Christians who believed in baptism but remained Jews and continued to circumcise.

Suddenly, in the sixth century, an even odder thing happened: the Jews and the Samaritans monopolized the role of drivers in the chariot races. Why and how this happened we do not know, and nothing quite like it ever happened elsewhere in the Jewish history of the times.

During the latter part of this phase, under the Emperor Justinian, the Samaritans in Palestine rose up against the Romans, crying out that they would restore Palestine as a Jewish homeland. The Samaritan role in history can only evoke heartache and pity. Remember, they were the descendants of the Joshua tribes, the Children of Israel or Beni-Yisrael, whose battles with the Jews are recounted in the latter part of the Book of Kings in the Bible. So long as they remained a national entity, the Jews shunned them, but their strange faithfulness to the Jews rarely wavered. Now, at the end of their time, in the sixth century, they would free all of Palestine from the gentile yoke and return it to their blood-brothers, the Jews.

The Jews would have had hearts of stone had they not responded to this, and in Constantinople, they rose up in sympathy. Thus in the last spasm of this trust in the sword, Samaria passed from the stage of history. She was literally put to death, and twenty thousand Samaritan corpses lay on the fertile fields of Ephraim, the males of the race executed, the women and children handed over to the slave dealers for a solid price—a price which was doubled when the women and children were bought out of slavery by Jewish communities throughout the Mediterranean. So at last the gulf between Jew and Samaritan was washed out, and the Samaritan women and children were taken to the Jewish heart, loved and cherished and no longer distinguishable from the Jew. In Palestine, only a handful of Samaritans remained—and even today a few of their descendants exist.

In Constantinople, Jew killed Christian and Christian killed Jew. There were more Christians and they were better armed, and the attempt to help the Samaritans turned into a massacre of the Jews. Their numbers were savagely reduced, their influence broken—but they were not destroyed as the Samaritans were.

The Constantinople experience of the Jews was strange, almost unique, for they would not bow their heads as Jews everywhere else did. The Arab Moslems swept up out of Arabia and conquered the bulk of what remained of the dying Roman Empire, but behind her great walls Constantinople remained secure. We have hints of battle within the city, of the Jews storming the great church of St. Sophia and holding it against the Roman soldiers, of peace pacts, massacres, further internal wars—but this is cloudy, a strange kind of history in which nothing is absolutely certain and most is surmise. The Samaritans were more warlike than the Jews and there were thousands of them in Constantinople. But then there is a gap in history, and the Samaritans are gone.

When that solid and informative traveler Benjamin of Tudela came by in 1170, there were only about twenty-five hundred Jews left, in their ghetto across the Golden Horn. And of these about five hundred were Karaites.

———•◆•———

Between the time of Benjamin of Tudela's visit to Constantinople in 1170 and its conquest by the Ottoman Turks in 1453, the Jews appear to have lived more peacefully in this city than anywhere in Europe. They were craftsmen and merchants and eventually shipowners, and they were increasingly allowed to work in direct competition with their Christian neighbors. Their numbers increased and toleration for them increased. They traded into Russia, across the Black Sea and up the Dnieper River to Lithuania and the Baltic, where there were Jewish trading posts that had traded with the Vikings for centuries.

This was one of the Jewish roads into Russia, but not in terms of permanent settlement—for usually language leaves a very apparent trail, and the language of these Jews was Greek, whereas Jews permanently settled in Russia and Lithuania and Poland spoke Yiddish.

Both Yiddish and Ladino—as the two great Jewish languages of modern times until the revival of Hebrew in Israel —will be discussed at some length. Since Ladino, the language of the Spanish Jews and their descendants, has an earlier beginning, it will be dealt with in the next few pages. Yiddish, the language of a great and populous people, with a unique literature and culture, will be dealt with in the story of the Jews in the European Diaspora. But while the sound and culture of Yiddish are so well known to the Jews —and many gentiles—of the modern world, American Jews in particular are almost unaware of the existence and history of Ladino.

The Turks conquered Constantinople in 1453, and it became Istanbul; and the Turks also conquered the entire Turkish peninsula as well as Greece. Against the Jews, the Turks, who were Moslems, took no specific measures; indeed, on occasion they went out of their way to help the Jews—as in 1492, when they generously opened their doors to thousands of Sephardic Jews who were expelled from Spain. The Turks gave the Jews full privileges of trade and manufacture, removed all travel stricture from them, and allowed them to worship in Jerusalem.

Under the Turks, the ghetto notion disappeared, and great and prosperous Jewish communities arose in Smyrna and Adrianople—as well as in Istanbul. This situation of freedom for the Jews did not appreciably change until the nineteenth century—at which point Turkey had the third largest Jewish population in the world, some 350,000 people. But many of these were in the Balkans, and as the Turkish Empire disintegrated, the Balkan Jews moved toward Europe and America. From 1850 onward, the Jewish population in Turkey lessened year by year. About forty thousand emigrated to the new State of Israel, and about a hundred thousand still live in Turkey.

———·•◦•·———

Before beginning the story of Spain and North Africa, a word must be said of Ladino. Even as Yiddish became the international language of the northern and eastern European Jews, so did Ladino become the international language that replaced Aramaic and Greek as the Jewish tongue in the Mediterranean basin—from Spain to Turkey. When the Jews were expelled from Spain in 1492, they brought with them the language, Ladino, already in use as a commercial tongue among Jewish merchants in the Levant, and the great numbers of Spanish Jews who were given refuge in the Turkish Empire brought their language with them.

Ladino is a Spanish dialect, which has its basis in old Castilian and even more ancient Spanish dialects; it is written in Hebrew characters and is liberally besprinkled with Greek, Aramaic, and Hebrew words. If Jewish history could be told in direct chronology, then one might describe in detail the formation of Ladino in the first centuries of our era. By the time of the Ottoman Empire in Turkey, however, Ladino was spoken all over Greece and Turkey and in Palestine as well. Thus the Mediterranean Jews were bilingual—just as the Jews of northern Europe were bilingual in Yiddish. And even today, Ladino is spoken in Turkey, North Africa, and in Israel among the Sephardic Jews.

Not only language, but history and culture connected the Jews of Spain with the East; and so ancient is the Jewish connection with Spain that if one is to talk of blood—a method of identification I consider rather nonsensical—one would have to say that there is Jewish blood in all Spaniards, or Spanish blood in all Sephardic Jews. Better to say that the Jews and Spain were interconnected—so deeply interconnected that Spain in tearing out its Jewry tore out its own heart, and thereby made a wound in itself from which it never recovered.

Jews whose ancestors came from Spain and Portugal are called Sephardim, as differentiated from Jews who either live in Europe and Russia or whose ancestors came from those places. Those Jews are called Ashkenazim.

Sepharad is a region the Bible speaks of, and while no one knows exactly where it was, there is a general belief that it was the area where Lebanon is today. This was the land of the Phoenicians, who were not only themselves of the Beni-Yisrael but deeply mixed with the tribe of Asher, who were specified in the Bible as belonging to Israel. If we refer to the hinterland of the Phoenician port cities as Sepharad, then we can say that there were Sephardic Jews there at least seven hundred years before our era. If they were not Jews of the tribe of the Yehudim, they were Yahweh worshippers; and after the destruction of the northern kingdom of the Beni-Yisrael, many clusters of Yahweh worship survived. In the course of time, as the Jews spread over Palestine and became the dominant population of Galilee, these Beni-Yisrael people became indistinguishable from the Jews. They had a natural affinity for each other, and as I said earlier, by the time of Jesus tribal records ceased to be kept and Jews no longer made any distinction in tribal ancestry, except for the Levites.

Now, how much of the Phoenician nobility was Jewish we do not know. David Ben-Gurion, I have heard, holds that the Jewish influence was great and that very likely Hannibal and his family were Jewish. The Romans did not take kindly to the preservation of Phoenician books and records, and therefore we know far less about the Phoenicians than we would like to know. Certainly much written about the Phoenicians and their "barbaric" religious practices, sacrifice of infants to Moloch, and so forth, is nonsense unless it applies to a very ancient period; for apparently the sacrifice of the firstborn male was practiced by many Semitic people early in their history. The historic Phoenicians were a cultured and civilized people, speaking the same language as the Jews, sailing everywhere with Jewish supercargoes, and certainly operating within a network of Jewish commercial finance. Phoenician colonies were planted in Spain perhaps as early as the time of Solomon.

When the Babylonians took Jerusalem and led the Jewish upper class into captivity in 597 B.C.E., many other Jews fled north toward Phoenicia and took refuge in the land of Sepharad. Already Jews lived there, and there is some reason to believe that several hundred families of these Jews decided to seek safety in Spain. They traveled there on Phoenician ships, and thus Spain became the new Sepharad, and thus the Spanish Jew and Sephardic Jew. Some of this is of course speculation, but there are enough indications to make it quite likely—and there is every evidence that Jews came to Spain around that time. It would also appear that they were joined by other Jews from Babylon. By the time of Jesus, the Jews were an integrated part of the Spanish population.

The Spaniards were a Mediterranean people, not homogeneous, but a great assortment of tribes and races living in various parts of the peninsula and talking a number of languages. For several hundred years, there was Carthaginian influence (the people of Carthage were Phoenicians, and in all likelihood Carthage was the Biblical Tarshish) in Spain. Jews were probably with the Phoenicians when they established Carthage, and we know that the Jewish cemetery of the Roman period had over three thousand tombstones. Carthaginian trading ports—which probably included Jewish synagogues—were well established at Gibraltar, Malaca, Sexi, Urci, Catonae, and of course, New Carthage— all of these cities in the south of Spain, where the Jewish influence was greatest. With Carthage destroyed as a result of the Punic Wars, Rome poured legions and settlers into Spain, especially the southern area, Latinizing it. The Jews were able to live with the Romans, and indeed conversions to Judaism were probably very considerable in Spain.

When the Visigoths conquered Spain and North Africa, Jews in both places were treated with warmth and respect, and the Visigoths regarded the Jews as an indispensable civilizing force. Not only were there Jewish physicians, but all else that the conquering barbarians needed for their status shift into an established ruling class the Jews provided— teachers who would make them literate in Latin, merchants to bring them the jewels and silks and spices of the world, architects to build them palaces, ships for commerce. At the same time, for their first period in Spain, the Visigoths were not Catholics recognizing the overlordship of the Pope, but were of the Arian Heresy—a form of Christianity strongly influenced by Judaism, denying the divinity of Christ, and monotheistic.

Jew and Arian Visigoth lived well together, creating an oasis of learning and civilization in Spain. But in 589, the Catholic Church triumphed and the Visigoths embraced Catholicism. In 612, a council was called in Toledo which promulgated an official policy of anti-Semitism, and as with all converts, the Visigoths were driven to make up for their former laxity. A hundred years of senseless, vicious persecution of the Jews followed. Their ancient synagogues were burned and leveled. A whole series of laws were passed against them, and finally the very practice of Judaism was forbidden under pain of death—a defense the Church considered necessary in terms of the enormous inroads Judaism had made in the population.

In the year 711, the Arab-Moslem sweep reached Spain and conquered southern and central Spain. Some hold that the Jews aided this conquest, both with ships and from within, but we have no reliable proof of this. In any case, under the Arabs, the golden age of Spanish Judaism began.

Like all golden ages, it glittered mostly in contrast. By the tenth century, throughout Europe, and during most of the years that followed, the life of the Jew came to resemble a chronic toothache—it was beautiful whenever it stopped hurting. Basically, that is the trouble with the various and sundry "golden ages" that Jewish historians like to refer to; the gold was a thin patina, and the simple fact of existence was turned into a glorious privilege. Jewish history is like a mirror that reflects bigotry and mindless hate.

For three hundred years, in southern and central Spain, under the Arab hegemony, Jews existed in their latter day "golden age." This meant that they could not be murdered with impunity for the murderer; it meant that they could buy out of specific persecutions; it meant that they could travel; and it meant that they could rebuild the synagogues that the Visigoths had destroyed. In return for this, they gave Arab Spain the finest medicine and medical practice that any part of the world then knew—perhaps the only really scien-

tific broad practice of medicine. They translated all their
medical knowledge into Arabic, creating a science five hundred years ahead of their time. They instituted a science of
water supply and sewage. They designed and built buildings
that were beautiful and often quite wonderful. They created
a system of mercantile trade routes—I detailed this earlier—
that opened the whole world to Spain. They made Spain one
of the centers for the China silk trade, and they had great
fleets of ships built as a foundation for this trade.

In Hebrew as well as in Arabic, they created a literature
that was rich and delightful, poems, plays, travel journals—
a variety of feasts for the mind's delight. A good number of
these Spanish Jews became advisors to kings and princes in
Arab Spain, as for example Hasdai ibn-Shaprut, who was
vizier to the famous Caliph of Córdova, and whose fame was
all over the world of his time—and who established contact
with the Chazars, the militant nomadic Jews of eastern Russia; and Samuel ibn-Nagrela, who as grand vizier to the King
of Granada wielded such power in the city that the Jews
were the armed watch on the walls.

The freedom from pain was limited, and in 1136 the Moslem Almohades invaded and conquered Spain. We mentioned this in the reference to Moses Maimonides and his father's flight from Spain to Egypt. Most Jews, however, could
not escape by ship. They endured the bloody cruelties of the
Almohades and then they found a road to a sort of freedom
and a sort of second "golden age," as such things go. The
Christian kings of northern Spain, particularly of Castile,
had watched the astonishing role of the Jew in Arab Spain
and had even persuaded a number of Jewish physicians to
practice in their courts. Now they asked themselves why the
Jews' misfortune under the Almohades should not be
turned to their advantage—and they let it be known in the
south that Christian Spain and Christian Portugal would
welcome Jews. By the tens of thousands, the Jews came.

At first, it was a very promising sort of "golden age." The
enormous mercantile skill and know-how of the Jews had an
immediate effect, and both Spain and Portugal quickly

made long strides toward sea power. Rulers of Christian Spain, such as Alfonso the Wise of Castile, were fascinated by the wisdom of the Jews, by the fact that they alone could produce dependable maps of the world at that time, by their enormous practical mercantile knowledge, a knowledge that embraced China, India, Russia, Central Asia, Scandinavia—and Italy into the Teutonic heartland of Europe (a movement we will follow in the next section on the Diaspora). The Jewish connection with the world jewel and perfume trade made them an asset to any court. They knew every language. They could translate anything—and they were able to make the instruments for stellar observation —this very much the fashion among the new postbarbarian courts in Europe of the Middle Ages. Alfonso gave them place and privilege, and as a result the court and kingdom of Castile became a showplace of wealth and distinction.

But this was a short-lived "golden age," and even as the Jews were delighting in the privilege and open-mindedness of Christian Spain, the Order of Dominicans stepped into the picture and decided that this embrace of Jew and Christian had gone too far.

Denied the right to proceed directly against the Jews (the Dominicans had power only over Christians; it was they who operated the various Inquisitions), the Dominicans began a campaign of anti-Semitism, undertook the Jewish-Christian Disputation of Barcelona, instituted a round of sermons calculated to increase hatred, and finally—when at last the time was ripe—persuaded the Christian Spaniards to undertake mass extermination of all Spanish Jews, giving them, however, the alternative of baptism. This was in 1391. An equivalent movement was under way in Portugal.

Faced with a choice between death and baptism, the majority of the Spanish Jews chose baptism and became what the Spaniards and Portuguese called Marranos (in Spanish, "swine") and what the Jews who remained Jews called, with great tolerance and understanding, *anusim*, which is the Hebrew word for "coerced." Just how many Jews converted in Spain, we do not know, but the estimates range from 150,-

ooo to 300,000—in either case, a very large part of the Spanish population in Christian Spain of the time. Since most
of these converted Jews belonged to the nobility or associated seminoble mercantile class, one could say, as an observer did a hundred years later, that there was no aristocratic family in Spain that was not wholly or in part Jewish.
The breadth of this act of conversion in some measure permitted the unconverted stiff-necked Jews to survive.

This is the only time in Jewish history that a great mass
conversion of Jews to Christianity took place—and it is interesting to examine the reasons for it. In every other part
of Europe—and Asia too—the Jews lived in communities,
sometimes fairly free communities, sometimes small Jewish
villages, sometimes walled ghettos. In Spain, this was not
the case. The tens of thousands of Jews who moved north into
Christian Spain at the invitation of the then rulers integrated
themselves wholly into Spanish life.

For one thing, they were an older people in Spain than
the Gothic and Frankish invaders; the Spanish language was
their language from the time it came into being; they remembered no time of coming to Spain; ancient Sepharad
was more myth than reality; and the Spanish people were no
different from them in any physical manner. They dressed
no differently, and they had enormous wealth. In other
parts of Europe, the Jew was different in dress, in manner,
in speech—and he had his community refuge where he
could be a Jew rather than a German or Frenchman or Italian. In Spain, he had no community as such. He had no refuge, no hiding place—and thus in large part he converted.
But curiously enough, the majority of those who converted
could not remain Christian; and when one looks back upon
history, the inner agony of the Jew who converts to Christianity, either through threat or desire, becomes a continuing part of the Jewish experience.

The great mass conversion of Jews in Spain took place
between 1391 and 1410, although there continued to be conversions after the latter date. For seventy-five years after
these conversions the converted Jew, as aristocrat and mer-

chant-prince, infused Christian Spain with enormous vitality. Sword in hand, he joined the wars against the Moslems; he was physician, geographer, supercargo, mapmaker, engineer, and architect. Suddenly in Spain and in Portugal, as nowhere else in Europe, there was a nobility that was literate and sophisticated, commercially connected with the entire world, astronomically and geographically advanced, bursting with energy and a sense of destiny—suddenly Spain was the leader of Europe and ready to break through the walls of fear and superstition that had separated Europe from North and South America.

It is interesting to speculate on what might have been Spain's destiny had these thousands of Marranos, together with the remaining unconverted Jews, been allowed to live and work and exist as Spaniards. Certainly, it would have been a very different destiny than Spain finally found for herself. Yet perhaps what happened had to happen, for there is a deadly and implacable logic in the seeming insanity of history.

The nut of the matter is that most of the converted Jews remained Jews; they accepted baptism, they assumed the trappings of Christianity; and in the seclusion of their families, their homes, and their hearts, most of them did a thing that was then called "Judaizing"—that is, they whispered the old prayers, lit the holy candles on the Sabbath eve, treasured Hebrew books, and had somewhere in their homes Torahs, parchment scrolls on which, handwritten in Hebrew, were the Books of Moses, Genesis, Exodus, Leviticus, Deuteronomy, and Numbers. Christians today have forgotten a time when unauthorized possession of such a scroll could mean death—many hundreds of years before Adolf Hitler.

And not only did they Judaize, but in the feeling of power and security these Marranos had gained, they helped the Jews who had remained Jews, prevented a great deal of persecution, and gained favors for the Jews.

The social structure of Christian Spain at that time was only beginning to emerge from feudalism. A power struggle between the royal houses of Aragon and Castile on the one

hand and the feudal nobility on the other was in progress—
and here was where the Jewish concentration was greatest;
there were actually more Jews proportionately in Aragon
than anywhere else in the world at that time. The Catholic
Church, by its very nature and its inner drive toward unity,
sided with the royal houses, and while the Marranos tried to
preserve an uneasy balance, social forces drove them into the
ranks of the nobility. The Church hated the Marranos for the
obvious facade of their Christianity, and the Crown feared
the quickly growing power of the Marranos, sensing that a
Marrano-Jewish alliance would represent perhaps the most
powerful force in Spain. (Yet any such alliance was impossible. The Marranos were not of one stripe. Among them was
a minority who had wholly embraced Christianity—a small
minority—but one that was vehement and filled with anger
at the Judaizers.)

Within this situation—becoming more and more acute
—the kingdoms of Aragon and Castile, engaging in a war
to drive the Moslems from Spain, still with no real taxable
base in the feudal holdings and desperately in need of money,
conceived of a scheme to supply almost unlimited funds.
They joined forces with the Dominicans to have the Inquisition mount what was at first a cautious attack against certain
prominent Judaizers. Found guilty of heresy by the Inquisition, not only were the Marranos burned at the stake, but
their property was forfeit to Church and Crown, who made
agreeable arrangements for dividing the boodle. So simple,
so successful was this method—not only for raising funds but
for breaking the backs of the small nobility—that all caution
soon disappeared. Marrano was found to bear witness against
Marrano, and estate after estate was split between Church
and Crown. This process began in 1478; ten years later, the
moral fiber of Spain had been shaken to the core.

Once a land of verve and excitement and veritable destiny,
Spain had become a place of fear, horror, and silence un-
equaled anywhere on earth. The Marranos, having watched
hundreds and hundreds of their fellows burned at the stake,
whole families, men, women, children, babes in arms, and

the very old consumed in the flames of what the Catholic Church called so eloquently the *auto da fé,* or "act of faith," retreated into their own shells of silence and despair. No town or village in Castile and Aragon was free from the smell of burning human flesh. Art and science and culture perished almost overnight, and family after family of the Marrano nobility gathered what it could carry and fled Spain, some by ship, some on foot into the Moslem south or across the Pyrenees. Those who left by ship went to the Low Countries and to North Africa for the most part.

Yet the greed of Church and Crown was measureless and their appetite insatiable. After thousands of Marranos had been burned for Judaizing, the Crown realized that by depending entirely upon the Inquisition, it could act only against Christians accused of heresy. Against the Jews, the Spanish Inquisition had no direct power. Whereupon, in the year 1492, the year Columbus' three ships left to ultimately open the New World, the United Kingdoms of Aragon and Castile issued an edict expelling the entire Jewish population from Spain.

It is estimated that there were in Spain then unconverted Jews to the number of 150,000. These were the Sephardic Jews who took their ancient Spanish-Hebrew language of Ladino with them to every part of the Mediterranean world and even to South America. Those who eventually went to South America were the descendants of those expelled Jews, who went first to Holland and then to Brazil and finally, in 1654, to Manhattan Island in New Amsterdam, where they built the first synagogue in North America.

One must at least mention the scholarly battle to prove or disprove the Jewish origin of Christopher Columbus. Whatever the outcome of this argument, there is no disputing the fact that troubled Jewish and Marrano merchants and financiers were intimately connected with his expedition. We know for a fact that his interpreter, Luis de Torres, the first European to set foot on American soil, was a converted Jew.

Howsoever, the great masses of the expelled Jews found what poor refuge they could in North Africa and particularly in Greece and Turkey under the Ottoman Empire. The Turks gave them refuge without which thousands and thousands of them would have surely perished. In 1497, the smaller population of Jews in Portugal was expelled, and a year later, the Kingdom of Navarre, in northwestern Spain, expelled its Jews.

So the Iberian peninsula was finally free of Jews. After a residence there of almost two thousand years, Spain expelled the Jews and thereby hurt itself beyond measure. During the next two hundred years, the boldest, the toughest, and the most sensitive of the Marranos left Spain. They left family by family, some openly, some secretly, but in almost every case, these Marranos, some of whose families had been outwardly Christian for several hundred years, underwent circumcision and returned to the Jewish fold the moment they were out of the Inquisition's power.

Spain never recovered from this combination of madness, fanaticism, greed, and stupidity.

———•◆•———

At some point in telling the story of the Jews, one must deal with Cabala (*cabala,* Hebrew for "what is received"), and the point is almost arbitrary, since Cabala runs like a thread through Jewish history for two and a half thousand years, from the time of the exile to today, and has made so deep an impression on Jewish thought that even Jews who know nothing about it as Cabala are influenced by it. However, in the final two centuries of Jewish presence in Spain, Cabala was elevated and advanced and became perhaps the most important single philosophical current of the time— which provides a good reason for discussing it in the Spanish context.

Cabala is an esoteric and mystic doctrine, derived by the Jews out of the very ancient past, and like all esoteric doctrines, directed toward a limited rather than a mass group. Yet at times it permeated the thought and action of most of the Jewish people; and even when it was limited it left its residue among the masses. Cabala deals with God and the

universe, their relation to each other and man's relationship
to both. It is essentially a part of Rabbinical Judaism, for it
came into being as a trend after the exile and among the
rabbis—possibly under the influence of eastern religion,
when the way was opened from Babylon into India, and
likely enough under the influence of Buddhism, with which
it has many important points of identity.

In the first centuries of our era, after Hillel—who was certainly influenced by Cabala—a group of rabbis arose whose
lifelong training was in Cabala, who were called *ba'ale ha-
cabala* and sometimes *mekubalim,* and were generically
known as *maskilim,* Hebrew for "men of wisdom." These
mekubalim have no precise equivalent in our culture or
language, and I think that the only proper translation of
makubalim is in the Hindu word *guru,* which means a combination of teacher and religious leader; for unlike the
prophets, the *mekubalim* did not claim divine inspiration
but rather inner experience. The word itself is very ancient,
and like many Hebrew words which do not yield to precise
meaning, its meaning and origin are in dispute.

Cabala is a most complex subject. Taught at first as purely
oral commentary, half concealed, called in Hebrew *hokmah
nistarah,* which means "the hidden wisdom," it was pres-
ently turned into a written literature which existed alongside the Talmud, an enormous literature finally, the most
famous part of which is the *Zohar.* But the plain fact of the
matter is that Cabala lost itself in its own complexity, im-
mersed itself in symbolism which became meaningless without the keys to the symbols; and then, in the nineteenth century, when the European Jew burst out of the ghetto, shook
off his ghetto beliefs, came by the millions to America, and
gloried in the new rationalism, Cabala was relegated to the
world of mumbo jumbo, magic, and assorted idiocies. De-
nunciation of Cabala (and of most religion) became a part
of free entry into the Christian-revolutionary-industrial-
scientific world; and even those Jews who desired to retain
at least part of their ancient culture found Cabala a bit too
much, and their only reaction was to apologize for it as a sort

of gobbledygook that Jews had turned to when the persecutions of the world were too much with them.

Perhaps what many Jews envied most about Protestantism was the fact that it was an easier religion; there were no language difficulties; and church service was conducted with decorum and without that tremendous flow of emotion that was both Jewish and embarrassing.

Cabala in recent times became synonymous with nonsense; a person who lingered over meaningless points of illogic was a Cabalist; Cabala was spells, devils, a way to influence them, to call demons, and so forth. This is a pity, for Cabala included some of the most wonderful moments of Judaism; both Hillel and Spinoza were deeply influenced by it; Philo was in part a product of Cabala—as were so many Jewish saints and martyrs. At the same time, over several thousand years, there were many bypaths that Cabala took; it developed its own mythology and a great deal that strikes the modern mind as rather silly.

But let me see whether I can make the major directions of Cabala meaningful—and whether this great stream of Jewish mysticism can be presented understandably.

Firstly, what is mysticism and how does it differ from ordinary religious experience? Nonmystical religion demands faith. It presents a theology, God and his relation to man, and whatever else is needed for the particular religious structure. It calls upon the believer to believe without proof, to worship without reward, to pray without assurance. Faith covers the metaphysical substitute for scientific evidence.

Mystical religion holds that man can directly know God—that man can relate to God as a matter of experience rather than faith—and from this, the conclusion that man is a part of God. In that sense, most mystical religions—the most famous is Buddhism—are pantheistic, which is the belief that all of the universe, all manifestations of the universe, all that is within the universe is God.

Then the question must arise, as it did over and over during the centuries of Jewish Cabala: Is Cabala monotheism? Can God as *all* be equated with God as *one?*

Hillel said, "Love thy neighbor as thyself. That is the whole Law."

But according to the view of the time, the Torah was written by Moses and directly inspired by God. Led by the Sadducees, the cry went up that Hillel had dispensed with God, and only the great authority of Hillel and the love in which he was held prevented a charge of heresy. To Hillel, mystic that he was, God was *all*, and the clearest manifestation of God was the action of one man toward another. In the literal sense of monotheism, the Sadducees were the rigid monotheists, the rabbis—or "fathers" as they are called today—were, to a great degree, pantheists. But the difference between pantheism and monotheism was frequently the result of who was doing the defining. The later Karaites—whom we mentioned earier and who were latter-day Sadducees in position and belief—denounced the Cabala as heresy and pantheism; and thereby aligned themselves against the rabbis and Rabbinical Judaism as defenders of monotheism and the holy *"Shamah"* ("Hear, O Israel! Yahweh is our God! Yahweh is one!").

But that most rational and clear-minded Jew of his time, Moses Maimonides, fought the Karaites tooth and nail, denounced them as mindless ritualists, and specified their defense of the ancient Jewish image of God (or Yahweh) as being without content. Maimonides, of course, was influenced by Cabala.

We will specify Cabala, not in terms of the magic symbolism of the Middle Ages, but as a mystical form of Judaism which began in the distant postexilic past and matured in the Talmudic (rabbinical) period and in the Gaonic period that followed. (The Gaons were the highly esteemed rabbis of the Babylonian Jewish community from the sixth to the eleventh century, the title *Gaon* meaning "eminence" and sometimes defined with the Hebrew *nasi*, or prince.) From that point, to one degree or another, Cabala has remained a part of Judaism—being deeply meaningful at moments of great suffering.

It is possible that the Greek mystery rites of the last two

centuries before our era were deeply influenced by Cabala—
but such was the intimacy of the Jewish-Greek relationship
that it is difficult, within existing scholarship, to determine
in which direction the influence was strongest. Gnosticism,
which is remembered better as a Christian heresy than as a
Jewish Cabalistic deviation, was a curious result of Cabala—
and if one reads the four gospels of the New Testament
with some knowledge of Jewish Cabala as background, the
apparent influence of Cabala is enormous and intriguing.
Some authorities on the New Testament believe that the
initial preaching of Jesus was wholly mystical in content
and that the parables of Jesus can only be understood mystically; but any further discussion of this is beyond our scope.

The teaching and study of Cabala moved north with the
Jewish migration into Germany—which will be detailed in
the next part of the story—developed there, and then took
hold in Spain during the eleventh century.

To attempt an explanation of Cabala, we go to the mystic
rabbis of the Talmudic period. Highly rational, deeply religious, and faced with the disintegration of Greek civilization
under the seemingly mindless Roman impact, they sought
sanity in their belief. Jews of that time were fascinated with
a curious Old Testament synonym for God, *ha makom*, which
is Hebrew for "omnipresent." Philo, the Alexandrian Jewish philosopher, stated: "God is called *ha makom* because He
encloses the universe but is Himself not enclosed by anything." Eventually, Spinoza would refer to this in his belief
that the early Jews did not separate God from the universe;
and he was quite right that in this period the *one* that was
God was being developed in thinking into the *all* that was
God.

More and more, *ha makom* became the essence of Cabala.
God was the place of existence. Then this thinking went on
with the need to grapple with good and evil in a new manner,
and of course this led to endless discussion and argument.
The concept of God began to take on a sense of a radiance,
an emanation of matter—which led to the conclusion among
the most mystical of the early Cabalists that if all exists in

God, then the chief purpose of man is to feel and be as one with God.

This is certainly pantheism, and to anyone who knows a little of Buddhism, the resemblance is remarkable—but of course all pantheistic religions have a great deal in common and one cannot assert a connection between Judaism and Buddhism without more evidence.

Looking backward at their own mythology, as put forward in Genesis, the Cabalists shaped it to their thinking. By the time of the *Zohar,* the definitive Cabalistic work, which was finally assembled, edited, and in part written by Moses de Leon, in Spain in the early fourteenth century, the Cabalists had asserted their definition of God as the "primal will," containing within itself all that was and is and will be of the universe, a total continuum of time; and all of matter as radiation to be contracted at the will of God. The sheer mental grandeur of this concept is overwhelming, and those who desire to can find the roots of it in the mythology of the Torah.

Within this infinite first cause and final cause, man is free. Human beings play their own role as part of the infinite wisdom of God. The finite exists only as part of the infinite, and the will of God can also be comprehended as an infinite light or radiation.

This, of course, is the most cursory definition of Cabala— but it does allow for a beginning of understanding; particularly of a religious trend that gave man the confidence that he in his living life could experience the radiance and the nature of God. Between the fourteenth and the eighteenth century, Cabala took an enormous hold upon the Jews. Driven from Spain, Cabala grew and developed in Poland— where prayer itself became a means of inducing a condition of ecstasy. The Orthodox Jew, under the influence of Cabala, infused his whole life with a sort of rapture that made an incredible contrast to the misery of his condition. The radiance—the goodness of God—was with him and of him. The ancient Sabbath became a weekly condition of ecstasy; and all that surrounded him became a part of the infinite he worshipped.

A Cabalistic doctrine—strangely like the Karma doctrine of Mahayana Buddhism—presented a condition where man's destiny and God's will were shaped by acts of goodness. The saint, the holy man, the pious man, the just man—these were the movers of the universe, regardless of how war and pogrom and hate and horror surrounded them. Love was the translation of the unknowable will of God. The only path to God, the only key to God's nature, was loving kindness, reverence for life; and only through the combination of a loving heart, good acts, and great study could wisdom, that most revered of Jewish attributes, be achieved.

In this fairly recent condition of so much of European Jewry, all words and concepts pertaining to what we discuss here as Cabala were in Yiddish, Hebrew, and Aramaic. In the huge Jewish immigration into America, a broken English of necessity became the language of communication between the European Jew and his American-born children. In his limited English, there were neither translation-words nor descriptive concepts for the mysteries of his ancient faith. What came through was truncated and distorted—and when his children and grandchildren looked at Cabala, they saw nothing understandable or particularly admirable.

We cannot, however, leave the discussion of Cabala without noting its effect upon two extraordinary men. The first is the Dutch Jew, Benedict Spinoza (Baruch de Spinoza in Portuguese), whose father and grandfather escaped the persecutions in Portugal and found refuge in Amsterdam. Spinoza, one of the great philosophers of the post-Renaissance period, elevated the teachings of the Cabalists to a strange pinnacle of rationality; strange because in the history of Judaism there is nothing quite like Spinoza's thought. There is much that leads to it, but Spinoza put into words the concept of an infinite God that is the cause of itself. In deep essence, Spinoza was both a Cabalist and a pantheist, for he postulated the presence of every finite thing in God and God

in every finite thing. The God of Spinoza is nature and created nature and was and will be. Knowledge is all good and
wisdom is freedom; and while these positions were newly and
brilliantly conceptualized by Spinoza, he never departed from
the mainstream of Judaistic thinking.

As with all Jews who saw God and love and compassion as
aspects of the same thing, he leaned upon the Rabbi Hillel.
He took from Maimonides, from Rabbi Hasdai ben Abraham Crescas, the Crown Rabbi of Aragon who so brilliantly
criticized Aristotle's dualism, and of course from the songs
of the Unknown Prophet (the Deutero-Isaiah). The more be-
wildering, then, becomes the fact of the anathema directed
toward Spinoza by the congregation of Amsterdam; but this
is also a question of the moment and the thinking of the moment. Again and again, revolutionary currents disturbed and
reshaped Judaism; and the fate of whatever prophet pro-
pounded the new thoughts often depended on his position
and support. But as I point out elsewhere, there is no ex-
communication as such in Judaism, and to be a Jew or not to
be one was left to Spinoza, not to his congregation.

The second man who must be noted in this question of
Cabala is the German-Jewish historian, Heinrich Graetz.
One of the great scholars of modern times, he is properly
called the father of Jewish historiography, and his monumen-
tal *History of the Jews,* which was published in eleven volumes during the period from 1853 to 1875, was written from
all the original sources available to him. He established not
only the form for Jewish history, but the beginnings of the
science of history among the Jews. In that sense, enough
honor cannot be done him.

However, along with the positive act of writing history, he
clouded a very important part of Jewish history by ignoring
it. Graetz was born in 1817 and he died in 1891—fatal
years for the millions of Ashkenazi Jews in the Czarist Empire, whose story I will tell in the next two sections of this
book. During those years, Cabalistic thought touched to one
extent or another most of the Jews of eastern Europe; but
Graetz had no sympathy for Jewish mysticism and very likely

no understanding of what it meant, its history or its origins. He treated the Cabala vulgarly and superficially and he influenced hundreds of scholars who came after him. Precisely because of the magnitude of the German-Jewish historical scholarship that followed Graetz and because of the great contribution it made to Jewish culture—precisely because of this, that pall cast over the true meaning of Cabala was never dispelled.

PART NINE

into Europe and North

U nlike the Jew in Spain and Greece, the Jew in Rome of long ago was always a stranger—although Rome is the only place in Europe where the Jew has resided in unbroken continuity from 138 B.C.E. until today. But Rome before the Middle Ages was always a place which the Jew viewed with bewilderment—often with disgust. As much as the Jew was bound to the Greek and committed to a reverence for all things Greek, so was the Jew repelled by all things Roman. The marvelous Greek gift of doubt, of skepticism, of delight in things intellectual, of reverence for things mystical—the mind that was so creative that it bubbled in constant ferment—all this was absent in the Roman. The Roman was literal, and the Jew would have perished in the first decade of his existence if he had ever allowed himself to be literal.

In Rome, from the very beginning, the Jew established an island within, a castle unto himself into which the Roman never penetrated. Rome was Edom, and Rome hated the Jew because the Jew was beyond Rome's comprehension. Through all the years of civil war within the city, of unrest and invasion and political struggle, the Jew maintained himself as a thing apart and lived with a quiet dignity in a world that existed behind the walls of his own house. It is true that from within this house, he had a thousand tentacles stretched out to connect with all the world, but these threads were invisible, not like the roads of mighty Rome. The Jew had wealth, and sources of wealth. No matter how many Jewish and Samaritan slaves the Roman legions took, the Jews somehow managed to come up with enough money to purchase them out of slavery.

This and many other things Jewish annoyed the Romans. Of all antiquity, the Romans were the money people par excellence. Not until modern times do we find a society predicated so greatly on wealth and degrees and standards of wealth, and the fact that so much of this inordinate Roman wealth had been looted from Jewish Palestine always underlay Roman relations with the Jews.

While the barrier between Jew and Roman was large, there was also a curious bond; and as Italian Rome died in the years after Constantine had removed the seat of the

Roman Empire to Constantinople, this bond increased. The Jew remained in the Italian city of Rome. His existence in Edom was symbolic; it was also commercial—and economically the Jew was a man of commerce, a traveler and merchant trader—and to use a worn phrase pointedly, all roads led to Rome. The great Roman roads literally led there, and from Rome they led everywhere into the world of Europe, and the Jew traveled those roads, sometimes before the Roman legions, beyond where the Roman roads ended, over the paths and the cart tracks deep into the wild land of the Franks, the Goths, and the Teutons. Even while Jesus lived, the Jew was building his log synagogues in the German forests and his stone synagogues on the Baltic shore.

Most Jewish histories are tales of scholars and religionists who kept a lamp of faith burning and the eyes of civilization open; and without detracting from the unusual virtues of these saints and scholars, it must be noted that even saints and scholars must have roofs over their heads and food to sustain them and clothes to protect them. When the Jewish presence in Palestine dwindled and ceased to be of major importance in the overall scheme of things Jewish, the Jews ceased to be a peasant people. In any case, the wonders of civilization—limited though they may be—have not arisen out of the minds of peasants, but out of the minds of urban dwellers, travelers, people with a sense of the world and the things of the world; and both the history and the survival of the Jew are incomprehensible without understanding the role of commerce in the slow maturing of social man.

Unhappily, history resembles the police blotter in some frontier Texas town in the eighteen-nineties; it records an endless series of gunfights, most of them mindless, but offers little indication of who fed and clothed the trigger-happy ninnies who achieved fame. Many historians are far more interested in antique celebrities, wars, battles, and generals than in so unimpressive a fact that some unsung and unremembered genius in India learned to weave pure gold as thread. Indian cotton—the best of it, that is—was even more gossamer than silk, and frequently brought three to five times the price of silk; that is in the fifth, sixth, and seventh centuries. A pound of this miraculous cotton could return twenty pounds of pure gold, and to the Frankish and Gothic barbarian chiefs, the Teutons who were getting their first taste of civilization, and even the Vikings, this cotton was *status*, very meaningful *status*. The barbarian chiefs had looted the Gaulish and Roman towns and villas of all the gold and silver and pottery that they could ever use. When the Jewish trader spread out for their ladyloves a cotton scarf woven with gold, the miracle was worth any price.

As were the pearls that the Jew brought with him, the diamonds and rubies, the jade and turquoise—and of course the silk, the regal, magnificent purple-dyed silk that was the mark of royalty. Until the time of Constantine, the Roman emperors had declared a monopoly on the silk that the Jews brought in from China and made purple in the Phoenician dye vats. But once Italy began to crumble under the barbarian invasion, the Jews began to raise the silkworm, and colonies of Jewish silk weavers arose in Sicily, southern Italy, and Greece. There was no barbarian chief, no Viking who had not heard of the Tyrian purple, the "cloth of the gods"; no Frankish count's lady who would not give a year of her life for a dress of the "Jew cloth," as it was often called.

And the perfume—the "Jew smell"! The first attribute of the newly rich is the awareness of the odor of the lesser orders (and themselves) ; and all over Europe, a new ruling class of barbarian petty chieftains had come into being. They no longer rode from place to place in wooden wagons; they had stopped painting their faces and wearing rings in their flesh; they had the Romans to imitate; they were beginning to regard women as objects of romance rather than work-horses, and they desired to smell sweet. All over the Levant, Jewish perfume vats, rendering everything from rose leaves to citron peel, worked overtime—and the essence of the perfume, tiny vials, an ounce of which, mixed with water, would yield a quart of perfume, moved out across the Roman roads into Europe.

Earlier, I mentioned this side of the Jewish economy in

the Diaspora. We tend to think of Jewish-European life in the Diaspora as a sort of nightmarish hell, lived in ghettos under unending oppression. Indeed, by the fifteenth century it had become this in many parts of Europe; but before the Crusades, the Jews were the commercial lifeblood of European civilization—and this accounts for their survival and for their spread throughout the European continent, into England, into France and Germany.

Until the tenth century they moved everywhere with impunity; they belonged to no class or group that had meaning to the barbarians of Europe. They were not Italians or Spaniards or Franks. They had a language of their own—and soon they began to blend it with the language of the people they traded with—and ultimately an extraordinary thing called *Yiddish* (or "Jewish" in English) appeared. They dressed differently, in a sort of semi-Oriental elegance that was good for business; most of them had medical skill, and some were excellent physicians; and they could always produce a little package of pharmaceuticals—more precious than gold.

So did the Jew move up through Italy, along the Roman roads into Gaul and Germany, and by ship to the port of Marseilles, and from there into France.

———•◦•———

One must not fall into the temptation to make the Diaspora of the Jews worse than it was. A Jew could be killed only once, and the very fact that the Jews survived and increased their numbers is evidence that the massacres one hears of so much were intermittent, and genocidal only in Germany. We look back over two thousand years, which is a very long time indeed.

Take Sicily, for example. No one is quite certain when the first Jewish settlement in Sicily took place, but by the beginning of our era there were a number of synagogues there. Or so it is believed; Sicilian history is cloudy over the first few hundred years of our era, and most histories do not even attempt to analyze the population, Greek and Italian and Arab and Phoenician and Jewish—not to mention the peasants who had been there before any of the above arrived. In this place, the Jews were at home. Many of them, curiously, appear to have lived on the dole of the rich. Were these manumitted slaves of the Jewish wars with Rome?

We don't know. The Jew lived nonexplosively in Sicily, so he produced little history. There is a gap of five hundred years about which we know practically nothing. Then we hear of the Jews under the Norman rulers of Sicily. Jew and Norman, Jew and Viking—this is a very old relationship. We have been so beguiled by the picture of the Viking hacking off the head of his fellow man that we have tended to forget that he was a highly civilized and worldly man; and like the Jew, primarily a wandering trader who took his longships into the Mediterranean not simply to loot and burn but to engage in that more sensible, more profitable art of commerce.

The plain truth of it is that the Jew had rapport with seafaring commercial people; it was with the inlanders that his trouble arose. In Sicily the Jew fared well with Norman and Arabs—so well that we discover that suddenly, in the fifteenth century, there were one hundred thousand Jews in Sicily and that there had been more; for along with the Spanish Inquisitional frenzy, that old, diabolical charge was raised in Sicily —that the Jews murdered little Christian children and made matzoh of their blood. This nice bit of Christian lunacy that lingered into the time of Adolf Hitler appeared again and again, especially in Germany—used conveniently to promote a massacre of a local Jewish population. It appears in prosperous, cultured Sicily—a fruitful and lovely land where perhaps a quarter of the population was Jewish. There was a series of bloody, terrible massacres of Jews, and the more than one hundred thousand who remained were expelled. In the year 1492, Sicily destroyed herself—even more thoroughly than Spain. Her merchants, silk weavers, doctors, cartographers, bankers, hydraulic engineers (so important in so arid a land), engravers, goldsmiths, silversmiths—perhaps 90 percent of these were expelled.

For the few years after they left, there was a heady time in Sicily. The Jewish wealth that was surrendered was very great, and it enriched a substantial handful of the Sicilian people. But then Sicily began to die—and since then the process has not ceased. Nor have there been Jews in Sicily since 1492—a few families in the eighteenth and nineteenth centuries—but hardly enough to build a synagogue.

————•••————

If a history of the Jews cannot be written without indicting Christianity, then at least it must make a small bow to the Popes in Rome. Howsoever it went with the Jew in the rest of Italy, in Rome the Jew was protected, and until the year 1555, the various Popes forbade interference with the Jews' worship or violence against their bodies. In those years, the Vatican was a refuge, and there is some evidence suggesting that the savage and dreadful use of the Inquisition by the Dominican Order gave various Popes some anguish. Yet the anguish was not sufficient for any Pope to suppress the Inquisition at that time. But in Rome the Inquisition was held in hand, and until 1555, the papacy treated the Jews with humanity. Jewish schools arose there; and being Rome, it was an important center for Jewish trade.

Elsewhere in Italy, things and conditions affecting the Jews varied. In Venice, Jews were hated and feared. This was because Venice—more than any other city in Europe—was a mercantile-commercial social unit. We have only just noted the fact that worldly and seafaring mercantile folk got along well with the Jews; but the Venetians considered themselves in direct competition with them. Throughout the Middle East, the Jews outsold the Venetians, outbid them, cornered the pearl market again and again—a market the Venetians treasured—and monopolized the trade routes to China. The Jewish Chazars straddled the overland route through Asia into China, and first the Jewish Parthians (we speak here of an important part of the nobility) and then the Moslems controlled the passageways into the Persian

Gulf and the Indian Ocean. There was no sea route around Africa in those days, and the very lack of Jewish cartographers in Venice contributed to the Venetian exclusion from the New World.

Incidentally, the history of Jewish cartography has hardly been investigated. Most historians are content to refer to the school of cartography which was conducted by the Jews of Majorca, and to which seamen from every country came during the Middle Ages to buy not only Jewish maps but Jewish shoreline charts, which had been maintained from very ancient times. Perhaps none of the historians, eminent scholars though they were, has ever sailed a shoreline by dead reckoning and recognition, either with or without a shoreline chart. Frequently, the shoreline chart can mean the difference between life and death; and in a place like the Mediterranean, without modern instruments of navigation, commercial traffic would have been impossible without them. The shoreline chart provides two imperative needs of the mariner: it defines for recognition and places in proper relationship every recognizable landmark along the shore, as, for example, trees, towers, piles of rock, hills, houses, ruins, cliff-faces, and so forth, and secondly it furnishes the absolute ebb-tide depth at every point along the shore where it becomes a danger to navigation—particularly in an area of many islands, a condition frequent in the Mediterranean. If the Jews conducted a school of cartography on Majorca and provided shoreline charts for the Mediterranean and other waters, it meant that they had vast maritime resources to take soundings constantly as the bottom changed and to mark and note the changing recognition points. In ancient times only the Phoenicians had such charts—not even the Greeks, who, though they were bold and daring sailors, were indifferent cartographers—and by the first century of our era, Jewish shipping out of the Levant had replaced most of the Phoenician craft. Not only does this testify to a Jewish maritime continuity from biblical times, but it reinforces the inferences of great Jewish maritime power and wealth up to the time of the Crusades. The full story of how the Jewish cartographers originated and maintained their charts, once it is told, should be fascinating.

From her fear and hatred of Jews and her unwillingness to use Jewish knowledge and skills, Venice suffered more than the Jews themselves. The cities that were her most intense rivals in Italy—Florence, Genoa, Mantua, Ferrara, Verona —all of these were becoming obsessed with the enormous profits of sea and overland trade. But because their feudal lords were still of the treasure-chest mentality, and preferred the shares of peasant labor and boxes of coin and jewels in their strong rooms, the need for capital during the fourteenth and fifteenth and sixteenth centuries became overwhelming. During those times, city after city in central Italy invited Jews to settle there, not only to provide capital for mercantile enterprise but to circulate small-loan money.

In Venice, in 1509 a series of events took place that were to have a special meaning for Jews the world over and a special memory. The Germans attacked Venice. A fairly large number of Jews, most of them refugees from Germany, pleaded to the Venetians to give them refuge in the city rather than subject them to the mercy of the advancing Germans. As much as the Venetians disliked Jews, they were still Italians; they had a sense of mercy, and they disliked Germans more than Jews. The Italian word for "foundry" was *ghetto,* and the Venetians gave the Jews permission to move into the *Ghetto Nuovo,* or New Foundry. There the Jews were segregated, cut off from the rest of the city, and a new word and concept came into the languages of Europe.

Meanwhile, in southern Italy, the expulsion of the Jews from Spain had a marked influence. Sicily had expelled her Jews, and in 1541, the Jews resident in the Kingdom of Naples were expelled. This was a particularly cruel and senseless act, which the Jews have never forgotten—and even today Naples is avoided by Jews as a place of hateful memory. A handful of Jews came there during the Hitler period, and friends of mine who tracked down their synagogue there found it to be a tiny, hidden place—as if the memory of the old times cannot be expunged.

In 1555, Pope Paul IV, fascinated by details about the Ghetto that had been established in Venice—the idea already taking hold in Germany—decided that the Jews of Rome, after seventeen hundred years of unbroken residence and the protection of all Popes preceding him, should be driven into a ghetto. He himself hated Jews, and he issued a bull on the absurdity of coddling them. With him, the peaceful Jewish residence in Rome came to an end—and until the time of Napoleon, the Jews of southern Italy were as driven and persecuted as the Jews in most of western Europe.

Italy was also the road into Germany and Gaul. The Jews were traders, and where there is either a market or the source of what he desires, the trader will go. Throughout history, the force and drive of the trader excites the imagination. Unarmed, he will move where armies have been exterminated; he will endure all obstacles, overcome all difficulties, so long as he may buy and sell—and the Jewish home, tight, peaceful, isolated wherever it was, has always been a strange contrast to the trials and tribulations of the Jew in the mercantile world of the gentile.

The Romans built the roads, and the legions traveled the roads and fought the barbarians on the frontiers and established the outposts of Roman civilization. The Jewish traders went with the legions. They bought and sold what the Roman soldiers needed and they came to know the barbarians, the Franks and the Goths and the Teutons. The barbarians wore bracelets and neckpieces of gold and silver, often hammered cold. They had jewels that had passed through the German forests, after coming out of the Orient and across Asia. They had fine furs. The Jews also had jewels, and the Jews had cotton and silk.

Historians properly eschew surmise; they have proper evidence of a well-established Jewish community in Cologne on the Rhine in the third century of our era; they hesitate to surmise how many centuries before that the Jews were there. Yet having the various classical references to the Jewish association with the legion outposts, it is safe to say that where the legions went the Jews went at more or less the same time. There is some evidence of Jewish legionaries—more likely converts than originally Jewish. The legionary was enlisted— by draft or voluntarily—for twenty years. His life was in the legion. Home was forsaken, wife and child forsaken forever, or for what amounted to that. There were no chaplains in the legions, and the Jew was there with his religion. So conversion to Judaism is understandable.

Some historians hesitate to place too much emphasis upon the Jew's role in history, pointing out that the Jews are a tiny minority in the Western world. But this is true only if one sees the Jew as static, isolated, and unchanging. The reality was quite different, and up until the Crusades, the Jews were a dynamic force in terms of their numbers, being joined through conversion by untold thousands of pagans—and Christians too, although not so many as the pagans—and losing thousands more to Christianity. For a thousand years, they were a salt that Europe desperately needed—especially Germany and France.

By the fifth century of our time, there were Jewish communities and synagogues all over that great stretch of land which is today's France and Belgium and Germany and Switzerland. The Jews moved freely, nor were they ghettoized; and except for a provision in most places against the holding of Christian serfs and slaves, they had equal rights with the Christians. They were an infusion of Byzantium and Persia and India and China and Greece and Italy into Europe. The barbarian chiefs were newly rich and newly rational; they wanted desperately what the Jew had to offer.

The presence of the Jews in Europe was far from an accident, nor was it at this time any sort of a mass flight from persecution; quite to the contrary, it was a useful and necessary social symbiosis between the verve and vitality of the Jew and the explosive energy of the barbarian.

As the Burgundians and the Franks established their empires, this relationship with the Jews continued. The Catholic Church moved slowly into the great Frankish-Teutonic forest land but their hold was still too feeble to convince the new kings that the Jews must be persecuted and destroyed. The ecclesiastical world—and the endless permutations and arguments and shades of meaning that went with it—was still too new and uncertain for meaningful anti-Semitism.

Charlemagne's relationship with the Jews and their position under him during his long reign from 768 to 814 best illustrates Jewish life at that time in western Europe. He needed them, used them, and valued them—and thus there was a great increase of Jewish population, wealth, and power during those years.

Charlemagne was a man of strength and intelligence, and under him a large empire came into being. Suddenly, his vision was broadened and he had a desperate need to penetrate beyond the forests and fields of Germany and France. He was in love with civilization, with the pomp and beauty and comfort that civilization represented. He heard of Harun al-Rashid—and there he must send an embassy, a train of pomp and power; and how else could he even know the direction, except for the Jews? So the Jews made up his embassies; they were his advisers; they helped him to create a navy; they financed his undertakings.

You will recall the note about Charlemagne standing on a hilltop and seeing a ship and presuming that it was a Jewish ship. That was the time of Jewish merchant sea power, and Jewish ships were in every sea. It was to the Jews that Charlemagne must turn for his naval designers, for his charts, for his paths across the land and sea.

During this time, the time of Charlemagne and his successor, Ludwig the Pious and the Carolingian kings who followed, the Jews waxed strong, wealthy, and proud in the

Frankish and German lands. But anti-Semitism was already
moving toward the culminating horror of the Crusades. The
bishops harped shrilly and unendingly about "those who
murdered our Lord," preparing the population for the beginning of a frenzy that lasted for almost a thousand years.
The Christian Church organized anti-Semitism ideologically and programatically; but they were not the first anti-
Semites. One must admit that a dynamic interplay between
Jew and non-Jew in any given land contributed to the rise
of some anti-Semitism. Either the leading figures of the
country in question became Jewish—as in Chazaria and Persia and Parthia—or the population turned on the Jews. If
the Jews had been a poor, quivering, cowering, and poverty-
stricken group, this would not have happened; but even in
their worst circumstances, the Jews encased themselves in
a pride and aloofness that irritated the gentile.

This was especially true in Europe of the Middle Ages,
where a rigid class system arose. There were the nobility, divided into upper and lower groups, the craftsmen set into
guilds, the Church as a clerical class, the mercenary soldiers,
and the serfs. There was always a certain amount of elastic-
ity, a shifting from one group into another—an upward
struggle by men of force and character—but by and large,
the class lines were set. The Jew, however, moved outside of
and apart from these classes; and since he controlled so much
of commerce and finance, he was wealthy or wealthier than
the nobility, without any of the power or social prestige of
the nobility.

To illustrate how this process worked, take the case of the
downfall of the famous Rabbi Gershom ben Judah, a
teacher and Talmudist who lived in the last stage of this
period. He was born in the year 965, and before the end of
the tenth century he was the head of a great academy of Jewish studies in Mainz in western Germany. Now it is very simple to state the fact and pass on; but what exactly does this
mean? We must first see Mainz as it was then, a town of
wretched early-medieval houses, muddy streets, squalor,
filth, meanness; a town where 100 percent of the nonclerical

population was illiterate, with no hope or desire to be anything else, where the townsfolk wore stinking leather jerkins
and trousers year to year, where to have two suits of clothes
was rare indeed, where the whole horizon was what a man
could walk in a day, where the ignorance of anything and
everything beyond that horizon was dark and absolute—
and above all a place where recent Teutonic paganism had
yielded only partially to a primitive and superstitious Christianity that would not be recognizable to any Christian of
today.

Into this setting, the Jews. The academy was a fine, large
brick and stone building. Attached to it was a sort of community center with a large swimming pool, the *mikvah*. The
Jews lived in the best houses in the city—only inferior to the
castles of the barons, but superior in taste and furnishings.
The Jews wore long silken robes, any one of which could
command enough money to support a family in the town
for a year. They walked like kings. They were exempt
from all military service. They had slaves to serve them—
slaves imported from the distant Levant, a place the townsfolk could not even visualize. Their women did no work and
were reverenced even more than the women of the nobility.
Their children were kept explicitly apart from the German
children—clean, well-fed Jewish children who went to
school for hours every day. The Jews had a language of their
own. They regarded the local Germans with a sort of tolerant contempt—and they gave the local Germans an uneasy
sense of being savages. They prayed in their own secret language. Though they were not of the nobility, they were
apparently respected by the nobility. They had books; they
read and wrote; and they were the very same people who
murdered God—the good, warm, beautiful German God
whose name was Jesus and who had replaced the old gods,
Wotan and Loge and Siegmund and Siegfried and the
others; and in the cloudy vision of these townsfolk, perhaps
the Jews were also responsible for the fall of the old gods,
and some said that the new good German God whom they
murdered was also a Jew—but anything could be believed

of these dark people with their silken robes and their cropped beards and mustaches and their Hebrew—a magic tongue that no one understood who was not of them.

We must realize the above and understand the minds of the people the bishops preached to. Even in the lifetime of Rabbi Gershom, the thing exploded and the triumph of hate began. His academy was burned and he and the other Jews were robbed, many of them killed, and all of them driven out of Mainz.

———•••·———

I mentioned earlier the flux, the expanding and contracting beat of the Jewish people through history. We pick a single spot—the town of Würzburg in Bavaria. There is some indication that several Jewish families lived there in the tenth century. No indications in the eleventh century. A very considerable population by the year 1114. In 1147, anti-Semitic riots, a number of Jews killed, and still fewer remained. But a time came when the Jews were gone—not to return for hundreds of years. Such was the flux of Jewish population through this period which covered the period of the Crusades. The Crusades destroyed Jewish hegemony over large areas of European-Levantine trade. Through the centuries up to the time of the Crusades (1096, the beginning of the First Crusade) countless thousands of Jews accepted baptism and became Christians (but never in a national sense, as we saw in Spain) and countless thousands of Christians became Jews. There was perhaps a degree of freedom in this pre-Crusade exchange of faith.

Moving north from Italy, across the Alps into Germany, from Marseille north along the Rhone River, northwest toward Normandy, northward from the Alps along the Rhine River, through the German forests to the endless fens of the Low Countries, and then northeast into Bohemia and Saxony and Prussia and then across Prussia to the lands of the Poles and the Lithuanians—such was the course of the Jewish people into the European Diaspora over a thousand years —from the third century to the thirteenth century.

There were other routes and movements—but minor compared to these. A few hundred Jews crossed over into England from Normandy with William the Conqueror. During the next two hundred years, their numbers increased to about five or six thousand, and for so few people, they made a curious impact upon British history. Jewish communities existed in Norwich and London and York and Bristol and a few other places. Coming originally at the invitation of the Norman barons—with whom they had lived amicably for centuries—they found themselves caught in the strife and tension between Norman and Saxon, Norman churchman and Saxon churchman, Saxon peasant and Norman knight, baron and king—a period of two centuries from 1066 to 1290. In this vortex, England was extended far beyond her financial strength, and the Jewish financiers were bled dry and then cast aside. When the Crown and the great barons withdrew their protection from the handful of Jews in England, anti-Semitism flowered. Riots and burnings. Ritual murder charges. And then the opening of sources for funds in Milan and Florence, among the Italian bankers and moneylenders. In 1290, the Jews were expelled from England—and not until the time of Cromwell were Jews allowed to establish communities there again. But more on this later.

Another direction was north through Greece and Macedon into Hungary. From there into Poland and Bessarabia—and then back, an ebb and flow that went on for centuries, depending upon the possibility for existence in either place.

From Bessarabia, the area north of the Black Sea that is watered by the Dniester River, Jews moved across the north shore of the sea toward the Crimea. But the largest movement of Jews into Russia was a flow north from Germany and through Poland.

The conversion to Christianity of the Frankish-German population that stretched from the North Sea and the Bay of Biscay eastward to the Polish plains and the Slovakian highlands was no quick or simple task. In this great area were literally thousands of tribal islands, each ruled by its own feudal chief, duchies, baronies, manors, kingdoms, principalities, nameless plots of land defended by single castles, walled free cities, walled free ports, leagues of towns, leagues of petty chieftains, and so forth—each with its own degree of Christianity during a period of hundreds of years. There were parts of Germany that were not actually Christian until the tenth century, and the Prussian Teutonic Order of Knights was attempting to bring Christianity to the Lithuanian heathen via mace and sword and the well-tried bleeding process as late as the fourteenth century.

It was in this situation, over a period of almost a thousand years, that the Jews spread across Europe and into Poland and Lithuania and Russia. They tended to move as a fringe on the edge of Christianity, not only because there was so much less hatred and oppression among the pagans but because commercial opportunities were always better where a robust barbarian people were taking the energetic initial step to civilization. At the same time, the movement was never a fringe as such, but a fringe with a blanket behind it; and so long was the presence of large and vital Jewish communities in the Frankish-German lands that a fascinating, viable language evolved among the Jewish people, a language called Yiddish which is still spoken by hundreds of thousands of Jews today.

———•••———

But before we examine the origin of Yiddish, we must see the situation that ended the Jewish commercial network to so large an extent, and which began the isolation of the Jews. Yiddish was a part of the response to this situation—which history calls the Crusades.

Like all large movements of mankind, the Crusades had both an ideological and an economic base. Economically, the French feudal leaders, the French shipowners, and the Italian feudal leaders, shipowners, and bankers had come to the conclusion that the united strength of England, France, Germany, and Italy could break the Moslem hold on the Levantine trade—and thereby break and destroy the Jewish monopoly of such trade in Europe, as well as the Jewish-Moslem trade understanding. We must note that the above is couched in modern terms; medieval thought, however, was not modern thought, and most of these feudal princes—not to mention the men they led—were little removed from their superstitious semibarbarian ancestors. There were great extremes: the culture and sophistication of the Italians and many of the French, as against the barbarism of certain Germans; there were also sections of the feudal nobility that wanted no part of the adventure. Nor is this to say that those with economic interests sat down and plotted the vehicle of Crusade. The time was ripe; Crusade was in the air—and they simply gave it their blessing, financial and otherwise.

To unite those who would have to do the fighting, the ideological notion of a Crusade for Christianity was put forward. On this question, curiously, the Church was split. There were Catholic bishops who supported the Crusades and preached a kind of insane hatred of the infidel, Jew and Moslem alike; and there were other Catholic bishops who opened their homes to the Jew and died with the Jews. From its onset, the first Crusade was immediately directed against the Jews and secondarily against the Moslems; nor were the Crusades a sudden notion. The freedom of the Christian sanctuary from the Moslem hold had been discussed for decades; the idea was ripe when the Italian and French merchants decided to act.

At the Council of Clermont, Peter the Hermit preached to a great gathering of the "flower of French chivalry," with Pope Urban II listening approvingly in the background. Such was the chivalrous spirit of the "flowers" that one, Godfrey of Bouillon, fired by the glory of the moment and the hope of redeeming Jerusalem, the city of Jesus, from the infidel, took a mighty oath: "I will avenge the blood of little Jesus on the blood of the Jews—and God willing leave not one of the cursed lot alive." This was a profitable and negotiable position that Godfrey took, and being a reasonable man, he accepted protection money of five hundred silver marks (about twenty thousand dollars in today's purchasing power) from every Jewish community he visited. Peter the Hermit, vying with Godfrey in his own hatred, exacted larger sums. Volkmar—a knight of noble memory—swore a mighty oath that he would not leave Lorraine until he had slain at least one Jew. He had to compromise with an old woman. A detachment of German Crusaders, scorning Godfrey's cheap price, murdered twenty-two Jews at Metz, raped a number of their women, beat out the brains of a teen-age boy who protested, and came out of it with over twenty thousand marks. This was in the spring of 1096.

In May of that spring, in the town of Speyer, a certain Bishop John prevented the Crusaders from burning a synagogue packed with Jews. They had to be content with fourteen Jews, two of whom they crucified. The spirit widened: in Mainz, where, as we noted, Rabbi Gershom ben Judah had established his academy of Jewish studies, the Archbishop Ruthard, sick at what was happening, promised protection to the Jews. He brought them into the monastery, but the Crusaders forced the gates and killed hundreds and hundreds of men, women, and children. The Jews fought back, but poorly armed and with no knowledge of warfare, they were almost helpless before the mailed knights. In Worms, all the Jews were killed. Killing the infants, the Crusaders cried out that they were saving the souls of the children for Christ. There as in most places, the Jewish houses, synagogues, and community buildings were burned.

In Cologne, where the Jews had lived since Roman times, where the whole city population benefited from their charities, and where they had fed the poor and hungry for centuries, the Christians took the Jews into their own homes and told the Crusaders to pass by or take the city with fire and sword. The Crusaders had little stomach for storming the city, so they held off. Meanwhile, the burghers and Archbishop Hermann of Cologne decided that the Jews would be safer if they were distributed among seven neighboring villages. But the Crusaders got wind of this, and surrounded village after village, killing the Jews to the last woman and child in each place. In Neuss, the Crusaders were drunk, and in the spirit of good fun they flung more than twenty women and almost a hundred children into the river, seeing how far two men could fling a screaming child. At Mors, almost a thousand Jewish bodies were observed floating in the Rhine. At Altenarh, the humane Archbishop Egbert attempted to defend the Jews and was beaten half to death. In Regensburg, the Jews were cut down in the streets. A Count Agthar likened it to rabbit hunting. A great pile of Jewish bodies was dragged into the main square, and Crusaders amused themselves by beheading the dead. Over four thousand Jews were killed in this Rhine district alone.

But crusading in the name of Christ went on everywhere. and lest it should be thought that this was simply a German aberration, one must recall our earlier mention of the Crusaders in Jerusalem, and one might note that England was also involved. Aware of the distance between England and Jerusalem and convinced that a bird in the hand was worth two in the bush, or a Jew in England worth two infidels in the Levant, the followers of Richard the Lion-Hearted turned their attention to the Jews of Lynn. Killing all of them they could catch, stripping the bodies naked, and then pillaging the Jewish houses, they went on to Stamford. Ten days later they were at Colchester—then Thetford, then Ospringe, where they got a bit out of hand and killed a dozen Christians. In York, a half-insane mob, led by some drunken Crusaders, marched to attack the Jews. About five hundred of them fled to the Royal Keep, which at that moment was empty, the Royal Warder being away. The Jews took refuge there, barricaded the stout doors, and listened from behind them to the threats and infamies of the mob. Days passed. Weak from hunger, parched by thirst, the Jews chose an alternative to the tortures and crucifixion that the mob promised. They killed each other, submitting willingly. Their gentle Rabbi Yomtov was the last, and he died by his own hand.

So was Jesus honored in a mighty Christian effort called the Crusades. One could go on and on, detailing the horror that happened in almost every community in Europe, not to

mention those in Asia. Indeed, a meticulous observer could
have created an encyclopedia of bestiality out of that madness which history remembers as the "Holy Crusades."

There came a time, in the year 1320, when the Crusades
were finished, but the nightmare they created was not finished for the Jews of Europe until the nineteenth century
—and in Germany it was not finished at all.

————•••••————

How many thousands of Jews fled Germany during the
Crusades we will never know; but they fled to the kinder
heathen in Poland and Lithuania and they took their language with them. So was Yiddish plucked out of Germany
and born as a Jewish language, a language rich, soft, and
lovely to the ear.

Yiddish, of course, was not a language with Jewish or
Semitic roots. It probably began in the Teutonic dialects of
the various Germanic tribes and in the legion encampments,
where by the third century most of the soldiers were German. Probably by the seventh century, it had centered itself in the Middle Rhineland in and around the city of Cologne, where the largest Jewish community in Germany had
come into being. There and in the surrounding towns, it became the Jewish language; it spread; it took on elsewhere;
and after the Crusades it moved north and east with the
Jews in their mass movement out of Germany.

In its growth, it structured itself curiously but logically.
In the great Frankish-Gothic-Germanic heartland of Europe, a trading dialect had to have a Teutonic base, and
that broad base was brought into a sort of order in the Rhineland. Germanic lettering was varied and primitive in those
days, and frequently unreadable in its Gothic complexity;
so the Jews wrote the language in the script and lettering
they had used for two thousand years, the Hebrew alphabet. The base was Germanic, but the Teutonic dialects were
the speech of semibarbarian tribesmen, a speech limited to
objects familiar to these tribesmen and hardly capable of any
kind of philosophical abstraction—not to mention the

words basic to the vast historical and geographic world that was a part of the Jewish life and memory. French and Italian were more sophisticated, so the Jews filled missing spaces with various selections from these two languages; but for Jewish life and communication hundreds and hundreds of words were needed which existed in none of those languages and could only be found in the Hebrew.

So the language came into being with a German base, French and Italian (very early forms) additives, and a philosophical, geographical, social, and religious superstructure of Hebrew. Written in the same Hebrew alphabet that every Jewish child was taught, useful in simple speech with the Germans of pre-Crusade times, it became a part of the Jewish character.

After the Crusades, Jewish life in Europe changed radically. Jews were isolated—and in time the ghetto idea came into being. But even before the period of the ghetto, the Jews were cut off from all normal intercourse with the people among whom they lived. Their great commercial network was smashed by the Crusaders; and once the way to the Levant was opened, Italian and French shipowners destroyed the entire Jewish maritime structure, blatantly confiscating or sinking the thousands of Jewish cargo ships and galleys. An unending period of permissive lawlessness—lawful so long as it was directed against Jews—had begun; and serious debates took place on the question of whether any sin was involved in the murder of a Jew and whether it was more sinful to kill a Jewish child than a Jewish woman or man. All the dark tragic frustrations of the European serf, the visionless peasant, were directed against the Jew. The feudal lords and the feudal clergy directed this frustration and used anti-Semitism as a means of control. All legitimate hates and resentments and demands could be steered off against the visible Antichrist, the Jew who was put forward as Satan among them.

This was not universally the case; as we saw before, this or that duke or count must perforce protect the Jew on occasion for his own needs; but it was very widely the case.

In this situation, Yiddish, the language of the Jews, shared
in the isolation. The medieval German basis of the language
froze, so to speak, for in the fourteenth and fifteenth centuries, the language was for the most part directed inward.
German spoken by non-Jewish Germans changed and became
modern German—and so separated more and more from
Yiddish; until today, except for very simple kitchen talk,
Yiddish is hardly understandable to German-speaking people; although strangely enough, people who speak Yiddish
well understand simple German. Yiddish became reticent
where German is aggressive; as the language of the closely
knit oppressed, it tended toward far greater use of intimate
forms; and without the hard discipline of German education to maintain it rigidly, it tended to soften, to become gen-
tler, more easily slurred than German. It moved and grew as
the product of the Jewish mind—which was very different
indeed from the German mind—and it shaped itself to the
intimacy of the Jewish social structure in the dreadful years
that followed the Crusades.

Far more than Ladino, Yiddish became the language of a
specific people. The Spanish Jews were Spaniards—perhaps more Spanish than ever their oppressors became—
but the Ashkenazi (the Hebrew word for *German,* and applied generally to European Jews) Jews never became Italian or French or German or Polish or Lithuanian or Ukrainian or Russian; they remained Jewish, and throughout the
lands of their greatest numbers, their language was simply
called Jewish (or Yiddish).

They became a people unto themselves within this place
and language; they developed their own literature out of it;
and at the highest point of their integration as a Yiddish-
speaking social-collective—in the twentieth century—they
numbered over twelve million people speaking the same
language. In this language they translated all their great clas-
sics; in this language, they created a theater both vibrant
and skilled, and a whole library of theatrical work. In Yiddish, they created hundreds of newspapers, a school of the
short story perhaps unmatched in our time, novels, poems,

philosophical works—and so extraordinary and varied a group of original literary forms that space prohibits even the itemization.

Mainly, Yiddish was the language of the masses of Jews who fled Germany into eastern Europe; but in time, the language was brought from Poland into France and from Lithuania into England. When the Jews came from Russia to the United States by the millions, they brought their Yiddish language with them. It went with them to Mexico and Latin America, and by other routes into other countries—until it became the language of the Jews the world over.

It is true that in the reconstitution of Israel as a Jewish state, Hebrew was chosen as the national language—and for very good reasons. The Jewish continuity in Palestine, that is, the Jewish communities that had lived there through all the Diaspora, spoke Hebrew; and among the immigrants were thousands of Ladino-speaking Jews from Greece, Turkey, and North Africa—as well as those Jews from the Arab nations who spoke Arabic and frequently Hebrew as a second language. The majority of the first immigrants came from the Yiddish-speaking Ashkenazi Diaspora of eastern Europe, but as they die off, Yiddish will diminish in Israel and possibly disappear entirely as a spoken language.

In the United States, during the sixty years from 1880 to 1940, Yiddish was spoken and read as a second language by over three million people, and among perhaps a million and a half, it was a first language. More of this when we talk about the Diaspora in the United States.

Today, however, Yiddish is a dying language—for the six million Jews who were put to death by Nazism were for the most part Yiddish-speaking, and they were about 40 percent of all the Jews in the world. Yiddish was the language of a European people under the pressure of terrible oppression and isolation. Neither the pressure nor the isolation ever existed in the United States, and therefore there was small inclination among American Jews to perpetuate the language. The social structure of the United States is not such as to invite a multiplicity of languages among its many na-

tionalities of immigrants, nor does it force into being structured enclaves of language such as exist in so many places
in Europe.

The first generation of eastern European Jews in America
spoke Yiddish among themselves and transmitted it to their
children—just as other immigrant nationalities did with
their children; but the second generation had English as
their prime language, and there was no incentive to keep
Yiddish alive in the home and pass it on to a third generation. Schools were set up here and there to teach Yiddish—
for the language is such in its warmth and beauty and in the
fact that it evolved as the tongue of a people in almost un-
endurable anguish, that it broke the hearts of sensitive and
creative Yiddish-speaking Jews to see it pass into a decline.
But the artificial promulgation of a language against a vital
existing language is next to impossible, as the Irish and Welsh
have discovered; and today, among third and fourth and fifth
generation American Jews of eastern European descent,
Yiddish is rarely spoken, and soon it will be spoken in America only by scholars and Yiddishists.

It is also understandable that Germany offered no fertile
soil for the survival of Yiddish—except during the later
medieval period and the time of the Reformation. So close
is the language in its base to German, that once out of the
ghetto, the German Jew turned to German almost immediately. It was with the Jews who left Germany that Yiddish
flowered and flourished.

————•◆•————

After the Crusades, Germany became for the Jews a place
of unremitting horror. Hatred for the Jew became a part of
German being, of German culture—and even of German
"excellence," as the German mind saw it. In 1298, Rindfleisch, a German knight, promoted a series of dreadful massacres in the district of Franconia. This stemmed from that
frightful invention previously mentioned that has had such
a hold on the German mind through the centuries—even up
to modern times—namely, that the Jews murder little gen-

tile children—preferably blond—and use their blood for ritual purposes. This piece of malicious nonsense is somehow fixed to the Germans' picture of the Jews, and a great mob-army of Germans, led by the Baron Rindfleisch, murdered the Jews in 146 communities. As always in these German affairs, women and children were murdered along with the men. (And I cannot help noting that nowhere in ancient warfare, among so-called pagans and barbarians, do we find anything to match this grim Christian wrath.) In the 146 towns and villages, not a single Jew was left alive.

In 1336, a movement arose in Germany that was based on the single fact of killing Jews. The members wore a short jacket of red leather and were called the *Armleder,* the name possibly referring to an overlay of leather armguards. Feeling themselves divinely motivated—within the German understanding of Christianity—they massacred the Jews in almost a hundred communities, most of them in Swabia and Alsace.

Twelve years later, Europe was scourged by the disease remembered as the Black Death. Living under the strict regime of their dietary and lavatory laws, the Jews were to a very large extent exempt from the disease—which naturally led to the conclusion on the part of the Germans that the Jews had caused the disease by poisoning the wells. Over 210 communities of Jews were utterly annihilated. So hideous did the slaughter become that Pope Clement VI issued a bull pleading for mercy for the Jews. The Emperor Charles IV negated this by granting the right to loot and kill to all those who brought one third of their boodle to the Crown. This was a period in German life of contest between the guilds and the petty nobility. Not only were the craft guilds moving toward a larger share of state power, but they needed money for various types of expansion and construction. This money was to a large extent borrowed from Jews, and during the Black Death massacres, there was a wide attempt—quite successful—to cancel all indebtedness by the murder of the debtors. Although 210 Jewish communities had been wiped out, almost 400 others were attacked and suffered deaths. The toll of how many thousands of Jews were murdered by the Germans during this sad time has never been precisely calculated; but this was the worst holocaust of the Middle Ages, not to be equaled until Adolf Hitler turned the tools of modern science, in the hands of the capable German citizen, to the same end.

Considering this part of the long, strange march of the Jewish people through history in context with the beginnings of Yiddish as a Jewish language unique in Jewish history, we begin to comprehend the forces that drove the Jews out of Germany proper into those lands where simpler and less "civilized" people lived. This exodus, which began after the first Crusade, continued for the next three hundred years— until the only Jewish communities remaining in Germany existed in the ghettos of Worms and Frankfort on the Main. While the ghetto in Venice had been established as a refuge for Jews fleeing the German horror, the ghetto at Frankfort had been established almost a hundred years before. It was a walled-in area, with entrance or egress only through heavy gates; and the opening and closing of these gates were not at the will of the Jews but of the Germans.

In these German ghettos, the Jews lived for generation after generation, maintained themselves and their community, carried on trade and finance of sorts, maintained synagogues and schools of Jewish study, carried on their charitable endeavors—even to feeding the gentiles in periods of famine—and eventually produced many of the great modern Jewish merchant families, as for example the Rothschilds, who originated in the ghetto of Frankfort on the Main. In fact, there are few incidents in the history of mankind that testify so much to the stamina of man as the Jewish experience in Germany.

When the Protestant Reformation began in Germany, the Jews had great hopes for their emancipation—or for at least a lessening of the oppression, but Martin Luther, after a time of tolerance toward Jews, reverted to anti-Semitism.

Not until the late seventeenth century did some rays of sunlight for the Jews lighten the German scene. The small, competitive German states, after the Thirty Years War, struggled for magnificence in a mercantile world. They needed capital desperately, and only the Jews could show them how to get it and how to build an apparatus for trade. For in this area the Germans had small experience, while those Spanish Jews who had settled in Holland and Belgium, as refugees, had become a significant and knowledgeable force in European trade and finance. Thus the court Jew came into being. Spanish Jews found their way to Hamburg, where a new Jewish community was founded. A Jewish community arose in Berlin.

During the eighteenth and nineteenth centuries, the German Jews breached the ghetto walls and began to enter the mainstream of German life. They entered with brilliance and personal distinction—and soon drove to prominence in almost every field. Anti-Semitism was still present; hatred for the Jew abounded; but momentarily the Germans had embraced culture and tolerance, and during this interval the German passion for mass murder and the German delight in death was temporarily eschewed.

Beginning with Moses Mendelssohn, Jewish names appeared everywhere in German life—in music and literature, in science, in the new art of prophylactic medicine, in commerce, and in finance.

Mendelssohn himself was the founder of a great German-Jewish family. He was born in Dessau in 1729, and he died in 1786. As a young man in Berlin, he studied philosophy, mathematics, history—and a variety of languages, enough to make of himself an important linguist of the time. In a sense, he was the father of the new German-Jewish cultural-mercantile explosion, literally as well as figuratively; for while he was in himself a vigorous and brilliant spokesman for things Jewish, he fathered a distinguished family: Joseph, born in 1770 and founder of the famous banking firm of Mendelssohn and Company, Abraham, who would become the father of the famous composer, Felix Mendelssohn—Bartholdy, and Dorothea, Recha and Henrietta, three rather extraordinary women.

Gotthold Ephraim Lessing, who was born in 1729, poet, playwright, and critic, was a close friend of Moses Mendelssohn and modeled the protagonist of his rather astonishing philosophical play *Nathan the Wise* after him. Lessing was the most noted of a whole group of writers, mathematicians, and philosophers, Jews who burst upon the German scene in the first flush of the emancipation.

Of course, one cannot speak of the new freedom in Germany without referring to the House of Rothschild. The founder of the house, Mayer Amschel Rothschild (the name means "red shield" and derives from the specific location of the house the family lived in—at the Sign of the Red Shield—at Frankfort on the Main), began as a dealer in antique coins. During the wars of the French Revolution, Mayer became financial agent for the Landgrave of Hesse-Cassel, the same landgrave whose poverty became legendary in his sale of mercenaries to the British to fight in America against the Continentals—it is to be hoped that Mayer demonstrated to him simpler ways to solve his problems. In any case, Mayer became not only wealthy in his own right, but the founder of one of the greatest banking families on earth —a family which cherished its Judaism and established a tradition of charity and humanity.

A momentary lapse among the Germans into a passionate anti-Semitism and violence occurred in 1819. Some thorough German scholar had discovered the ancient anti-Semitic battle cry of the Crusaders, "Hep! Hep!"—an abbreviation of *Hierosolyma est perdita* ("Jerusalem is destroyed")—and this was picked up by the German youth of the time, to be shouted at every passing Jew and to be the battle cry for beating and mugging and often killing Jews—mostly elderly—caught by gangs of hoodlums. But this lapse led to no mass slaughters, and while anti-Semitism was always a principled position for the German people, the nineteenth century proved to be a time of freedom and enlightenment. This extended into the first two decades of the twentieth century, and then came to its tragic end.

As a cause once removed, the German barbarism toward the Jews played the major role in bringing into being the culturally Yiddish Jews of the great Polish-Lithuanian-Russian area, Jews whose social existence can be so totally embraced by the word *Yiddish*. The importance of this segment of the Jewish people can be best understood if we realize that of the eleven million Jews in the world today, almost nine million are descended from the Ashkenazi Jews of this area, and of the six million Jews the Nazis murdered, well over five million were from this area.

Since in all the years of emigration from Germany into Poland as the gateway to eastern Europe and the Baltic area, no more than half a million Jews could have passed through (and this is a large estimate), one must realize that the life of the Jews in Poland was rich and fruitful at times, as well as sad and cruel at other times. At the beginning of the twentieth century, there were less than half a million Jews in all of Germany; there were more than ten times that number in eastern Europe. This does not mean that Russia and Poland did not persecute the Jews; intermittently, they persecuted them savagely; indeed, the Russians proved second to none in their ferocity—but where were the Jews to flee? Further north was only cold and darkness—and the rule of the Czars stretched to the polar ice cap itself. So the Jews developed the art of survival. They remained and they multiplied.

Jewish historians love to dwell on the delicious mystery of Chazaria and the Chazarian Jews. It is easy to understand how so bookish and essentially gentle a people as the Jews would look with romantic delight upon a Jewish nation of fierce nomad horsemen, who could put forty thousand cavalry into the field, and who ruled a vast area of central Asia, wide as the Black Sea, inclusive of the Crimea, and stretching northward for seven or eight hundred miles, the Volga basin eastward to the Dnieper River. But there is no permanence to a nomad people; they sink no roots into the earth; and if their flocks perish, they are blown away like the wind. And while the Chazars were pagans who had adopted the Jewish religion and circumcision, whether they were Jews in a cultural-social sense is another matter.

The legend behind the conversion of the Chazars to Judaism goes thus: in the seventh century, King Bulan of Chazaria won a great victory over the Arabs. Believing that this had been granted to him through the mercy of the supreme God, he called to him representatives of the three religions that worshipped this God, namely, the Jews, Christians, and Moslems. Each put forward his belief; but when the King spoke to them separately, asking each to choose between the two other faiths, only the Jew refused to make a choice. The Christian chose Judaism as preferable to Mohammedanism, and the Moslem chose Judaism as preferable to Christianity —whereupon King Bulan chose Judaism as the religion of the Chazars. Of course, this is a legend, and the reality was probably quite different.

Be that as it may, it is doubtful that any but the nobility took their Judaism very seriously. Jews they were, but they built no synagogues, and in their great black tents or on their war-horses, they could hardly plant that basic unit of Judaism, the Jewish home. In any case, during the eleventh and twelfth centuries the Russian Varangians united with the Bulgars and the Crimean Goths to destroy the Chazars. Like the horsemen of that other Jewish-led nation, Parthia, the Chazarian cavalry was not easily defeated. Indeed, Hannibal, during his invasion of Italy, proved that well-led cavalry cannot (in terms of pre-gunpowder war) be defeated by foot soldiers, so long as feed and remounts are available.

No one knows precisely what happened to the Chazars, but the likelihood is that they were driven out of the Volga basin onto the eastern steppes. In terms of origin, we know only that they were a Turkic-speaking people; and thus probably related to the Turkic-speaking nomads of the great Asian steppes. There, cut off from any further intercourse with the Jews, they either forgot their religion or brought it with them to Hungary—for there is some speculation that they were a part of the Hun invasion of Europe.

But the plain fact is that they passed off the stage of history.

Many Jewish writers propose to see in the Chazars a considerable portion of the Jews who subsequently settled in the
Ukraine, but I must reject this completely. The Ukrainian
Jews, like the Polish and Lithuanian Jews, were Yiddish-
speaking, Ashkenazi in Hebrew usage and ritual, and Yiddish
in culture. I know of no Turkic words in their speech, no
memory, not even the vaguest, of Chazaria, no real knowledge
of Chazaria, and no mood or tendency among them to suggest
a nomad-warrior background. In fact, the strongest pacifist,
nonviolent tendencies ever to arise among any people in
history were the product of Yiddish culture in eastern Europe.

As for the early Jewish trading posts on the Baltic shore,
they perished after the Crusades destroyed Jewish trade.
It is very possible that these Jews joined the Lithuanian
communities; and since they were few in number, they would
be readily absorbed. But the plain fact of the matter is that
the Yiddish-speaking Jews of the eastern European Diaspora
came out of Germany, bringing their basically German language with them—in flight from the German massacres of
the Crusade and post-Crusade period.

But the memory of the early Jewish traders helped to
dispel the mysteries of the Polish-Lithuanian area. Most
likely, the Jews were the first Mediterranean people to enter
Poland and Lithuania—and the Jews came as they came everywhere, with their miracles of silk and linen and cotton, their
cloth of the legendary royal purple, their bales of Chazarian
fur, their jewels and perfumes and spices, their medicines
and their extraordinary skill as surgeons and physicians.
This was in the eighth, ninth, and tenth centuries—when
the Jewish trading posts still existed on the Baltic shore,
when trade with the Viking longships was brisk and profitable. But this was no movement of peoples, only of individual
traders—perhaps enough for a synagogue somewhere on the
Baltic. The movement of peoples began after the Crusades.

It is frequently thought today that the Christianization

of Europe was a short process—that Pope Gregory gave his blunt command to go out and convert the heathen, and lo, the heathen was converted. Not quite; it took well over a thousand years to bring Christianity to Europe, and even as late as the beginning of the fifteenth century, there were pagan people on the northern Baltic shore. By the tenth century, the tide of Christianity had been halted at the Polish borders, and all to the north and the east was pagan, Scandinavia and Poland and Lithuania and much of the great stretches of Russia. If, as legend has it, Poland granted the first charter to Jewish immigrants from Germany in the year 905, then these Poles were pagans, and like pagans everywhere they welcomed the Jews with pleasure and great interest. As the Crusades rolled across Germany, the influx of Jews into Poland increased, and after the First Crusade, there were probably thousands of Jews and perhaps dozens of important Jewish communities in Poland. That the Jews were a civilizing influence cannot be denied—although we have very little written material of the time, this because during subsequent periods Jewish synagogues and libraries were destroyed—particularly in the Tatar invasion of 1240, when the Jews fought side by side with the Poles in defense of Poland. So deeply and importantly had the Jews become a part of Polish life during the thirteenth and fourteenth centuries that many of the Polish coins of the period bear an inscription in Hebrew as well as in Polish.

The Jewish population in Poland increased as the German bloodletting increased, and some Jews moved north into pagan Lithuania where they repeated their economic integration; yet Poland itself was either pagan or ambivalently Christian during the twelfth and thirteenth centuries. So long as the bishops in Poland were unsure of their ground, so long as the native feudal princes were able to resist complete control by the Church, their anger might more likely be directed against the new religion than against the Jews. Many an early bishop in Poland found himself at the whipping post for too much zeal, and thereby the anti-Semitic movement was slow and careful.

A great deal went on in that border area between Germany and Poland that is only vaguely remembered, and one of the reasons that we are unable to describe the movement of the Jews precisely concerns the Order of the Teutonic Knights. This was a German order of knighthood, modeled after the Knights Templars, but like so many things German, unique in its own way, particularly in the art of savagery. The Teutonic Knights pledged themselves to Christ and the redemption of the pagan.

The valley of the Vistula River and the lands on either side of it to its mouth on the Baltic Sea were inhabited by a people called the Prussians. Though they gave their name to the area, they were not German, nor were they Christians; most likely, they were a Slavic-language group with strong Viking influence. It is hard to be specific about the Prussians. There is evidence that the Jews had trade relations with these people as far back as the third century, and by the twelfth century there were important Jewish communities among the (Slavic) Prussians.

The Order of the Teutonic Knights moved against these pagan people early in the twelfth century, in what was called the "Prussian Crusade." The Teutonic Knights exterminated the Prussians and the Jews among them. The Pomeranian barons cooperated with the Crusaders and hunted down any Prussians who fled into their area. The Teutonic Knights methodically surrounded every community and slaughtered the inhabitants, who were no match for the heavily armed and armored knights and the mobs of eager Germans who followed them—and this methodical slaughter went on for a long time, until the Prussian people had vanished forever from the pages of history.

There were two explanations that the Teutonic Order offered for their actions: firstly, that since German bishops rode with them (armed with maces instead of swords, so that they, as clerics, would not break the Catholic Church's injunction against a priest shedding blood, and would therefore not be guilty of sin) and gave the dying an opportunity to embrace Christ and thereby be saved from hellfire, their

deeds were missionary; and secondly, it was not fitting that
pagan barbarians should hold the fertile lands of East Prussia
when so many of the Teutonic Knights were landless.

This action on Poland's border took place almost at the
same time that Poles and Jews were fighting the Tatars; and
when that war against the Tatars was over, much of Poland
was in ruins; the people, Jew and gentile, were exhausted and
had too much to do and rebuild to speculate over what had
happened in Prussia. Poland was in a vital ferment now, and
the kings of Poland opened their doors wide to all Jews who
desired refuge from the Germans. Boleslaw the Pious issued
a charter of protection to Jews in 1264, and so important
did the Polish kings consider it that it endured for the following two centuries. In 1334, Casimir the Great, ruling over
a larger and united Poland, signed the Statute of Kalisz—by
which the Crown guaranteed protection and the right to a
full life to Jews all over Poland. In 1364, the burgeoning
Polish power conquered White Russia and Little Poland—
and the edicts protecting the Jews were extended to those
areas. Poland was at the height now of power and young vitality, and in 1388, Lithuania came under Polish rule,
whereby Lithuania was opened to the Jews, with full rights
and protection for them. And within this period, Polish armies
marched into the Ukraine, subduing it and guaranteeing the
rights of Jews.

It is not difficult to see what happened against this outburst
of Polish vitality—which was, to a very large extent, Jewish
vitality as well. By the thousands, the Jews poured out of
Germany and into Poland, carrying with them their Yiddish
language, their precious Torah and Talmud, their memories
and their anguish, their hopes and fears. The German Jews
left home and wealth and property—anything and everything
—only to leave the land of horror for the freedom and essential decency of Poland, so much of it still pagan or half
pagan.

The Jews poured into Poland, and reestablished there the
trade routes to the East that had been wiped out in the rest
of Europe. They helped to design and build cities, and soon

they numbered almost half the population of urban Poland. They built schools and new community centers, and suddenly they were able to raise their heads again and to begin to forget the mindless horror that was Germany. So grateful were they to Poland that they spared no effort to contribute to Polish greatness and prosperity; and as Poland gained hegemony over other Slavic lands, the Jews moved in as administrators, builders, merchants—into Lithuania and White Russia and into the Ukraine.

But through all of this, the Jews made no effort to become Poles. The gulf separating Jew and German and Jew and Pole created a new era in Jewish Diaspora history: a Jewish national entity, landless, yet bound together with links of blood and suffering, speaking its own language and living within its own culture, a thousand years away from the blue Mediterranean and the sun-soaked hills of Israel, and two thousand miles distant from their beginnings. They had created their own Yiddish language, and they loved it and cherished it, and for the next six hundred years it would be the language of their home and hearth, the language of their schools and trading centers and their literature.

Even their religion had undergone change. The ringing tones of the Torah, the great commanding figure of Moses in the desert, King David and his men of valor—all this remained in their memory and mythology; but only the wisdom of the *fathers,* the teachings of the rabbis, enabled them to survive—and only the Cabala, with its mysticism that joined them to God, enabled them to make some sanity out of their experience.

Their place now was in the cruel cold of northern Europe. The long, dark winters, the abundant snowfall, the howl of the winter wind—all these meant a change of character, an inwardness. While in the first flush of the Polish sanctuary, the Jewish traders experienced a brief revival; by the late fourteenth century the German merchants and traders had grown strong enough in Poland to drive the Jews out of the field. This much the new Polish bishops were able to accomplish in their patient building of a structure of anti-Semitism;

and while the Polish kings and noblemen valued and protected the Jews during their first three hundred years in
Poland and Lithuania and the Ukraine, by 1400, the Catholic
Church in Poland had triumphed and, except for the deep
reaches of Lithuania, was in a position of unshakable power.
Now the dreadful old saws that had come out of the peculiar
German mind were revived in Poland—the ritual murders,
the desecration of the host (which meant that the Jews had
stolen the Christian matzoh, which is offered and consecrated
at the Mass, and substituted for it Jewish matzoh, made with
the blood of Christian children, kidnapped and drained of
their blood to use in the baking every Passover); and if anyone
should doubt that this incredible nonsense was believed, one
should remember that this was revived and believed in Hitler
Germany.

This created a curious situation for the Jews in Poland. The
barons and kings, being Polish and not German, would not
tolerate massacres German style, yet they retreated before
the attack of the Church and the new German merchant
class—and bit by bit, the Jews were isolated and their privileges removed.

But by the fifteenth century, the Jewish population of
Poland, Lithuania, and the Ukraine had increased greatly—
and was many times as large as it ever was in Germany. Over
the bridge of a thousand years, from the scattered Jewish communities of the Mediterranean Diaspora, here was a great
nation of people, spread over an area that stretched from
the Polish border and the Baltic Sea, north to Latvia and
White Russia, south to the Carpathian Mountains and into
Rumania, and eastward to the valley of the Dnieper River,
numbering almost a million people as the fifteenth century
came to an end and soon to be many, many millions. Knit
together by their own language, they turned inward more
and more. Intermarriage was a rarity—as was conversion
to Christianity. More and more isolated, a curious and new
phenomenon occurred—for here in this cold, dark, windy
land, Jewish villages came into being, the Jewish community

not as a part of a Christian city, but a small town in and of itself.

Part of this was the result of ever increasing anti-Semitism. As Poland became increasingly Christianized and linked itself more and more closely with its western neighbor, a new merchant class came into being, often in partnership with the German traders who had flocked into Poland along with the Church. These combined forces to break the Jewish hold on trade, and in the effort they spared no effort to make German anti-Semitism an integral part of the Polish scene. To a large degree, they succeeded, and by 1454, most Jewish rights and legal privileges in Poland had been abandoned. This led to the expulsion of many Jews from the Polish cities Warsaw, Cracow, Lvov, Posen, and many others. Some of these expelled Jews sought other urban centers, but a great many went into outlying districts where the Polish inhabitants were few and still unbitten by the virus of anti-Semitism, and where the hold of the Church was still new and often indifferent. Here they settled in small villages, most villages wholly Jewish, and began an isolated and different existence, wrapped in the mantle of an increasingly mystical and Cabalistic religion.

However, one must note again that this condition was unlike the Jewish experience in Germany, and in 1500, there began a period of 150 years, under the reigns of King Sigismund I and his successors, during which time the Jews returned to prosperity and national influence in Poland.

———•◦•◦•———

It is important to understand that Poland itself was the cradle and the salvation of modern Jewry—and only through Poland in its national vigor did the few thousand Jews who fled from the medieval horror and soul-sickness of Germany grow into the millions of Ashkenazi Jews who comprise the great majority of the Jewish people today, in America, in the Soviet Union, and in Israel. Jews who know their history only fitfully are inclined to point to eighteenth and nineteenth and twentieth century anti-Semitism in Poland, but this is after hundreds of years of Polish history in which Jew and Pole stood side by side. While many forces joined together throughout European history to use and promote anti-Semitism, the fact must be faced and stated bluntly: that anti-Semitism in the European Diaspora of the Jew was the child and the ideology of the Roman Catholic Church and the Greek Catholic Church. In the ecumenical spirit of today, many Jews feel it is best to tone down such matters and forget; but history cannot be both written and forgotten; and still others, sensitive Christians, say, "But surely you cannot blame the Nazi murder of six million Jews upon the Church. Surely the Church never countenanced it."

Far worse; the Church from its very inception organized anti-Semitism in modern, clerical guise, spared no effort to inoculate the entire Catholic population with it, and gave it to the German pagans along with Christianity—as if to provide a perennial outlet for a blood and murder sickness that has been a part of Germany as long as Germany was a part of history. (It is only fair and somewhat hopeful to note here the recent revisions in the Catholic litany to eliminate some of the more scurrilous anti-Semitic references.)

In Poland—as in some other places—the kings and the nobility resisted anti-Semitism and resisted the Church. They were able to do this for hundreds of years, but they were not able to keep the Polish people in general from learning this particular lesson of Christianity, and therefore, from the fourteenth century onward, there was a slow, steady growth of anti-Semitism among the Polish people and among the other peoples who were subject to the Polish Crown and the Polish barons.

We are used, today, to thinking of great Ashkenazi Jewish populations in many different countries, such as White Russia, Lithuania, the Ukraine, Galicia, and Transylvania—as well as in Poland; but almost all of this area was once under the Polish Crown, and Jews went to these lands and settled there as part of the political and social evolution of Poland.

In sixteenth-century Poland, the Jews became, to a certain

extent, the force behind the social and political structure of the Crown. They were the revenue collectors and local judiciaries; they were the bankers, financiers, and merchants. They controlled the leather, fur, silk, cotton, and perfume trades.

So far did the Jewish privilege under the Polish kings of the House of Jagiello reach that in 1551 Sigismund II, who was called Augustus, gave the rights to Polish Jews to have their own courts, to appoint and elect their own judges, and to choose a chief rabbi. The chief rabbi and the judges would preside over any and all cases where Jewish law or crime was concerned and to a reasonable extent the Jews would exercise self-government as a nation within a nation. This is possibly the only time such a situation arose in the Diaspora, with the exception of ancient Alexandria.

The process of self-government went even further. It was a Polish custom to hold annual fairs in every district of the kingdom, where produce and manufactured wares were offered for sale. Jewish merchants always attended these fairs—and thereby an opportunity was afforded for Jews from various parts of the kingdom to come together and discuss problems. Out of this arose a sort of council, called the Vaad, which began to specify the amount of general taxation to be borne by each Jewish community in what were called the Four Lands—districts of Poland, White Russia, and the Ukraine. So strong and respected did this Jewish council become that it was virtually the parliament of the Polish Jews. It sent observers to the Polish Diet in Warsaw; it enforced upon the Jews royal edicts of taxation and legal rights; it became a sort of general board of education—and to some extent it touched upon every aspect of Jewish life in Poland. The council also set up schools for medical training and for cartography, to facilitate Poland's new interest in sea power. In Poland, during the reign of the Sigismunds and the rule of Stephen Báthory within the Sigismund period, a time, as we noted, of 150 years, the Jews came forward as a great executive force, yet in a hostile environment; for they allowed themselves to be used as administrators and governors by the

militant Polish dukes in the Polish conquest of White Russia
and the Ukraine.

Force bred counterforce, and in 1648, led by a great army
of Cossacks under Bogdan Chmielnicki, the Ukrainians rose
up against the Polish landowners and the Catholic clergy,
liberated themselves, and then began a brutal, systematic
murder of Jews that made the word *Cossack* a symbol of
horror to Jews for a long time to come. In the infamous
Chmielnicki massacres 744 Jewish communities were wiped
out—and once again the back of Jewish independence in
Poland was broken. This point marked the beginning of the
fragmentation and dissolution of the Polish Empire—and
the beginning of the taking over of so much of it by the Czars
of Russia.

It also marked the end of real hope for a future in Europe
among the Polish Jews. From here onward, they fell into increasing isolation—especially in the Ukraine and in Car-
pathian-Galicia, where they retreated into their village life,
into the comparative peace of their isolated settlements, turning more and more to the Cabala and its warm mysticism, to
their homes, where they made the primitive sod huts into
little shrines of light and beauty every Sabbath eve, exalting
the Sabbath as it had never been exalted before, dreaming,
through the long, dark winter nights, of the sunny hills of
Palestine, praising God and hopefully awaiting the Messiah.

While the urban Jews in what remained of Poland, and
those in Lithuania, continued to have a hold in trade and
banking, and while they were able to build schools and
important academies of Jewish studies, in the villages there
was the desperation of a people lost on the edge of darkness.
Anyone who has experienced the northern European winter
knows how depressing it can be, how heavy on the soul—
especially of those who were wanderers; and the Jews of
Poland (old Poland), now numbering almost a million, had
long ago assumed the mental attitude of wanderers. They
were in the Diaspora. They were exiles. There was no hint
of reality in their dreams of the ancient land of Israel, yet
their greeting to each other came to be "Next year in Jeru-

salem!" The Messiah, the redeemer of all mankind, would come to lead them there.

This time, the last of the seventeenth and the beginning of the eighteenth century, was the time of Messiah hopes and false Messiahs, and of one strange figure who was less than a Messiah yet a most extraordinary man. His name was Israel ben Eliezer.

———•••———

He was called the *Baal Shem-Tov,* which is Hebrew for "master of God's good name." *Baal Shem* was a category of Cabalist rabbis, "masters of the name," men who believed that miracles could be achieved through the use of the letters that formed the various Hebrew names for God. It must be remembered that among other achievements of the people who called themselves "the Children of Israel," the Beni-Yisrael of olden times, was the invention of the alphabet—from which all other alphabets are derived. Thus the majestic Hebrew letters, each one heir to a thousand meanings and shadings, have always been held, to some degree, sacred —just as the *book* in itself has been a sort of holy thing among the Jews.

So these Cabalists were not dismissed as foolish magicians; for within a closed system—which the Jewish world often was—magic can work as well as science. But since they were Cabalists they were more than magicians, essentially mystics and thereby kin to all mystics.

Israel ben Eliezer, the *Baal Shem-Tov,* was born about 1700, in Podolia, a province of the Ukraine which seemed destined for martyrdom. Again and again, it was attacked and bathed in Jewish blood by the Cossacks. Here came thousands of German-Jewish refugees of the Thirty Years' War, only to be wiped out by the Cossacks in the Chmielnicki massacre.

(No one knows exactly how many Jews the Cossacks and Ukrainians put to death, but estimates vary from a quarter of a million to half a million. It must be noted that almost a thousand Catholic nuns and priests were also murdered by the Cossacks. This incident is regarded with honor in Russian history, and even the Soviets continue the celebration of Chmielnicki as a Ukrainian hero. Gogol's book about the Cossack uprising, *Taras Bulba,* still published and praised in the Soviet Union, is perhaps as vicious a piece of anti-Semitism as exists in "respectable" literature.)

Subsequently Podolia suffered grievously in the Czarist period of the pogroms, in World War I, again in attacks by the "White forces" in the Russian Revolution—and came to its end in a methodical slaughter of extermination by the SS German troops in World War II. In between these various holocausts, the village Jews of the area lived as best they could; and to them, as a sort of a redeemer, came the *Baal Shem-Tov.*

He came from poor people, but as Sholom Aleichem, the great Yiddish writer, often pointed out, there were only poor people in these Jewish villages. From his childhood, when he was introduced to the Cabala, he studied and read, and meanwhile worked sometimes as a teacher, as a lime burner, and as a ritualistic butcher of meat. His was a gentle, winning personality, and in his thirties he began to achieve miraculous cures, mostly, one supposes, of hysterical paralysis and associated symptoms by the laying on of hands. One cannot write of the *Baal Shem-Tov* without being reminded of Christ and of the ancient Jewish belief in the *Lamed Vav,* which I told about earlier.

At the age of forty, he moved to the town of Medzibozh, where he lived and preached for the rest of his life—which town, by 1750, had become the focus of interest for the European Jewish world, as the abode of a saint.

There have been endless arguments as to whether the *Baal Shem-Tov* preached pantheism, just as there have been endless discussions as to what hold pantheism had upon the Jewish religion; but howsoever one names it, Israel ben Eliezer preached the mystical union of man and God. The universe was God's vestment, and as a part of the universe, man can witness God through ecstasy. And ecstasy could be achieved through prayer or through study with fervor.

His teaching was permeated with a kind of joy—in a place and time as joyless and hopeless as ever the Jewish people occupied. He preached the joy of religion, the joy of obeying God's commandments in the Torah, the joy of trust in God and love of God.

His movement found followers by the thousand—and became one of the important directions in Jewish belief. Called Hasidism, it declared itself the highest area of religious thought and put all its trust in its leader, the saintly Rabbi. It appeared at a moment when the isolated masses of the Ukrainian and White Russian and Galician and Polish Jews needed it most desperately, and in its vital time, it became the major current among those Jews.

But with the destruction of the eastern European Diaspora, it foundered in transplanting, and while islands of Hasidism exist in America and in Israel, the expansive vitality of the movement is gone.

———•━••━•———

Russia became the inheritor of most of Poland's territory, and thus, by political and military conquest, of millions of Jews. White Russia, Lithuania, the Courland peninsula, the Ukraine—all these vast territories that were once Polish now became Russian. It was no small band of refugees driven out of Germany that the Czars inherited, but a people who numbered millions, a people who made up half and sometimes more than half of the urban population of Polish and Lithuanian cities, a people who occupied several thousand villages, a people who included small peasant farmers, great landowners, merchants, physicians, professors, scholars, bankers—a people who had built uncountable schools, academies, universities—a great, indigestible mass of vital and energetic human beings, with a language of their own, a culture of their own, a way of dressing that was their own—and, most irritatingly, a religion of their own that was a bone in the throat of the entire Christian world; only by now, a most enormous bone.

What were the Czars to do? Limited men, prisoners of

their own position, none of them a man of insight, sympathy, or brilliance, they approached the Jews without policy,
intelligence, or understanding. Unlike the Polish kings and
nobility, they had no memory of the Jews that went back into
remote antiquity. Russians had never fought side by side
with the Jews in defense of their land; quite to the contrary,
Jews and Poles together had conquered Russian lands. Jews
were outsiders, strangers, yet there were so many of them
that they demanded a policy in and of themselves. The
Czars used the Cossacks against the Jews, instituted pogroms,
used the Jews and persecuted the Jews to take the revolutionary pressure of their own people off their backs,
contained the Jews, confined them in an area which came to
be known as the "Pale of Settlement," and refused them
living space in Moscow and St. Petersburg.

(The geographical area designated as "the Jewish Pale of
Settlement" was set aside in 1791, by decree of Catherine
II, Empress of Russia. This consisted of twenty-five provinces
of the Czarist Empire, an area that covered parts of Poland,
Lithuania, White Russia, the Ukraine, Bessarabia, and
Crimea. Only in this area were Jews allowed to live—with
certain exceptions. Under very special conditions, Jewish
doctors, lawyers, merchants, jewelers, and scientists, plus a
few other categories, were allowed to live apart from the
Pale, that is, in the great cities of Russia. Jews found to be
illegally outside the Pale were tried without jury or counsel
before the particular governor of the place where they were
apprehended, and the governor had total power of punishment, fine or whipping or prison or even death. Not until
the revolutionary uprisings of 1917 was the Pale of Settlement finally abolished.)

The pogroms, deliberately planned by the Czars, were ap-
palling and unforgivable, but the Jews survived; and as a result of these mass murders of the 1880's, the great immigration of Jews into the United States took place; and even in
Russia a sort of slow and painful progress was made. But it
was small progress within an overwhelming horror. The Russian government under the Czars fostered a hateful kind of

anti-Semitism, a sickness that struck so deep into the Russian masses that even today, a Russian government that calls itself Socialist is still riddled with anti-Semitism.

We must return here to the whole of this story of the European Diaspora, and note that we have yet to hear the story of the Jews in those lands where civilization thrived and where neither slaughter nor mindless persecution was permitted—Holland and England from the seventeenth century, and the entire Scandinavian peninsula—but these were places where comparatively few Jews lived. They were outside of the mainstream of a movement through history. The wandering Jew wandered everywhere, in every part of the earth, but that story is mankind's story; our tale is of the great mass of a people who fled north through Italy to escape the results of the Emperor Constantine's edict against them, who entered Germany and Rhineland France, coming there only in the thousands—who fled from the horror of Germany by the tens of thousands, who found hope and safety in ancient Poland, who increased there into hundreds of thousands and spread throughout the whole Polish Empire, who came then under the domination of the Czars of Russia, who fled from them to America and to western Europe—but who were nevertheless so numerous that after most of the emigration had taken place, at the outbreak of World War I, there were almost six million Jews in those lands ruled by Russia.

Then we arrive at a question that puzzles most people, who look upon the Jews as the Palestinian people of the Book and then find them by their millions in eastern Europe: since only a small minority of the Jewish people went into the German and Frankish lands, how is it that their descendants number perhaps 90 percent of the Jewish people in the modern world? Certainly there were more Jews in Spain than ever lived in Germany in the Middle Ages, and probably there were more Jews in Greece, or in Turkey, or in North Africa at various times after Constantine. But when we look at the Levant today, we discover that in spite of the great slaughter of Jews by the Nazis, the Ashkenazi Jew and his descendants outnumber the Sephardic (mainly Levantine today) Jew by many times. Why?

The answer to this question is hardly as mysterious as it appears at first; but curiously enough, it is the opposite of what most people—Jews included—believe. That belief is to the effect that there was much conversion toward Judaism in eastern Europe at one point or another; but the plain fact of the matter is that there was little or no such conversion. Still other people have held that there was a great influx from Chazaria, but we have shown that there was probably no influx whatsoever. We must accept the fact that the Jews of eastern Europe are all—with so few exceptions that they matter little—descended from the Jews of Medieval Germany and France, and that their increase is numbers is due to a natural increase and a high birthrate over the centuries. Possibly this increase was larger, proportionately, than the increase among the Poles, since the Jews had better medical service available and since the dietary laws imposed a higher degree of sanitation upon the Jews; but the Jewish increase was not too much larger than the non-Jewish increase in the same areas.

However, why was there no corresponding increase of Jews in the Mediterranean and Levantine world? The answer is that the people of this area were racially (to use an unhappy word for which there is no proper substitute) the same as the Jews, historically related, and of such social nature as never to force isolation upon the Jews. As we have shown, Spain experienced the conversion of tens of thousands of Jews to Christianity, and conversion to a lesser extent took place elsewhere in this area—conversion to Mohammedanism as well as to Christianity. Conversion took place through the centuries of the Diaspora because it was socially possible. The rich Jewish trader of Spain or Greece differed little from his Christian contemporary; the Jewish physician and the Arab physician worked side by side, taught in the same schools, ate the same food. The Jewish olive or mulberry farmer in Italy and Greece differed little from the Christian farmer in the same area. Remember, it was not the Jew

B. G. Phillips, photographer / Immigrant women arriving at Battery Park, 1890's / Museum of the City of New York

Jacob A. Riis, photographer / Ready for the Sabbath Eve in a coal cellar, Ludlow Street, early 1890's / The Jacob A. Riis Collection, Museum of the City of New York

Byron, photographer / Scene at the intersection of Hester and Ludlow streets, Lower East Side, 1898 / The Byron Collection / Museum of the City of New York

Jacob A. Riis, photographer / Jewish children in a Lower East Side public school, early 1890's / The Jacob A. Riis Collection, Museum of the City of New York

Jacob A. Riis, photographer / Jewish afternoon parochial school on Hester Street. Such schools did not substitute for public schools, but taught Hebrew and the Bible to Jewish children after school hours / The Jacob A. Riis Collection, Museum of the City of New York

Jacob A. Riis, photographer / Jewish workers in a sweat shop, about 1889. / The Jacob A. Riis Collection, Museum of the City of New York

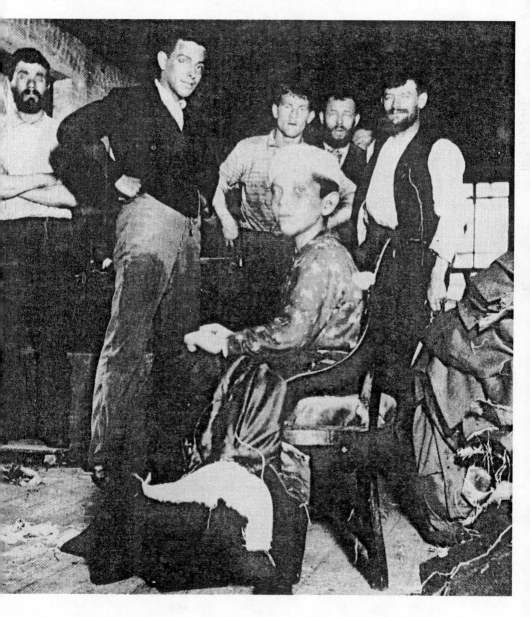

Facing page: The Adler Family was one of the great families of the Yiddish Theater. Right: Jacob Adler as Shylock; far right: Celia Adler / YIVO Institute for Jewish Research

One hundred and fifty-four workers, most of them Jewish, died in the Triangle Shirtwaist fire in 1911. Below: a body is carried to the morgue for identification / Culver Pictures, Inc.

Facing page: A postcard depicting Rudolph Schildkraut in his many roles in the Yiddish Theater / YIVO Institute for Jewish Research

Right: Theodore Herzl in the prime of his young manhood / Zionist Archives and Library

Below: Herzl en route for Palestine, 1898 / Zionist Archives and Library

From a letter by Theodore Herzl: If I were to sum up the Congress of Basel in a few words — which I would be sure not to use in public — then I would say: in Basel, I founded the Jewish State. If I were to say this out loud today, I would be greeted by universal laughter. In five years possibly, and at any rate in fifty, no one will fail to see this. A State is established essentially in a people's will to a state, or even in that of a sufficiently powerful individual *(L'état c'est moi,* Louis XIV). Territory is merely the concrete foundation; the State itself, even when possessing territory, is always something abstract. The Papal State exists even without territory; otherwise the Pope would not be sovereign.

Thus, in Basel, I created this abstract thing, which because of its abstractness is invisible to most people. And I did it with rather infinitesimal devices. I gradually drove the people into a "State mood" and invested them with the feeling that they were the national assembly / *Zionist Archives and Library*

A group of Jewish students from Russia studying farm work in Rishon-leZion, 1905. David Ben Gurion, future Prime Minister of Israel, is in the first row center above X / Zionist Archives and Library

Facing page — Top: Dr. Chaim Weizmann (left) and Lord Balfour (right) / Zionist Archives and Library

Facing page — Bottom: Henrietta Szold, hand on hip, greets the first Youth Aliyah arrivals in Palestine, 1934 / Zionist Archives and Library

Above: Nazi pickets outside Jewish store, Germany, 1933. Signs read: "Germans, be on your guard. Don't buy from Jews!" / The Bettman Archive, Inc. Right: Flight of Jewish family from Nazi Germany / The Bettman Archive, Inc.

*Jewish resistance fighters rounded up by Nazis in Warsaw Ghetto uprising /
YIVO Institute for Jewish Research*

Captured Jewish fighters being led to their death through the flaming streets of the Warsaw Ghetto / YIVO Institute for Jewish Research

Two prisoners of the Nazis in Nordhausen Concentration Camp / The Bettman Archive, Inc.

Mass grave at Belsen Concentration Camp / The Bettman Archive, Inc.

Refugees en route to Palestine / Zionist Archives and Library

Haganah ship illegally carrying Jewish immigrants to Palestine / Zionist Archives and Library

Former inmates of the death camps of Breslau and Tulzin ghettoes on their arrival at Athlit, Palestine, 1944 / Zionist Archives and Library

Refugee woman and child / Zionist Archives and Library

Daughter reunited with mother, 1944 / Zionist Archives and Library

Above: Dr. Chaim Weizmann's inauguration as first President of Israel, February 17, 1949 / Zionist Archives and Library

Right — Top: Jewish farmers and their children dig air-raid shelter trenches at outbreak of First Arab-Israeli War / Free Lance Photographers Guild, Inc.

Right: Israeli tanks on the road to Suez / Free Lance Photographers Guild, Inc.

First Arab-Israeli War — a battle-weary Israeli unit raises flag at the Wailing Wall / Free Lance Photographers Guild, Inc.

who came to Spain, it was the Christian; the Jew was already there and had been there for over a thousand years. The Jew did not flee to Greece or come to Greece as a merchant; the Greeks were superb merchants and still are; the Jew was there, as he was in Italy, in Syria, in so many other Levantine places where he had been for long ages of man.

Jew and non-Jew speculate endlessly on the mystery of Jewish survival and give it all sorts of metaphysical overtones; but the story of the Jew is enchanting enough without metaphysics. Jewish survival took place—in a broad "peoples" sense—in eastern Europe, because the Jews there lived among a population so different, so unlike them physically and historically, that absorption was impossible. Also, the Jews of eastern Europe had come there through the "hell" of Germany—a memory that did not incline them toward the strange feudal Slavs, whose condition was so physically wretched and whose outlook was so different. Also, the Jews were able to survive as "islands within," and so often in history what happens is simply what is able to happen.

We forget, however, that if we were to subtract the millions of Ashkenazi Jews from the Jewish people, there would be no talk of Jewish survival. This is not to compare the Sephardic and Ashkenazi Jews to the detriment of either, but simply to state a fact of population figures. Without the Jews of eastern Europe and their descendants, there would be perhaps a million and a half Jews in the whole world today, including Israel. There would still be Jews, but their presence in Africa, Greece, Turkey, and Yemen would hardly raise the same discussion concerning their survival. They would be a small sect, a curiosity rather than an enormous, vital force in the current drama of man's life on earth.

———•◦•——

English anti-Semitism has never been a matter of violence and murder; and the love and reverence of so many Jews for all that is English is not unconnected with the fact that England is one of the very few countries that adopted a civilized attitude toward the Jews. We have referred to the tragic incident of the Jews of York in the Middle Ages, and while there were other incidents of beating and synagogue burning, there was never anything like the inhuman massacres that were a constant occurrence in Germany.

In 1290, the Jews were expelled from England—that is, some four or five thousand of them. There is some reason to believe that perhaps twice that many lived in Cornwall and Devon and were simply absorbed into the population, as happened so often in the Mediterranean area and the Levant. After this expulsion of 1290, a trickle of Jews returned to England, family by family, and these were not molested. Under Cromwell, a larger immigration of Jews began and continued through the years up to today, when the Jewish population of Ireland and England and Scotland is over half a million—most of these Ashkenazi Jews from Germany and eastern Europe.

But no ghetto system was ever introduced into England, nor were the Jews, since Cromwell's time, ever again molested, restricted, or treated with any kind of violence. Quite to the contrary, the Jews in England have been treated with extraordinary justice and decency, even during the heat of the postwar situation in Palestine. In England, as in Holland, the Scandinavian countries, and the United States, there came into being in the nineteenth and twentieth centuries, a cult of Judaphilism, limited but with a real influence in literature as well as in life.

Like England, Holland treated the Jews with fairness and decency, giving them shelter after the Spanish expulsion. The first large influx came during the sixteenth century, Sephardic Jews from Spain at first and then German and Polish Jews, seeking freedom and able to move toward the West. Holland welcomed them. By 1700, there were over 10,000 Jews in Amsterdam, which made it the largest Jewish community in western Europe. After 1815, rabbis as well as ministers were paid by the Dutch state, and in 1797, Holland became *the first country in the world* to admit Jews to its parliament and to appoint them to high public office. In 1940, there were about 140,000 Jews resident in Holland

—as well as tens of thousands of refugee Jews. After the Nazi holocaust, only about 25,000 Jews were left alive in Holland.

In the Scandinavian countries of Norway, Sweden, and Denmark, Jews have been so few as to make them the exception to the European rule. Since no Jews lived in Scandinavia during the Middle Ages, none of the ghastly incidents that marked the rest of Europe were ever repeated there. The only great slaughter was that of Norwegian Jews by the Nazis—a horror that the Norwegians could not prevent, but which they attempted to avert with great bravery. Jews were invited into all the Scandinavian countries, and the few who came were well treated. The rate of intermarriage was the highest in western Europe, and because of this— and of course the quality of Scandinavian civilization—it was almost impossible for the Scandinavian Jews to maintain themselves as a community; an interesting comment, incidentally, for those who seek metaphysics in Jewish survival. In Sweden, where Jewish-Christian intermarriage has probably been higher than any other place in Europe, one can find only the statistics of the handful of Jews who remain synagogue-connected. Thus in 1956, Sweden had 13,000 Jews, or one-tenth of 1 percent of the world Jewish population, but this figure is misleading in the sense that it does not and cannot cover intermarriage. Intermarriage between the Jews on one hand and the Swedes and Danes on the other probably began with the Vikings, who had great rapport with the Jews, and the Jewish presence in Sweden dates back a thousand years in the commercial rather than in the communal sense. Jews who went to Sweden became Swedes, and a study of this would be most interesting.

(If the question is asked here: what is a Jew, and how does he cease to be a Jew and become a Swede, and why has not the same process happened in America?—the answer is hardly as mysterious as it sounds. Since the Jewish people began, a sizable number of them have ceased to be Jews at any given moment in history. This is a process. Where the conditions are possible for voluntary assimilation of Jews,

they will assimilate, and where the Jews are only a sprinkling among friendly people, they will tend to assimilate
more easily. But all Jews never assimilate, only a part of
them, and this assimilation can be of various degrees. Some
assimilation leads to Christianity, other assimilation does not.
Some assimilation is through intermarriage, and again some
is through a sort of ethnic forgetfulness, and some is a desire
for status, for integration. In the Scandinavian countries,
among a people civilized and gentle and singularly decent,
Jews have assimilated easily through the ages—yet a handful
seem to remain Jews. In America, which is still a land of national and ethnic groupings, customs, prides, with no identity of past history, no single national origin, the Jewish community has become a stable fact of the culture—at least for
the historic moment. American Jews assimilate, but so
great and so viable in its own sense is the Jewish population
in America that there is a particular opportunity and in-
ducement for most American Jews to refrain from assimilation. This is not to inject value judgments. I do not believe
that ethnic survival is either beneficial or necessary to the
human race. What is necessary and beneficial is ethnic understanding and toleration, so that we may eventually become
sufficiently civilized to establish the community of man. So
long as the Jewish people can offer the world and themselves
values singular and positive, they will exist.)

In Denmark, much of the same thing took place. During
World War II, there were less than six thousand Jews there,
and by a national act of unmatched courage and devotion
on the part of the Christian Danes, practically all of these
Jews were saved from the Nazi gas ovens and concentration
camps. But in Denmark, in 1967, an important and thoughtful Jew spoke hopelessly to me of Jewish survival in that
country. Intermarriage was too frequent; the climate of
opinion was most pleasant; and the people were civilized.
Within this, he saw no way in which the Jews could maintain
their identity as Jews—or be caused to desire to maintain
their identity.

France, during the Middle Ages, was never a part of the

European Diaspora in and of itself. Those areas that bordered on the Rhineland shared the history of the Germans toward the Jews, and those areas that bordered on Spain shared Spain's attitude toward the Jews. Indeed, the Kingdom of Navarre was one of the main forces in carrying through the expulsion of the Spanish Jews in 1492. Jews were numerous in Burgundy, Alsace, and Lorraine during the Middle Ages—and also in Provence and Languedoc; and in all of these provinces they were hunted and slaughtered mercilessly by the Crusaders. Many of the Jews of Provence fled to Italy and Greece, and from northeastern France many made their way across Germany to the safety of Poland.

Yet small communities of Jews managed to remain in France, many of them ghettoized, and during the fifteenth and sixteenth and seventeenth centuries, their numbers were augmented by Sephardic Jews from Spain and Ashkenazi Jews fleeing from the horrors of Germany. They were never very numerous—numbering probably less than seventy-five thousand at the time of the French Revolution. The French Jews in great majority joined with the revolutionary forces to the best of their ability, and the Revolution removed all restrictions placed upon them, giving them full equality before the law—a situation reinforced under Napoleon and continued thereafter. Thus the Jews in France were able to play a large and important role in the life of the country. By World War II, their numbers had increased almost to three hundred thousand; but unlike the Danes, the people of France—with the exception of the active resistance—watched with indifference while almost a hundred thousand French Jews were put to death by the Nazis.

We cannot leave the European Diaspora without noting if not detailing what will be dealt with later—the rise of anti-Semitism in the nineteenth and twentieth centuries as a modern political weapon—although much of the history of this usage of anti-Semitism took place during the period of the Diaspora described above. Thus, in the next part of this story, we return to Christopher Columbus and the year of the expulsion of the Jews from Spain, 1492.

PART TEN

They Discover America

There is no point in pursuing the argument over Columbus and his crew; how many were Marranos, and was he himself a converted Jew? Columbus is a symbol—better he remains thus, and we accept the fact that he knew Jews and associated with them and valued their backing and their advice. These Marranos—the converted Jews of Spain who eventually returned to Judaism—were an extraordinary group of men, brilliant, versatile, a combination of Spanish fire and *élan* and Jewish philosophy. Among them were the Jewish cartographers.

It is inconceivable that without the cartographers Columbus would have undertaken his journey. Let the credulous believe that he sailed boldly and witlessly into the Atlantic Ocean, thinking to reach a shore anywhere from nine to twelve thousand miles away, with food for four thousand miles at best. Columbus was not an idiot, nor were the men who accompanied him. He knew the sailing speed of ships; he was capable of calculation; and anyone who reads the detailed accounts of his first journey must come to the conclusion that he knew just where he was going and when his landfall would come, at least within a margin of error of no more than five or six days.

Furthermore, the Jews had known the size and shape of India and the Indo-Chinese peninsula for hundreds of years. They knew the China coast, and like all mariner people of antiquity, they knew that the earth was round. The ancient Greeks had calculated the size of the earth and the Phoenicians had done the same, with dead reckoning, in their journeys around Africa to India. So unless Columbus and his backers were utter imbeciles, they had a very good idea where he was going, and his charts were charts made by Jews, because in 1492 there were almost no others that were dependable. How the Atlantic Ocean became known to Mediterranean sailors, I do not know—unless the Viking ships that traded into the Mediterranean and bought their charts from the Jews in Majorca gave the Jewish cartographers the sailing directions—but known it was. Many mariners of the time acknowledged their debt to the great cartographers, the Cresques family of Majorca, to Jacob ben Makhir for his invention of the "Jacob's staff," a navigational in-

strument for measuring the sun's position, and to Abraham
Zacuto for his astronomical tables.

(Abraham Cresques and his son, Judah Cresques, known
in his time as Jacomo de Majorca, were two of the most intriguing figures of the fourteenth century. They were known
as "the map Jews"; and Abraham, the father, bore the title
of "Master of Maps and Compasses" to the Royal House of
Aragon. In 1377, Abraham completed the famous *Catalan
Atlas*, perhaps the greatest work of cartography produced
during that century. It was sent as a gift to the King of
France, and it can still be seen today in the Bibliothèque
Nationale in Paris. It is asserted that the Cresques family
had maps of every part of the world, including lands never
visited by the ships of Spain and Portugal.)

Of course the Jewish participation in the opening of the
New World was not celebrated; considering that it coin-
cided with the greatest wave of anti-Semitism and inquisi-
torial fear that Spain had ever known, it could hardly have
been noted as a memorable occasion. Nevertheless, Jews
knew and seamen knew and supercargoes, merchants, and
chandlers also knew. Many Jews had quietly become ship
chandlers, sometimes alone, sometimes with a Christian
partner. They were important from the Baltic ports down
through the North Sea, and of course most important in Marseilles; and there is very little about shipping in any age that
the chandlers and the cartographers do not know.

Jews were with Columbus and other Jews followed on
subsequent voyages, and as soon as eleven years after the
first voyage of Columbus we have evidence of crypto-Jews
(secret Jews—as Marranos in Spain, Chuetas in Majorca,
Jedid-al-Islam in Persia, Neofiti in Italy, and the Donmeh
of Salonica) in Brazil, as planters, merchants, and physicians.
During the next hundred years, a scattering of Jewish families—Marranos publicly—appeared in various parts of South
America and the West Indies, but only in Brazil did a substantial community arise at that time.

These Jews were still Marranos, so their Judaism was a secret thing, and the Inquisition was not as thorough in Brazil

as in Portugal. In 1631, the Dutch conquered the Pernambuco area of Brazil, far to the north of Rio de Janeiro, where there was a considerable Jewish community in what is today the city of Recife, and which was then a more important trading center than Rio. Recife, which most Americans have hardly heard mentioned, played an important role in the history of the Jews and of the Americas. When the Dutch conquered Recife, the pent-up frustration of the Marrano community exploded, and in a great celebration the Marranos returned openly to Judaism. Shouting and weeping, the new Jews pledged to their Dutch liberators that Recife would become the new Jerusalem; and indeed many immigrants, hopeful of this, sailed from Holland to Recife. But their hopes were dashed a generation later when Portuguese warships opened fire on Recife. Repossessing this area of Brazil, the Portuguese were firm. The Jews must go.

The Jews left as quickly as ships could be found to carry them, thankful that the Inquisition was not yet there—for every one of them was guilty of heresy (as the Inquisition saw it) and therefore faced death by burning. It is interesting, I think, that the Portuguese soldiers felt no need for vengeance or slaughter, but were content to allow the Jews to leave.

They left in Dutch and Portuguese ships, leaving their homes and plantations and paying out most of their wealth to charter the ships. One small group of these Jews—numbering about thirty—was led by a most extraordinary man, a man who had leadership thrust upon him, and whose character was so indomitable that he set his stamp on the presence of the Jew in colonial North America, shaped their position there, and to an extent defined the prototype of the Jew in the United States. He was a truly remarkable man, too little known.

———————

His name was Asser Levy van Swellem, and he had come as an immigrant to Brazil after the Dutch had taken the Pernambuco district from the Portuguese. He was a tall, strong,

well-educated man, born a Jew—not a Marrano—and a
butcher by trade (which meant that he had been trained and
educated as a ritual slaughterer, *shohet* in Hebrew, and was
versed in Talmud). He was a proud man who would brook
no insult to himself or his comrades.

With a small group of prominent Jewish citizens—probably the members of a single synagogue—he found a ship
to take them to the West Indies. There were about thirty
people in the company to begin with, young couples with
their children—the majority of them former Marranos, and
all of them Sephardic Jews of Spanish and Portuguese ancestry. First they made the long journey to the West Indies, a
place which Levy found as little to his taste as Brazil. They
had lost some people by death on the way and a few others refused to go on. Levy, however, had heard of the colony called
New Amsterdam, which the Dutch had planted in North
America, and according to all he heard, the Dutch colony
was surrounded by Protestant colonies that England and
Sweden had planted—and therefore beyond the reach of the
Inquisition. Levy announced that he had no intention of
living the rest of his life and raising up his children in fear of
the Inquisition. He and his party were Jews. He was not going to put down roots in any place where the Inquisition
could burn his friends and give their children the choice between Catholicism or death. Therefore, he was going on to
New Amsterdam, and those who wished could go with him.
Twenty-three people decided to accompany him. Again a
journey of thousands of miles, and as the fall of 1664 was setting in, Asser Levy's ship dropped anchor in the Upper Bay
of New York Harbor—then New Amsterdam.

The ship's boat took Levy and two others to shore, where
they were met by the Dutch governor, Peter Stuyvesant. Informed of his attitudes toward Jews—all hostile—and refused permission to disembark, Levy, who had influential
friends in old Amsterdam in Holland, raised the roof—and
two very strong and stubborn men fought it out then and
there. Levy told Stuyvesant how far they had come and that
they had no intentions of budging, even if they had to sit it

out all winter in the harbor. Stuyvesant gave in, and the Jews landed.

There is no record of any other Jews in New Netherland at that time. Levy's group therefore lacked the ten adults needed to form a congregation and synagogue—and when the number was finally obtained, every obstacle was placed in their way by the new British governor. Thus, New York did not have its first formal synagogue until 1693, although services were held in Jewish homes since the first arrival.

The year after Levy had arrived, Stuyvesant received orders to mount an attack against the Swedish colonies, which had been planted on the Delaware River. Stuyvesant then called for the enlistment of the able-bodied men in the colony, whereupon Levy and several of his companions promptly appeared and stated that they were ready to serve. Raging, Stuyvesant went to the city council and rammed through an ordinance that said: "Jews cannot be permitted to serve as soldiers, but shall instead pay a monthly contribution for the exemption."

Levy refused to pay and defied the governor. It had become Asser Levy van Swellem versus Peter Stuyvesant—and the mounting feud between the two became the talk of the town.

On November 5, 1665, Levy took a new tack and turned over to the council a petition demanding the right of the Jews to stand guard in the manner of the town burghers. Stuyvesant crumpled the petition and screamed at Levy that if he and the rest of his Jews did not like New Amsterdam, they had his permission to go elsewhere. In fact, Stuyvesant offered to raise the money for their passage. Levy told Stuyvesant that he was remaining in New Amsterdam, and he wrote another petition that he sent back to the directors of the Company in Holland—where the Levy-Stuyvesant feud became as interesting gossip as it was in New Amsterdam.

Levy then demanded from the council the right to be licensed as a butcher and made an agreement with a Dutch cattle raiser up the Hudson. Again, Stuyvesant intervened, and again they fought it through and Levy won. Levy and his fellow Jews had now acquired two sailing craft, and they were trading up the Hudson as far as Albany, which was then called Fort Orange. Stuyvesant now got an order from the council forbidding any Jews to buy or sell at Fort Orange—directed against Levy, who in turn sent the details of the whole affair to Holland. Levy had now become a *cause célèbre* in Holland as well as in New Amsterdam, and now the directors of the Company issued a public rebuke to Stuyvesant and stated that any person in New Netherland had the right to trade at the fort.

In a fury—now apparently constant—Stuyvesant got the council to amend this right to burghers only. Levy went to court and demanded that the Jews be made burghers. The battle went on—and Levy won. The Jews were made burghers.

Levy's name appears almost unendingly as a litigant in the Dutch courts. He fought everything, and he fought every step of the way. His position was that this was the beginning of Jewish residence in America, and that it would begin right or he would die in the attempt. And strangely enough, the Dutch burghers of New Amsterdam adored him. He was the first Jewish landowner in New York City—holding several parcels near William Street. He built a slaughterhouse on Wall Street, at the East River end, and there he provided kosher and non-kosher meat. When the British attacked in 1664, he contributed one hundred florins to the defense fund, and when New Amsterdam became New York, he continued as a local hero of sorts. By 1665, he was a rich man, trading with London as well as Amsterdam; and to lay the groundwork for a place of human decency where anti-Semitism would be eschewed, he put up the money for the building of the first Lutheran Church in New York City.

Not only did this action make Levy the toast of the city, but it reverberated to the credit of Jews everywhere in the colonies. When his son, who had taken up land in Connecticut, informed him that a Jew locally had been rather heavily and unjustly fined, Levy appeared in the Connecticut court in behalf of the Jew. The judge presiding was delighted to remit the fine, stating that he did so "as a token of its [the court's] respect to the said Mr. Asser Levy."

Asser Levy died in New York City, in 1680, a man rich in worldly goods and richer in the love and respect accorded to him by Jew and gentile alike. In a sense, he became the symbol and definition of the Jew's life in America, and his grandson appeared as an officer of a New Jersey regiment during the American Revolution. Not remembered too well in our time, in his own he was famous throughout the colonies, as the "New York Jew," and also as "Stuyvesant's nemesis."

———◆•◆———

Asser Levy founded the first Jewish community in America—that is, in the colonies which subsequently became the United States—but he was not the first Jew to come to the colonies. The first one came in 1621, full thirty-three years before Levy's ship made its berth at New Amsterdam; and two years after Levy arrived, that is, in 1656, there were enough Jews in Delaware to hold services. That does not mean that there were the necessary ten adult males to comprise the *minyan* that Jewish law calls for as a regular congregation. In other, more difficult circumstances a Jew is permitted to pray alone, or with one or two or three companions—or with anything short of ten. In Connecticut, in 1659, they appear to have had a full-fledged *minyan.* Rhode Island reports its first Jews in 1658, and also a *minyan;* in 1677, the Jews of Rhode Island purchased a plot of land for a burial ground—the first Jewish cemetery in the colonies. In the southern colonies, Jews appeared in the Carolinas in 1665 and in Georgia a good deal later, in 1733. There is some evidence that a Jewish physician was practicing in Virginia as early as 1700, before there was either a medical school or a quota for Jewish students.

Newport proceeded to build a synagogue the year the congregation was formed, in 1668, not the beautiful building that is a historic shrine today—that was built in 1733—but an earlier and less carefully constructed house. In 1734, Savannah, Georgia, built a synagogue, and the Jews of Philadelphia built theirs in 1745. In Charleston, the lovely synagogue still standing today was completed in 1750.

Though the great majority of these first settlers were Spanish- or Portuguese-speaking Sephardic Jews, from the very beginning there was a sprinkling of Yiddish-speaking Ashkenazi Jews, some from Poland, some from England and some from Holland, these latter not fleeing from persecution, but seeking a new land of opportunity where little or no anti-Semitism existed. These came singly rather than in groups, but by the time of the American Revolution the majority of the congregation in perhaps half of the synagogues was Ashkenazi, not Sephardic, though they followed the Sephardic ritual. There was another factor, of course; the Spanish gentleman has always been a great grandee, with excellent manners and bearing, and the Sephardic Jews were more Spanish than the Spaniards. The Ashkenazi Jews, with their beards and side-curls and distinctive Jewish dress, were astonished to find these lordly colonial gentlemen, resident in the country for over a hundred years by 1776, speaking perfect English, living in the new beautiful Georgian homes, intermarrying with prosperous Protestant families—indeed, if not for their devotion to the synagogue and their faith, the antithesis of anything Jewish, as these Ashkenazi Jews saw it. The Sephardic Jews, on the other hand, were rather repelled by the strange, Yiddish-speaking immigrants who looked to them with nothing short of worship. Yet the Spanish Jews did not turn the strangers away; they helped them and provided for them—as I mentioned much earlier—and by the time of the American Revolution, the Polish and English and other Ashkenazi Jews were all over the colonies, engaged in commerce of every description—and with few exceptions on the colonial side against the British.

There are a number of indications that these early Jews spoke Yiddish among themselves (but of course this bears no connection with the Yiddish of the mass immigration a hundred years later, since so many of these early Jews intermarried with Christians, and since the language was abandoned then after a generation) and there are also references to their praying—which references would appear to indicate a connection with the Hasidim. How many Jews there were in the colonies at the time of the American Revolution we are not certain, estimates varying from 2,500 to 3,500. Somewhere between the two would make the Jews one-tenth of 1 percent of the total population, yet their involvement in the war was far greater than their numbers would call for. Where a Cohen or a Levy turns up in the regimental rolls, it is hard to determine whether we have a Sephardic or Ashkenazi Jew. There are very few private soldiers, but a surprising number of officers are on the rolls. Ashkenazi Jews of Hasidic background or influence could no more take up arms than a Quaker, but we find them in every area of support, furnishing food, finances, uniform cloth, even ships. (The name of Haym Salomon, an Ashkenazi Jew, has become rather more famous than his actual role deserved, although he was a brilliant financier and again and again found money for Washington's army. Many other Jews participated in the same work.)

From their very beginning in America, Jews have been prominent in the fur trade. They were the only group in early America who traded successfully and constantly with the Indians, without resorting to either arms or whiskey. This was almost an Ashkenazi monopoly, since the only capital required was a mule or donkey and a bag of trifles, mirrors, ornaments; while the Sephardic Jew moved more actively in shipping, importing, and so forth. This fur trade spread the Jews through the West and gave them commercial footholds wherever the West was opened, a factor that would influence their development in America greatly. I have come across many fascinating manuscript notes of these early Jews—as for example, the first Jew to come into the settlements of the canebrake country of Kentucky, while it was still a stockade society, a good-natured fur trader who allowed the settlers to feel in his hair for the horns that appeared on Michelangelo's Moses and which many people suspected were standard equipment on all Jews. In another case, in manuscript again, women survivors of the Wyoming Valley (Pennsylvania) massacre tell how after two days of terror-stricken flight, they came to a Jewish fur-trade store, where the Jews fed them and took care of their wounds. There are many such notes; they are oddities, of course, but they help to show the Jewish beginnings in America—the land where half of the world's Jewish population lives today.

———

At first, the Jewish growth in America was slow, and as in Spain, the Jew was not set apart in costume. Even the Polish Jews would doff their distinctive Jewish garb, and those from Holland and England were already a second or third generation away from Poland. A trickle of Jews from the two great ghettos of Germany reached America, and by 1825, nine functioning synagogues could call themselves communal centers, and by their membership count, there were six thousand Jews in the United States. But such a count did not include intermarriage where synagogue connection had been suspended, nor did it include Jews who had become Christians—of whom there were many hundreds, possibly thousands. In Philadelphia particularly, where there was one of the oldest and largest communities, intermarriage and conversion were frequent, not only because the Sephardic Jews had already married into several highly placed Philadelphia families, but because Philadelphia was the heart of Quakerism in America, and because then as now, among the Jews the Quakers were the most admired and beloved of all the Protestant sects.

Also, among the New England Presbyterians and particularly among the Congregationalists, there was much conversion to Christianity by Jews who joined these two sects. In such a situation, particularly in New England, where Jews were treated with a forthrightness and decency they had never before experienced among Christians, there was a situation not unlike that in Sweden, where the Jews were few and the freedoms were many. So it is hardly possible to state exactly what the Jewish population was in the United States then—any more than it is possible to do so today, as we shall see.

Of course, here we come to another problem, which has never been solved satisfactorily: namely, what is a Jew? Faced with this in our own time, under the necessity to make a general law for the admission of all Jews who so desired into the Republic of Israel, the Knesset, Israel's parliament, debated the matter at great length. But the only conclusion they could come to was to admit that he who says he is a Jew, is a Jew. Naturally it was not this simple, and under the legalistic demands of an immigration, a hundred technical puzzles arose. Since the ancient Jewish law traces descent through the mother, was the child of a Jewish man and a gentile woman a Jew? Or could one claim Jewishness by conversion? Or could a Jew become a gentile and then return to Judaism? Or could a half-Jew make his own decision, or a quarter-Jew, or an eighth-Jew? Was one to be ruled in policy by these ridiculous mathematical distinctions, so reminiscent of Nazi ideology?

There is no simple answer to this problem; but so basically is Judaism a religion—or way of life or culture or philosophy, if you will—that specifies man's right to a direct confrontation with his God, as himself, as an individual, with no need of priest or any other clergy as an intercessor, that whatever the answer may be, it is based upon an individual response. I am a Jew within myself—and no other human being on earth can change that fact if I so decide. No Jew can be excommunicated in the sense that a Catholic can. Many years ago, in Talmudic times, a thing best called *Anathema* was employed by certain Jewish communities against members who for one reason or another were considered a danger to the community. But this was a form of the ancient practice of ostracism, a secular rather than a religious action, which involved severance of social, personal, business, and communal synagogue relations with the individual until he repented.

In the light of the above, it must be recognized by the reader that all Jewish statistics are rather amorphous, and that even two statements concerning intermarriage may have very different meanings.

But large mass immigration of Jews into the United States
—the type of thing Jewish historians call a major shift in the
Diaspora—did not begin until 1848. That was a year of revolutionary uprising in Europe—the most tragically unsuccessful revolution taking place in Germany. Then, to the permanent weakening of every decent force in Germany, a
mass of her brightest and most resolute citizens sought a
better life in the United States. Germans by the thousands
poured into America, young, vital people for the most part,
determined to live their lives and raise their children in
conditions of freedom. With them came German Jews—a
steady stream that did not slacken until 1871, when the Jews
of Germany were to a large degree emancipated. By that
time, the Jewish population of the United States had grown
to over a quarter of a million, perhaps three-quarters of them
German Jews or descendants of German Jews.

The Jews by now had spread out to every state and territory of the United States. They reached California with the
Forty-niners; they set up trading posts all over the plains and
in the Rocky Mountains. With the Civil War, they were
found both as officers and as private soldiers in both armies.
The New England Jewish communities, old and traditionally
American by the time of the Civil War, were strong supporters of Abolitionist movements; in the South, most of the
Jews supported the Confederacy. They were for the most part
already integrated, and took no separate or singular position
as Jews. Except for the original Sephardic synagogues, established in the colonial period and Orthodox in ritual, the new
synagogues were of the Reform ritual—except for New York
and Boston, where Polish Jews had begun small and painfully
poor Jewish congregations. As most of these immigrants in
the 1848-1871 period were German, they spoke little or no
Yiddish, and by the Civil War, Yiddish had ceased to be of
any consequence, if indeed it was spoken anywhere in the
United States.

These German Jews were quite extraordinary. Well-educated, thoughtful, aware of the play of forces the world over,
they were for the most part descendants of Jews who had sur-

vived the ghettos of Frankfort and Worms and other cities of Germany. They had great energy and drive, and for the first time, they made the Jewish presence wholly felt throughout the United States. They created, in 1859, the Board of Delegates of American Israelites, set up charities, homes for Jewish poor and aged, clinics, hospitals. They founded the Hebrew Union College, the first rabbinical seminary in America, and began community Hebrew-American schooling. They realized that the ancient form of Jewish Diaspora community could not and should not be revived in America, and they set the pattern for the Jewish existence in the United States.

They established newspapers and magazines, at first in German, then in English with a German-Jewish point of view. They began the process of Jewish scholarship in America, working with and drawing upon German-Jewish sources —and they brought to the Jews already resident in the United States a sense of communal Jewishness.

Their own rise to positions of wealth and influence was rapid. They brought to America their knowledge of finance and mercantilism, which was already being exercised by a handful of German-Jewish families in Europe, such families as the Rothschilds, the Bischoffsheims, the Sterns, and in England the Salomons. They became bankers, financiers, traders, and they founded in America the institution of great retail stores. By 1871, when the German-Jewish immigration dwindled to only a trickle, there was hardly a branch of American endeavor in which they were not to be found. They —together with the Polish Jews—invented and instituted in America mass production of clothing, an industry that was to grow enormously and be emulated eventually by other countries.

Today, the names of many of these German-Jewish immigrants have become important family names that are a part of the American scene, a rather old part in so new a country. We take for granted the great art collections, the parks, the hospitals and schools and libraries that represent such old German-Jewish names as Altman, Lehman, Speyer, Straus, Loeb, Rothschild, Untermeyer, Lewisohn, Hellman, Warburg, Lawson, Guggenheim, Abraham—not to mention the writers and artists and scholars who emerged from these families. Coming to the United States in 1846, Rabbi Isaac Mayer Wise became the leader of Congregation Beth El in Albany, New York, where he began his process of altering the Orthodox Jewish service—a process which resulted in the founding of the great system of Reform synagogues in the United States. German Jews supported and underwrote this movement.

By 1871, there were synagogues and Jewish social institutions in Chicago, Cleveland, Detroit, Cincinnati, San Francisco, Portland—and elsewhere. There was little anti-Semitism, and the German Jews were pouring all their gifts and energies into the body America, even as the Russian and Polish Jews would begin to do a decade later.

———•·•·•———

The Protestant Reformation, which might be said—as a matter of destiny—to have begun on the eve of All Saints Day in 1517 with Martin Luther's posting of his ninety-five theses on the door of the castle church, while it did not as such immediately liberate the Jewish masses of Europe, did break the great and monopolizing religious power of the Catholic Church—which ideologically was the base for attitudes against the Jew. The eternal accusation that the Jews had killed Christ or God was no longer tenable except among children and the most ignorant, and no longer a weapon acceptable to civil governments. The fact that for centuries western Europe should have responded to the charge of deicide, constantly resurrected by the Catholic Church, is so sorry a comment on the condition of mankind that one cannot elaborate upon it. Yet the base for anti-Semitism, the masses of people in continental Europe, was there, and in the later part of the nineteenth century, statesmen began to be aware of the advantages of a new type of anti-Semitism, something to be built upon the base that the Church had historically provided.

As a matter of fact, the actions against the Jews which have occurred since Constantine were never particularized as *anti-Semitic* in the sense of the word itself; since the designation *anti-Semitic* was invented in 1879 by a German journalist, Wilhelm Marr, who was obsessed by his hatred of Jews.

The expression itself was based upon a peculiar theory of the races of mankind, which arose basically because of the partitioning of Africa and parts of Asia among the great colonial powers of Europe. "The white man's burden," as it was so neatly put, was European colonialism claiming destiny's approval (or God's approval), a kind of tribal approval that the European powers appeared to need at that time—and subsequently too; a kind of modern "divine right" directed toward the darker people of the earth. Two Frenchmen, Ernest Renan and Joseph-Arthur Gobineau, who became amateur anthropologists of a sort, began to develop a theory that was eagerly seized upon as being the proper medicine for what ailed a burgeoning Europe. They began by separating the white race from the darker races, giving to white a superior status: namely human. The black was a little less than human. In the white race, however, there was superior white and inferior white—and the manner in which one separated the sheep from the goats was through language. They arbitrarily chose two language groupings, the Aryan and the Semitic. The Aryan was the language of the superior whites; the Semitic was the language of the inferior whites. At the apex of the Aryan pile were the "noble Teutons," blond, blue-eyed, wise and superior—indeed superman himself; and then as one went down the pile there were the millions who were supermen (because they spoke an "Aryan" tongue) though to a lesser degree, a part of the elite of the earth because they were at least a little watered by the "noble" Teutonic blood.

The Semites, on the other hand, were inferior from the word go—so inferior that there was no hope whatsoever for them—and the Jews were a sort of "fifth column" of the inferior Semites.

It all added up to a bag of silly nonsense; but on the other hand, even a casual study of history should convince the observer that there is no theory too silly or nonsensical or inherently vicious for the public to swallow. There is no great movement in our times that has not paraded an ideology of nonsense, perhaps not so blatant, but foolish enough; and it is shocking to poke around in the literature of the last of the nineteenth century and see how many writers fell for this tripe, which even ignored the fact that Sanskrit—the oldest surviving Aryan tongue—was spoken by millions of dark-skinned people. But from Jack London with his "blond beast" to Kipling with his beastly "burden," both literate and illiterate climbed on the Aryan bandwagon. The whole range from the "genteel" British anti-Semitism to the crudest of German sputterings was covered, and indeed in the minds of a great many, the Jews had become too arrogant and presumptuous in their new-found European liberation. Particularly in Germany, where the nineteenth century had created such a volcano of Jewish talent, enthusiasm, and vitality, was the new anti-Semitism welcomed and greeted. A German agitator by the name of Eugen Dühring leaped into print with a shaky theory of a Jewish seizure of power and intimations of various and sundry nefarious Jewish plots. Bismarck, fighting for power, saw a marvelous diversion in the new anti-Semitism. His liberal opposition contained the first set of Jews in German politics, and Bismarck met this challenge by climbing on the Aryan-racial-superiority wagon.

Two anti-Semitic political organizations were organized in Germany—the Christian Social Union and the Anti-Semitic League. A quarter of a million Germans signed a petition in 1881, calling for the disenfranchisement of all Jews and their forcible return to the ghettos.

Curiously enough, these German movements did not explode into violence, nor did they send masses of Jews into flight from Germany. In their new liberation, the German Jews felt that theirs was a supremely civilized country and that it was only a matter of time before sanity replaced idiocy. They pointed to the fact that organized anti-Semitism represented only a tiny fraction of the German people, and they said confidently that those evil days of the past were done with and could never return.

But in Russia—lord over the former Polish lands—a government that no one had ever marked particularly with the badge of civilization, the Czar and his ruling circle, watched events in Germany with keen pleasure and interest—as did certain circles in France. Events were building up that would have the most profound effect upon America—and the world, too. Here, we are simply noting the incidents that led to one of the great mass migrations of human history, the migration of the eastern European Ashkenazi Jews to the United States of America.

Anti-Semitic political leagues were set up in Hungary and Austria and Rumania as well as in Germany, and in 1882, an anti-Semitic congress was held in Dresden, which called for everything from incineration to forced exile for the Jews (as those might note who feel that the Nazi phenomenon had no precursor in Germany).

Let us pivot for a moment on the year 1881, simply noting the events that followed in the growing structure of modern anti-Semitism, and then returning once again to 1881: as for example—1882, anti-Semitic political party organized in the Austrian Parliament by Georg von Schonerer; 1882, ritual murder charges in Hungary; 1893, German anti-Semitic party gained fifteen seats in the Reichstag; 1894, the Dreyfus case exploded in France—one after another, steps toward a still unrealized end. This is a progression to keep in mind, while we return to the year 1881, and examine what happened in Russia.

The year 1881 is rather sadly called "the year the pogroms began." In a town called Elisavetgrad in the Ukraine, an argument started in a tavern. A few drunken Russian soldiers and peasants began to elaborate on the sorry old saw of the ritual murder of gentile children for their blood. Jews present and listening took exception and a fight started. Three Jews were killed then and there—and the tavern fight boiled into a full-scale riot. The riot wrecked the Jew-

ish quarter, set the Jewish houses aflame, while the rioters
counted the loot. Beer and vodka and vocal anti-Semitism
spread the riot to Kherson—and from there to Kiev. A week
after it began, a whole garrison of soldiers was loosed into
it, not to quell it, but to join in the killing and looting. The
Russian officers stood by and the Czar and his advisors read
the reports with delight. For them it was an opportunity to
turn all the social unrest and revolutionary agitation aside
and bury it under a national wave of anti-Semitism. The
Ukraine was a difficult and nationalistic place; the Czar
decided to let the Ukrainians take out their frustration and
hatred on the Jews.

The riots spread to Odessa and to a thousand villages and
hamlets between Kiev and Odessa. Tens of thousands of Jews
were robbed, beaten, raped; poor people were burned in the
shacks they lived in. Hundreds of them lay dead in the streets
of their tiny villages. A group of edicts called the "May Laws"
were passed under the Czar's urging—expelling Jews by the
thousands from the larger towns and cities.

Thus the Jewish Pale of Settlement in Russia—an area of
land where the Jews had lived for centuries in their tiny
hamlets and in the cities nearby—was destroyed, even as
the Jewish will to live and work in Europe was broken. The
most tolerant and patient people on earth had at last found
their condition intolerable and they began an exodus.

Very possibly, this movement of Jews over the next four
decades has no parallel in the history of mankind. Even the
westward surge in the United States was not on this scale;
and while larger masses of people have moved, it was never
under conditions that resembled the great trek of the Jewish
people out of eastern Europe, which had been their homeland for seven centuries, into a literal unknown. For these
were not the erudite, sophisticated cosmopolitan traders in
silk turbans and embroidered robes, men of wealth and influence; no, indeed; that was in a past so long ago that even
the scholars hardly remembered it. These were poor—indeed, unimaginably poor—peasants and woodcutters and
tailors and charcoal burners and Talmudists and peat cutters

and fullers and peddlers whose whole lives were circumscribed by the tiny villages they lived in, by the low, bare horizons of the sere Russian and Ukrainian prairies, by the howling blizzards of the long, dark northern winters—and whose only light and joy were the Sabbath candles or now and then the mystical ecstasy of the Hasidim. Unless they lived in the cramped ghettos of Warsaw or Vilna or Grodno, they lived in villages where Warsaw and Vilna were only names; yet in both cases, beyond Poland and Russia were places of mythology only.

Yet they picked up what they had and went into the unknown. They buried their dead, filled their pockets with what food they had, tied up their few possessions in quilts or bags—and left. Some had a little money; some had none; and the rich among them were "as rare as gentiles," as they put it in their wonderful, half-mocking Yiddish—for the only weapon they were armed with was a strange, ironic sense of humor—a caustic bitter-sweet humor that was like no other humor and which was more or less the result of the witless joke that history had dealt them, leaving them to dwell for almost a thousand years on the icy, dreary prairies of the north. Yet they had conquered the prairie, and they had found a way to laugh and mock at every blow life dealt them.

The essence of Jewish humor is the mockery of one's own bitter fortune, and it is possible that a very large element of Jewish survival lay in the Jews' ability to laugh at themselves. Perhaps this sort of self-directed, self-examining humor is a part of all persecuted peoples; and the Jew clothes it with a very ancient and patient wit and wisdom. That the humor so often takes on the quality of non sequitur is due perhaps to the amount of non sequitur in the Jews' effort to live in a seemingly insane world, as for example:

Two Jews brood over their tea. One says to the other, "You know, my friend, when one considers the fate of the Jew, the Egyptians who held us in captivity, the Romans, the Crusades, the endless persecution, and then Hitler and his murder machine, one can only conclude that it is better never to have been born than to be a Jew."

To which his friend replies, "That is so true, so profound—but who has that kind of luck? Not one in fifty thousand."

This story sets the style of the humor. It is intellectual, complex, and gentle in its complaints. The German Jew under the Nazis, taken severely to task for feeding his single remaining chicken whatever he feeds him, finally says wistfully to the gauleiter: "I don't feed him any more. I give him a few pennies and he buys his own food." A poor Jew promises Baron Rothschild immortality; he need only go to their little town in the Pale of Settlement; in all of its history, no rich man has ever died there. Nonsense is a large element; for the Jew is ever the outsider, looking at a world pervaded with nonsense. He listens to a street argument between two strangers and finally demands: "Why do you involve me? Do I need this?" The earth puzzles him, history puzzles him, fate puzzles him, and most of all he is puzzled by the strange trick God played upon him by making him the chosen people; and thus his humor is puzzled, gentle, probing, self-mocking, and full of despair for the human race. He is annoyed with God but never wholly angry, and his humor grasps wistfully at the tiny crevice of light that sometimes appears and for an instant makes the entire drama understandable.

The Jews moved westward. The railroad platforms were crowded with them where there were rails, and they filled the third-class carriages. Some had wagons or hired wagons. Many of them walked, and most of them had no destination, only *west*, because west meant a degree of freedom and perhaps safety from the mobs and the Cossacks. There was even hope in the west, because somewhere, as far away as the end of the world, was a place called America, and the legend of America was that there was the only place on earth where a Jew was a man like other men, and where no one cared that a man was a Jew or a Catholic or a Moslem.

They piled up at the frontier posts, at the customs points, at the seaports. They filled whole fields in places, and they sat and waited and waited and waited, by the thousands and tens of thousands, because, as they put it, they would wait and die but they would never go back.

Later, there would be money and tickets sent back by those who had already reached America and England, but for the first of this great movement, there were no connections and little money indeed. Yet they came to the seaports with the little money they had, and from the German and Dutch and British Jews, there came aid and help and chartered ships. In the centuries, so far apart and away, the eastern European Jews had become like another race, as different from the German, English, and Dutch Jews as any people could be, dressed in their strange clothes, bearded, speaking their soft medieval German-Hebrew that was called Yiddish, frightened, bent with oppression and labor and undernourishment; yet they were Jews, and the other, more fortunate Jews of the world held out their hands to them.

So from the Baltic and Prussian ports, the exodus continued.

England swallowed as large a mouthful of these refugees as a small country could digest. In a few years, a hundred thousand additional Jews were living in the teeming East End of London, along with the forty thousand and more who had been there before. It was as much as England could take, and anyway, to the Jews, England was only a way station. The destination they dreamed of was America, and now the ships laden with these penniless, desperate Jews steamed toward America.

And what ships they were! Old, rotten, rusty tramps that could barely stay afloat, ancient passenger ships, schooners resurrected from oblivion, any hulk or bottom that could stay afloat, and the steerages of the great liners as well. How many Jews have I spoken to who looked back upon that desperate crossing with unmitigated horror, telling of the black, endless hours in the steerage, the families huddled together, the children weeping with the nastiness of smell and darkness, the inadequate toilet facilities, the vomit and filth! There were no five-day crossings then, but ten to forty days—yet the Jews endured—and the day came when the ships steamed past Sandy Hook and through that golden haze that appears almost as a permanent fixture over the Lower Bay, and through the Narrows into the Upper Bay—and then they were on deck, jammed as tight as human beings can be, to see ahead of them the point of Manhattan with its great crown of high buildings—even then in the 1880's, a miracle to these Yiddish-speaking people of the cold Russian prairies.

And they came and they came. Day and night, American Immigration processed them through, but the procession was endless, and the rusty, stinking ships piled up on each other, dropped anchor in the bay and the North River to wait their turn with Immigration, while the children squalled and the women wept piteously that they could endure no more, and wailed to know why they had ever left their tiny prairie villages and sod huts—so lovely in retrospect against the misery of the ship.

Most of them entering the Port of New York came through Ellis Island, twenty-seven acres of rocky land in Upper New York Bay, just to the southwest of the lower tip of Manhattan Island. For many years, Ellis Island had been used as an army arsenal, but in 1892, under the pressures of the enormous flood of immigrants, it was pressed into use as an immigration station—in which capacity it gained almost legendary fame. A few years before this, in 1886, the Statue of Liberty, a colossus 152 feet high and symbolizing all the immigrant dreams of the promise of America, had been completed and opened to the public. It stood in the Upper Bay on Bedloe's Island, not far from Ellis Island, where every immigrant could see it. Engraved upon its base, the lines from the Jewish poet, Emma Lazarus:

Give me your tired, your poor,
Your huddled masses yearning to breathe free,
The wretched refuse of your teeming shore.
Send these, the homeless, tempest-tossed, to me:
I lift my lamp beside the golden door.

The Immigration officers worked manfully, day and night, yet they never quite caught up with this human tide. The wealthy, dignified, and intellectual German and Sephardic Jews of New York did not become Immigration officers, and while many of the gentile officers managed to pick up some Yiddish, there were half a dozen separate Yiddish dialects confronting them now: the soft Yiddish of the Ukrainian prairies, the nasal, singular Yiddish of the Carpathian highlands, from whence came thousands and thousands of Galician Jews, the hard, precise intellectual Yiddish of Warsaw, the lisping, singsong Yiddish of Lithuania, the Prussian-influenced Yiddish of Courland. How to understand it or deal with it? Many of them had never seen a Yiddish Jew before 1881 —yet their patience and decency with so ragged and strange a race is worth remembering. Suddenly these Jews met people, Christians, who were indifferent to them as Jews, who shouted at them, ordered them here and there, questioned them— and renamed thousands of them Cohen and Levy, two Jewish names Immigration found it easy to spell—but never degraded them as Jews.

Above all, these Jews were poor—not poor in any terms we understand today—but rock-bottom poor, penniless, possessionless, homeless, landed in a strange country, unable to speak a single word of English, unable to read even a street sign, since the literacy of almost all of them (and almost all were literate) was in the Hebrew alphabet, the alphabet in which Yiddish was written. Their first steps were guided by people the established German Jews provided; their first shelter on the lower East Side of New York was provided by the German Jews; and the food that kept starvation from destroying them during their first days in America was provided by German-Jewish charities. There were no public welfare funds then, nor could the Jews go to the poor-kitchens, since the food there was non-kosher and these Jews were deeply religious and ritualistic (except, of course, for the small but volatile minority of atheists, Socialists, bundists, anarchists, Spinozaists, writers, actors, agitators, and so forth) .

But the compassion and charity of the rich German Jews

were boundless, even as their willingness to socially accept the Ashkenazi Jews was limited. They saw no avenue, no bridge even, to these incredible, ragged, bearded paupers, who spoke only their own strange language—*jargon,* the German Jews called it—who were crude and dirty and voluble, who took snuff and wore the long, dark garments of Ukrainian peasants, and were without manners (western style), and shouted and sang and went into a state of ecstasy during their religious ritual, and wept in public—and who worked with their hands as common laborers, street sweepers, factory hands, porters—and anything else that would buy them the bread and salt to exist for another day of their incredible poverty.

At first, a lodging for a boatload on the East Side; a house, a stable converted into a dormitory, a kosher soup kitchen—then five hundred were a thousand, and a thousand were ten thousand and ten thousand were a hundred thousand—and suddenly there was a ghetto (but like no ghetto Europe ever knew), a ghetto of exploding, changing, permanently excited and anguished humanity.

In time, these eastern European Ashkenazi Jews would live in every city in America, but with a few exceptions, the beginning was in New York City.

———•◆•——

As I pointed out earlier, Polish Jews had been coming to America since the 1680's, but they were either single men or single families. Never had there been enough of these Polish Jews in a group to maintain a separate identity for more than a generation. Either they married into the American Christian world or they married into the Sephardic Jewish community and later into the German Jewish community.

You will recollect that the Polish Jews had for the most part come under the rule of the Czar, and thus the majority of them were now called Russian Jews and gave Russia as their place of origin. A minority came from what was left of Poland, and from the lands—once Polish—that had been incorporated into the Austrian-Hungarian Empire, and from

Rumania and Moldavia. However, they were knit into a single people by their Yiddish language, by their tendency toward religious mysticism (Cabala), by their Orthodox observance of Talmudic dictum—dietary laws, and so forth. For the sake of simplicity, I call them Ashkenazi Jews, for no other term embraces them properly. The German Jews would also technically be Ashkenazi, since the word means German, but they are set apart during this period by their longer residence in America and by their strong admixture with the Spanish Sephardic Jews who came to Germany in the seventeenth and eighteenth centuries.

Yet it would be wrong to imagine that the first great flow of refugees in 1881 were the first of the Ashkenazi (eastern European) community. The congregation B'nai Yeshurun was organized by German Jews in New York City in 1825, and it had over fifteen members who were Polish Jews. In 1852, there were enough Polish Jews in New York to organize their own modest synagogue, with a straightforward Ashkenazi ritual—as opposed to the Reform Movement, which had been brought to the United States by the German Jews and had become predominant among them.

(The Reform Movement in Judaism began after the Napoleonic period, chiefly in Germany. It consisted of shortening the service, translating key parts of it into the local language —first German, then, in America, English—introducing instrumental music, usually an organ, and having the sermon in the local language. The Reform Movement surrendered those parts of Jewish ritual which—to put it bluntly—made many Jews uncomfortable in open gentile society, such as covering the head at worship, observing the ancient dietary laws, using phylacteries, and deifying the Sabbath. It also did away with most of the mystical elements in Jewish worship and leaned toward rationalism. At the time of this writing, the Reform Movement in American Judaism is no longer predominantly German-Jewish—in terms of descendants— but is dominated by the descendants of the Ashkenazi Polish-Russian Jews. There are over 550 Reform synagogues in America, with a membership of well over a million. But among the Ashkenazi Jews, this is for the most part a post-World War II development.)

So when the great migration of the eighties and nineties started, there was a nucleus of Ashkenazi Jews already resident, a core of them in the East Side area which was to become the Jewish ghetto. In all of New York, there were perhaps twenty-five thousand Ashkenazi, but scattered, many of them with half-grown American-born children—and then came the year 1881.

In 1881—about 22,000 arrived; in 1882, 24,000 in the one year; in 1883—some 17,000; in 1884—19,000; in 1885—30,000; by 1890—35,000 in a single year; a year later, double that number, over 70,000; then dropping to the 40,40,30 thousand mark, then in 1900 leaping to 60,000, 75,000 in 1903; well over 100,000 in 1904, past 130,000 in 1905; and then, in 1907, in the single year, over 150,000 Jews entered the United States, almost all of them through the Port of New York—and then, year after year, this floodtide of humanity continued. Fifty years later, there were four and a half million Jews in the United States—almost four million of them of Ashkenazi (eastern European) birth or descent.

History reveals no other migration quite like this. In the hundred years after Plymouth Colony was founded, only a tiny fraction of this number entered North America; the migrations of antiquity are dwarfed by it. Here a whole nation of millions of human beings took their language and culture and religion from dreary prairies, wild mountains, and Polish ghettos, and transported it with themselves to the heart of a new city in a new land—into a new kind of ghetto, a place they went to because only in this place could they learn the language and way of life that were necessary for life in America.

People who make history are usually more interested in their immediate survival; the nation of Jews that was arriving in America had no idea of what they would contribute to the vigor of the United States; their interest was survival and survival in the Russian Empire was almost intolerable.

Later, their children would empathize with the first settlers and with the pioneers who opened the West, but I doubt that life was as cruel to either of these groups. The Ashkenazi Jews had a common poverty that is difficult to describe. In 1967, the Jewish Museum in New York City had an exhibition of photographs that traced the history of this Ashkenazi Jewish nation that squeezed itself into the East Side ghetto; it was a pictorial record of such poverty and filth and degradation and sheer human suffering as is hard to describe in any words, and I saw old men and women looking at the pictures and weeping over the memories they evoked. But no Czar or tyrant or reigning madman or organized movement of hate had put these Jews into the wretchedness of Rivington and Broome and Allen and Hester and Delancey streets. They put themselves there, and retrieved their dignity out of the degradation, and began to build a world. They had nothing but liberation, which—as history so often records— was enough.

They worked with their hands; they worked eighteen hours a day to have their children live, and they dropped dead from work. Often, they were exploited by their fellow Jews, and so they banded together to begin what would be an important part of the American trade union movement.

We find that as the twentieth century began, these Ashkenazi Jewish workingmen and women had organized the Amalgamated Waiters Union, two hundred members, out of which fifty were Jewish. (From the beginning they realized that Jew and gentile worker must stand together. They were no masters at the art of organization, but neither were they tyros. Their journey to freedom was a sort of masterpiece of loose organization.) They organized the Bakers Union in Brooklyn and Harlem, with five hundred members, of whom two hundred were Jewish. An interesting development— which we will enlarge on later—was the Yiddish theater; thus we have the Bill Posters and Ushers Union, fifty members, forty-five of them Jewish. (The five gentile members worked on the Sabbath.) The Boys Waist Makers' Union, two hundred members, of whom sixty were Jewish.

But their two great efforts were the United Garment Workers of America, ten thousand members, of whom nine thousand were Jewish, and the Cloak and Suit Tailors' Union, six thousand members, out of which three thousand were Jewish. Along with this, a fantastic variety of unions, desperately brought together as a means of survival: Suspender Makers' Union, Shirt Makers' Union, Mattress Makers, Knitters, Ladies' Waist Makers, Ladies' Wrapper Makers, Paper Box Makers—all of these predominantly Jewish. Organize—the word went out. For the first time in history, half a million penniless Jews were working in factories, sweatshops, tenements, with their hands. The fever spread, and the Yiddish theater joined the workers, forming the Hebrew Actors' Protective Union (before Equity was dreamed of), seventy members, of whom thirty-five were Jewish. One wonders who were the thirty-five gentile actors in the Yiddish theater, and what they did. But musicals and music being even dearer to the hearts of the Jews, we find that over one thousand Jews joined the large, existing Theatrical Musical Union.

Nor was the trade union organization impetus confined to New York City. Samuel Gompers, who was London-born, and who was already organizing the Cigar Makers before the great Ashkenazi migration began, was Jewish, and in 1886, he was elected president of the newly formed American Federation of Labor; but he and the many other individual Jews who worked with the Knights of Labor and the subsequent American Federation of Labor, were in a sense apart from the Ashkenazi migration. The Yiddish-speaking Jews built their own unions, and then they moved out of the ghetto and sent their organizers into New England, into New Jersey, into the Piedmont factory lands of the South. Able to speak only the most broken English, frequently derided, mocked at, tarred and feathered, beaten, abused, jailed—they exhibited a most indomitable spirit and a keen awareness of the fact that the tiny unions they had started in the ghetto sweatshops could only survive if they were joined to the masses of American workers. Indeed, these men and women played no small role in determining the destiny of the

American labor movement—and to a degree, of America as well.

———— .—•—•—.————

The trade union movement was only one direction; the explosive, viable mass of Ashkenazi Jews burst forth in every direction—as if the energy and talent they contained had been cumulatively growing during their thousand years of indignity. For one thing, their language, the expressive and malleable Yiddish, sprang into maturity. There were no Cossacks here to whip them and ride them down if they answered a question in Yiddish, no Russians to deride them, no Prussian policemen to sneer at their "jargon." Their language was at last resolutely their language. Here in this massive, dirty, wonderful, freewheeling city of New York, it was expected that the Italians in their Italian neighborhood would speak Italian, that the Germans would speak German, and that the Jews would speak Jewish. It was natural, obvious, as natural as that the Armenians in their neighborhood spoke Armenian and the Poles Polish and the Hungarians Hungarian. There was some sort of newspaper in every language imaginable; in Yiddish, twenty years after the migration started, there were six daily papers, eleven weeklies, perhaps forty monthlies—the lives of weeklies and monthlies were unpredictable—trade union papers, religious papers, atheist papers, and even a sort of short-lived almanac.

There were writers in Yiddish, novelists, reporters, short-story writers, poets, playwrights, historians, prophets, frauds, and seers. (It must be understood that while hundreds of thousands of the Ashkenazi Jews became workers, thousands became entrepreneurs, manufacturers, publishers, merchants, and so forth.) Not only were their works published, but the beloved Yiddish writers of eastern Europe, Solomon Ettinger, Isaac Meir Dick, Abraham Ber Gottlober, and, of course, Mendele Mocher Sephorim, Isaac Peretz, and Sholom Aleichem—the latter two among the most gifted short-story writers of modern times—were published in America and widely read.

Upon this base, a whole body of American Yiddish literature came into being, most of it translated into English and read eagerly by the native American audience.

As a correlation to this, and with a great vitality all its own, the Yiddish theater in America was born. America was not the beginning of the Yiddish theater; in Cracow, for example, there was a Yiddish theater giving nightly performances as early as 1830, and there were Yiddish theater groups in half a dozen Polish and Lithuanian cities. When the great tide of Ashkenazi migration began, it was hardly to be expected that people as emotional and as effervescent as actors and directors and playwrights would be left behind. They bundled up their costumes and scripts, and along they came—and within a decade after the beginning of the migration, the Yiddish theater in America had burst into life. In fact, Boris Thomashefsky, the great Yiddish producer, writer, and actor, arrived with the vanguard of the migration in 1881. He was joined by Jacob P. Adler, Jacob Gordin, and Sigmund Mogulescu—and soon there were half a dozen Yiddish theatrical productions concurrently running, academies for actors— and most important of all, a style of acting, rich and deep, that was to influence the entire American theater. From these beginnings an exciting new generation of American English-speaking Jewish writers, actors, and directors emerged, many of them trained in the Yiddish theater.

But the Yiddish influence did not stop there. A language so gay and alive and descriptive could not reside in America without changing the American-English Americans spoke. Words, phrases, juxtapositions, inflections, attitudes of Yiddish became a permanent part of the American language.

(Here are a few examples of Yiddish words more or less incorporated into the American language: *schlemiel,* a fool; *shlep,* a drag; *mavin,* an amateur expert; *mishagas,* nonsense; *mishuga,* slightly insane; *gesundheit,* good health; *gansa geshichta,* the whole story, which can be alternately the *gansa megilla; lachiam,* health; and, of course, *chutzpah.* One can only define *chutzpah* by citing the example of the man who murdered his mother and father—and demanded mercy of the court on the grounds that he was an orphan. That, indeed, was *chutzpah*.)

And the instinct, the feeling for theatrical showmanship led the Jews—even those born in eastern Europe—toward the creation of the American film industry, a thing not the making of the Ashkenazi Jew alone, but so much of his making that it is hard to conceive of it without him.

———·━•━•━·———

No other nation of people came to America as the Ashkenazi Jews did; to them it was not a residence or a place or a nation—it was a lover. They embraced it; they adored it; they wept for it; and they married it. When they criticized it, they criticized with worship; they did mental somersaults to convince themselves that they had been in America since the first settlers; they looked at it with clouded vision; and they poured into it their total capability.

And they adapted almost immediately. During the two thousand years they had spent in the Diaspora of Italy and Germany and Poland and Russia, the Ashkenazi Jews had refused to adapt. With few exceptions, they had not intermarried; they had kept themselves and their culture apart— and in Poland and Russia, they maintained their own language as well. Yet here in America, the process of adaptation began almost in the few blocks between the pier and the ghetto. They breathed in the air and began to change. They worked all day and sat up nights, fighting their way through the English-language books. They jammed the night schools. They literally forced their frightened children to enter the public schools, where they sat terrified at the strange language, strange faces, strange ways of teaching—so different from the tiny schoolhouses where Jewish children of all ages were taught by a single teacher. And then, apparently overnight, the children were talking English, spending hours in the free libraries, where the librarians complained frantically that the Jews had cleaned every book off the shelves, leaving the shelves empty and the library useless. But there were never free libraries less useless.

Five, six hundred years had passed since the Jew had been physician to Europe, and to these penniless Ashkenazis, even the memory of that period was gone; yet by 1895, so great was the Jewish Ashkenazi pressure on the medical schools that the quota system—a limitation of Jewish applicants to colleges— came into being, and during the next thirty years, it was extended to hundreds of colleges throughout the country. It was a form of anti-Semitism, yet quite different from anything that had been devised in Europe. American college authorities pleaded that they had no room for the surge of Jewish applicants—that to admit all of them would turn the universities into Jewish institutions. This was certainly untrue, and as the great mass of the Ashkenazi increased, spreading across the country, moving into city after city, state after state, anti-Semitism came into being for the first time (as a national mood) in the history of the United States. At its worst, it never resembled the European product; it was exclusive in certain industries, in colleges, in social institutions—country clubs, fraternal organizations, many learned societies—in neighborhoods where Jews were barred from home purchase by restrictive covenants and other methods, in summer hotels, and in many other places; but except for the South with its Klan, this exclusiveness rarely turned into violence of any sort, and perhaps the majority of Americans were little touched by it.

(The cheap and stupid forgery entitled "The Protocols of the Learned Elders of Zion," which was written in 1904 by Serge Nilus, a Russian monk, was for the most part copied from a French attack upon Napoleon III, in 1865. With little originality and by changing names here and there, the monk turned the French book into what purported to be the secret minutes of a Jewish group who planned to overthrow the Christian countries and establish a Jewish dictatorship over the world. This childish book was picked up by Henry Ford in an English translation, and in 1920, a series of articles based upon acceptance of the "Protocols" as truth was printed in the

Dearborn Independent, a newspaper owned by Ford. This began a schematic and rather lunatic projection of anti-Semitism based on the invention of an endless and tedious plot by the Jews to take over the world. It remained a lunatic fringe affair, touching only a tiny minority of the American people, and it still continues.)

Yet it would have been strange indeed—and the American people would have been saints—if the incoming of the Ashkenazi had not aroused resentment in America; the wonder is that there was so little resentment, and taking the country as a whole, the resentment was small indeed.

Yet the Jews took nothing without giving. From the beginning they took care of their own and asked nothing of the government—the charity of the German Jews making the word *Jew* in America synonymous with *charity*—and as the Ashkenazi masses took hold of their lives in America, they built charities of their own. As thousands of Jewish doctors emerged, the Ashkenazi Jewish philanthropists built hospitals, laboratories, research centers, old-age homes, temples, orphan homes. Children of the penniless immigrants became dentists, and soon the Jewish contribution helped to make American dentistry the finest in the world.

Ashkenazi Jewish businessmen, capitalized with pennies, improved the new way of making clothing—mass producing it for the women of America—and twenty years after these same businessmen had come out of steerage in their rags, their industry promised to be one of the largest in America.

And suddenly, these same Ashkenazi Jews, the first generation of children of those who had crossed the ocean, were graduating from the universities, secure in a culture their parents had never dreamed of. A nation had moved from one world to another, from one culture to another, and had survived and had joined itself to a polyglot people called the Americans.

———•◦•———

At each stage of the development—or one might say simply the movement—of the Jewish people through history,

they took on a new form and shape and even a new ideology
to fit the circumstances of their situation. Often enough,
there was wide variation in the world outlooks of different
groups of Jews in different situations—so enormous a separation in terms of culture, language, and social-functioning,
that it almost passes one's understanding that the groups are
linked together. We have seen this again and again, the cultured Alexandrian with his contemporary, the Hasmonean
peasant; the Spanish gentleman as opposed to the fifteenth-
century Polish villager; the Sephardic aristocrat in nineteenth-century Philadelphia as opposed to the Ukrainian
woodcutter; the German merchant prince of New York as
opposed to the masses of Ashkenazi refugees; and after World
War II, the incredible intermingling of cultures and back-
grounds that took place in the State of Israel.

One might argue that Christians, like Jews, represent extremes of culture and class; but Christianity is a religion and
Judaism is that and also a way of life and particularized world
outlook. Again and again throughout history, the class re-
lationships of Christians have been based on alienation and
fear. The Christian planters of the South did not build hospitals and old-age homes and schools for their Christian
slaves, nor did the barons of the Middle Ages establish funds
for the education of the children of their Christian serfs.
One could come up with an endless list of comparisons; but I
do not think one can overstate the fact that the Jewish experience is singular, and that the specifics of this singularity
carried them through each new social and national situation
that they encountered.

The Norman Baron and his Saxon serf had absolutely
nothing in common, in spite of the fact that they professed
the same religion; it was not simply their culture that was a
world apart, it was the absence of any singular world outlook.
It is quite true that the idea of social obligation finally blos-
somed among the Christian rich, but perhaps it is not too
cruel to suggest that this sense of social obligation only
matured when the anger of the oppressed had reached a
dangerous level. Among the Jews, the situation was quite

different, and the interplay of social obligation is supported by the very roots of the religion-culture, the sense of total identity before God and total identification by the Christian world. Many Jews will hotly deny that they possess either of these two attitudes, but it would appear to me that consciously or not, all Jews partake of such identification to one degree or another.

The shift, however, of the Ashkenazi nation from eastern Europe to the United States of America was unique—in that it put the Jews into a new existence almost instantaneously. It is true that this historically instantaneous transition would take place in Israel later, but never with equivalent masses of people and not in any parallel set of circumstances.

(We must note that in speaking of what I call the Ashkenazi nation—for convenience—I do not mean to imply that all of the Ashkenazi Jews of eastern Europe picked up and moved to the Western world. Theirs was an extremely high birthrate in Europe, and in any such voluntary movement of people as this, it is the young, the strong, the most oppressed who move. As severe and untenable as the oppression of the Russians was, the Ashkenazi Jews lived across a vast area, and there were many parts of this area hardly touched by the pogroms and the mob violence. So that in spite of this great migration to the United States, before the advent of Hitlerism, the majority of the Ashkenazi Jews remained in eastern Europe. The statistics of the 1930's, the pre-Hitler era, show that there were over three million Jews resident in Russia and another four million resident in Poland, Rumania, and Lithuania. At that time, the total Jewish population of Europe, including the above areas, was over nine and a half million; and of these more than six million were murdered by the Nazis and several hundred thousand more perished from other causes during World War II.)

The shift of this mass of population from eastern Europe to the United States resulted in an unforeseen and unmatched generation gap (though the expression did not exist at the time). Between the parents and the children was a gap, not only of language but of era and comprehension. All former Jewish experience in some part or era of the Diaspora was among Moslem or Christian nations, the non-Christian, non-Moslem areas being so minor as to have no permanent historical effect. The United States differed in that it was not a Christian nation in the European sense, but rather a nation in which the majority of the people were Christians. The United States lacked the organized pressure for baptism that existed in Germany, the national chauvinism of France, the blanketing ignorance and ignorant hatred of Czarist Russia.

With the Ashkenazi Jews, the American process worked. They burst out of the ghetto in one generation, and they also burstout of the walled-off world that the Ashkenazi Jew had chosen to live in ever since he first entered the lands of the Teutons at the beginning of our era. Since then, he had borne himself as a thing apart. He was not simply *Ashkenazi,* which means German; he was *Yehudim Ashkenazi,* the German Jew in the literal beginning, and then the *Yiddish-Yehudim,* or the Yiddish-speaking Jew. In America, in a single generation—and often enough in a single year or month— he became an American. Thousands and thousands of American-born children of the immigrants closed their minds against the gentle, intimate language of their parents; they refused to speak or think in Yiddish; they were having a love affair with the American language, devouring English and American literature, worshipping at the shrine of the American folk heroes.

This is not to advertise the legend of the "melting pot." The "melting pot" is an interesting symbol, but it is questionable whether it ever had more than symbolic validity. Generation after generation, New York City swallowed a gigantic mass of immigrants, Germans, Irish, Jews, Italian; and the children of each generation were a product called American. The title had validity; these were Americans; but they had not been put through a melting pot. Rather had their culture and folkways been added to the American whole, but without surrendering ethnic meaning and pride in a subjective sense. When such meaning and pride were surrendered, they had to be reclaimed before the immigrants could feel that they were whole people in the American scene. What type of society thus comes into being has not yet been sufficiently defined, but it is new and different.

America was not and is not a land of religious symbolism, and the American generation of the Ashkenazi—in the great majority—rebelled against the ritual of their parents. The older generation of Yiddish-speaking Jews had no words for the ancient mystical rites of their religion; ritual had been so interwoven into their lives in the eastern European Diaspora that they had never known a need to spell it out, to attempt to rationalize what was beyond rationalization. The Ashkenazi nation did not dissolve with the passage of years; it disintegrated immediately. The new generation grappled mechanically with Hebrew and then for the most part abandoned it. Some of them related to the new synagogues that were building in America; some did not. But the great majority of them tolerated rather than embraced. When war came, in 1917, the children of the Ashkenazi immigrants—in whose lives and thoughts violence had once been impossible, incredible, and bestial—enlisted by the thousands, and many a short-order Jewish philosopher declared that the need and reason for Jews had, in America, finally disappeared.

———•◦•———

The Ashkenazi American-born (and foreign-born) Jew might well have replied, in the words of Mark Twain, that the news of his death had been greatly exaggerated. He broke out of the ghetto and into the cities and neighborhoods of America to discover that the situation was far more complex than he had imagined it to be. So long as he had lived in the ghetto, there were few restrictions against him. Outside of the ghetto, there were a good many.

There were four and a half million Jews in America now, in the 1920's—perhaps more. (The number of Jews in America has always been a perplexing statistical question, for no national census has been directed toward religion, such

direction being by implication a violation of the First
Amendment to the Constitution. Religious statistics are come
by through the membership in the various churches and estimates to accompany the membership; but in the case of the
Jews, the simple truth of the matter is that *no reliable or
exact or confirmable* statistics have existed since the time of
Moses, where the dispute between the Biblical "higher crit-
ics" and the traditionalists goes on constantly; and the situation has scarcely improved since Moses. That serious and indefatigable traveler, Benjamin of Tedula, in his journeys during the twelfth century, would sometimes count the Jews
of a town, head by head; but even he was driven to guess-
work. At this writing, in 1968, a popular figure for the number of Jews in the United States is somewhere between five
million and five and a half million, depending on what almanac, yearbook, or atlas you examine. This is to a very large
extent based on synagogue and Jewish community center
membership and religious attitudes, but this is a dubious
method at best. I know personally many Jews who have
no synagogue affiliation, and I have heard sober estimates of
fully 25 percent of the 1967 Jewish population being without
synagogue or Jewish-center affiliation. At the same time, what
constitutes a Jew in America? Is it being half-Jewish, one-
quarter Jewish, or precisely how much? Or is it an attitude,
a sense of oneself? We have examined this question before
to no firm conclusion. How does one deal with the thousands and thousands of Jews who have married Christians in
America over the past two hundred years—and their descendants who may be in the millions? So we must remember that the statistics used are for the most part arbitrary and
within a rather broad spectrum.)

In the 1920's, thousands of these Jews had returned from
military services. Other were physicians, lawyers, businessmen, pharmacists, labor leaders, artists, writers, actors, scientists. The Jewish workers had already discovered
that the gentile summer resorts were closed to them, and
they began to build vacation areas of their own, the largest
concentration being in Sullivan County, in the Delaware

River region of New York State—the Catskills, as the area is called. The middle-class Ashkenazi Jew—of whom there were then already hundreds of thousands—was not satisfied with a nonghetto vacation interval. He was ready to step into the mainstream of American life. He desired to live in the better neighborhood, and then the best, to go to the same places as the gentile, to use the same facilities—and he began a struggle to do so.

In this struggle for complete equality, he had some but far from complete success—perhaps because he fell into a new pattern of Jewish Diaspora life, which, for want of a better or existing name, I will call *equivalency*.

Powerful now, increasing in wealth and position, he began more and more to move toward equivalency. He desired to live on Park Avenue and Fifth Avenue in New York City. When the owners of wholly Christian-occupied buildings refused to rent to him, the Jew bought the building. Or he bought land and built his own apartment houses. Through the twenties, he had become the major factor in New York City construction, and he built with an energy as explosive as his Americanization. He went to the suburbs and found areas barred to him. He built equivalent areas alongside the barred areas, and the two were indistinguishable—and in most suburbs there was a gradual interlocking of Jewish and gentile enclaves. Barred from gentile golf clubs and gentile city clubs, he built his own in precise imitation. But once these middle-class Ashkenazi Jews accepted the process of equivalency, they found that they had virtually agreed to live as a sort of mirror image of middle-class American society, and middle-class American society was socially church-grouped.

Thus the first and second generation middle-class American Ashkenazi Jew found himself directed back toward Judaism—his ancient religion—by the very dynamic of a society he had plunged headlong into, momentarily willing to leave his religion behind him. He began to build synagogues, not as the early American synagogues were built, as urban houses of prayer alone, but as central social suburban units, equivalents in size and purpose to the Catholic and Protestant churches he could see from his own doorstep. The Jewish Orthodoxy of the prairie villages of the Ukraine and of the Polish ghettos, the mysticism of the *Baal Shem-Tov,* the ecstasies of the Cabala—these were beyond revival in America (and most often beyond the memory and knowledge of the first and second generation in America), so a new form of Judaism had to be created for the new patterns of equivalency.

There already existed the Reform Movement of the German Jew, which the Ashkenazi of the second and third generation embraced in large numbers in the post-World War II period, but this was still too alien, too far removed from traditional Jewish Orthodox worship for the Ashkenazi Jews of the twenties and the early thirties. Instead, equivalency was satisfied by the creation of "The Conservative Movement" in Judaism, a sort of halfway step between the Reform and the Orthodox, which would serve those middle-class Jews who could not yet make the step to Reform Judaism.

This suburban pattern was repeated by the urban middle-class Ashkenazi and their children, who frequently combined the synagogue with neighborhood religious schools and youth centers—a combination that existed in the suburbs as well.

———•—•—•———

The large Jewish working class—who had come in the great migration—took another direction. Either out of the bitterness and soul-destroying misery of the sweatshops, they broke with the synagogue entirely—as many Protestant factory workers did with their church—or they remained with the Orthodox worship. A small core of them, numbering only a few thousand, recreated an island of Hasidim, eventually buying rural pieces of land wherein they attempted —and still attempt—to continue the mysticism of the *Baal Shem-Tov.*

But the masses of the Jewish working class, who were in

great majority the Ashkenazi immigrants and their children, remained for the most part in the great East Side
ghetto, or left for one or another less wretched ghetto in
Brooklyn or in the Bronx. Either they broke with the synagogue or they lived out their lives as Orthodox Jews, praying
in the old manner, attempting to observe the complex Jewish ritual as best they could, leaving part of it here and there
by the wayside—for life in America did not make it easy for
an Orthodox Jew to follow every detail of his Orthodoxy.
But among the working-class Jews—whether they were
Orthodox or atheist—there was one thing held in common:
a driving ambition that their children should be educated
and should climb out of the working class in a single generation.

Not all of them, by any means, succeeded; they worked
themselves into early graves, many of them; they saved and
scrimped and sacrificed and all too many of them were defeated by the great festering slum in which they lived. They
raised up not only Jewish doctors and lawyers and judges and
legislators and scientists and teachers and members of almost
every other profession and small business men and big businessmen; they also found some of their children turning into
thieves and prostitutes and gangsters and petty shysters and
swindlers and common bottom-rung street hoodlums. Their
problem was not exclusion nor was their solution equivalency; their problem was simply survival in a world that was
free of government oppression and anti-Semitism of the
European kind, but cruel and merciless in what it demanded
of plain working people for their survival. As we noted,
the great and lasting contribution of the very poor Ashkenazi
Jews to America—aside from their children—was a trade
union beginning that laid the basis for the present-day organizations of the American working people.

Yet, while there are thousands of Jewish workers in America today—many of them the last great wave of the Ashkenazi, who came here just prior to World War I—no longer
is there a wide working-class base. A majority of the children
of the immigrants have moved up, from the working class

into the middle class, and into the upper middle class. The beginning of the great Ashkenazi immigration was the year 1881, and from the early immigrants, there is a fourth and increasingly a fifth American-born generation. Now (1968) eighty-seven years have passed since then. Some of those who came here as small children at the beginning are still alive, and of course a great many of the later immigrants are alive, but they are looked upon rather askance by the younger generations, whose presence in America is matter-of-fact, and certain.

Almost two thousand years ago, the Roman philosopher Seneca observed that of all the people in his world, only the Jews understood the meaning of their religion and its rites. This could hardly be said in America today.

———•—•—•———

In the next part of this book, when we observe the events leading to the destruction of more than one-third of the entire Jewish people, we will note the further steps of development and motion in the United States. Certainly, the American Jew of the forties and fifties and sixties is quite different, in both mood and outlook, from the American Jew of the first four decades of our century. Indeed, from the first appearance of Nazism, a process of reexamination of self and substance began among American Jews. At that point, in the 1930's, the distinctions between the Ashkenazi eastern European Jews and the earlier-arrived German Jews and what remained of the still earlier-arrived Sephardic Jews had begun to blur, and they have blurred still further in the years since then.

As Zionism (which will be dealt with later) changed from a narrow curiosity to a matter that left no American Jew untouched, the process of Jewish self-examination was further deepened. The ease with which not only the Jews in America, but the Protestants and Catholics as well, have been able to discard religion or consign it to an utterly mechanical and mindless observance began to be suspect, and many thoughtful Americans, of various religious groupings, have begun to examine the gilt-edged, shiny, and often rather terrifying gimmicks and devices that have replaced religion.

The small Jewish advantage is that even with his new and American method of precise equivalency, he still remains something of an outsider and thereby retains some objectivity. A people so old does not easily lose its memory, and Adolf Hitler underlined the pain if not the meaning of Jewish existence.

PART ELEVEN

the Holocaust

Now and then in history, a place, a moment, an event, and an idea coincide, and then a little of the human race's journey through time is changed. Usually, the coincidence is fortuitous, as it was in the fall of 1894. A journalist, an Austrian Jew, Theodor Herzl by name, thirty-four years old and the correspondent of a Vienna newspaper called *Neue Freie Presse,* happened to attend the trial of a French officer who was charged with treason—with the sale of secret documents to the German Government. The officer was a captain, and his name was Alfred Dreyfus. He happened to be Jewish, but that was not primarily what brought Herzl to the trial; Herzl was simply covering a sensational case for his newspaper.

Captain Alfred Dreyfus was a year older than Herzl, and like Herzl a product of the nineteenth-century emancipation of the western European Jew. Proud, dedicated to the French Army with religious fervor, much more eager to be a Frenchman than a Jew, he was an ironical choice for the victim in a nasty frame-up—a man caught in a web he never really understood. As nearly as the plot can be unraveled, a certain Major Esterhazy of the French Army, an alcoholic and a rather spineless human being, had allowed himself to become a spy in the pay of Germany. A group of Jesuits, meanwhile, had conspired with certain enemies of the Third Republic to charge that the Republic was in the hands of the Jews, who were committing treason and selling military secrets to Germany. Esterhazy forged a document that was attributed to Dreyfus by the above-mentioned conspiracy—and Dreyfus was charged with treason and placed on trial before a court martial.

Ultimately, most of the important personalities of France, and almost all of the intellectuals, were drawn into a national struggle that revolved around the Dreyfus case—which became a much broader matter than the role and fate of Captain Dreyfus himself and which involved issues as far apart as civil rights, the race question and foreign policy. The French military, the Catholic Church, and a national coalition of the right wing joined in the attack on Dreyfus and thereby the Jews. The defense came under the moral leadership of the French novelist, Émile Zola, who wrote his famous article "J'accuse" in defense of Dreyfus. (Interestingly, drawn into this affair, the playwright Rostand wrote his famous comedy-drama, *Cyrano de Bergerac,* with its marvelous defense of the independence of the intellectual inserted into sentimental theater fare of the time.) The Dreyfus affair not only contributed to the separation of Church and State in France, but proved a vital force for the growth of French socialism.

It is not our purpose here to go into the specifics of the trial of Dreyfus but rather to examine the effect it had on a dark-eyed, handsome, and sensitive Jew named Herzl. As Herzl watched and recorded the trial, he had a flash of deep and intuitive understanding, and above all things, he saw the Jew used, singled out, degraded even as Jesus was degraded, dehumanized, and turned into a hate emblem for reaction.

There are few Jews who have not known such a moment— a moment of the utter despair of a man lost and surrounded by a ravening mindless mob. For days after the trial and conviction and degradation of Captain Alfred Dreyfus, Herzl brooded upon what had happened—and then, bit by bit, he began to form a solution for the Jewish problem in his own thoughts. What the Jews needed above all else, he decided, was to be a nation within an area of land which they owned and governed. Day and night he lived with this idea, talking about it to all of his friends, testing it, promoting it, feeling it himself on ever higher levels of excitement and conviction. He even approached the Jewish financier Baron de Hirsch, a famous philanthropist who had already allocated funds for the establishment of Jewish agricultural colonies in Argentina and other thinly settled countries.

Herzl was attractive, intelligent, and charming, but even Baron de Hirsch backed away from the notion of a Jewish state. Not that the idea was new. Ever since the Babylonian captivity, twenty-five hundred years ago, Jews had spoken of the *Aliyah,* the ingathering of the exiles; but the expression had become wholly ritualistic, and the emerging class of influential Jews of western Europe looked upon the whole notion of a nationalist ingathering as a part of the "crazy messianic dreams of the Polish Hasidim," whom they regarded without understanding and with some impatience, shame, and distaste. While the enormous Ashkenazi nation that had transported itself to the United States was working twelve to eighteen hours a day in sweatshops and assorted hellholes so that their children might climb out of the pit of poverty and ignorance, the emancipated Jews of western Europe, of Germany and France, whose condition had never been so wretched as that of the Ashkenazis on the Russian prairies, were moving into positions of esteem and influence all over Europe. They were dazzled by the breadth of the horizons open to them, and they saw their future in a civilized, cultured, and tolerant Europe where no bars or roadblocks of any kind were placed in the path of Jewish equality.

This being the case, it seemed to them that Herzl's suddenly acquired mission could only present new hooks for anti-Semites to cling to. The Jew, as they put it to Herzl, was no more connected to ancient Palestine—or modern Palestine—than the English Anglo-Saxon was connected to Holland and Belgium, nor would a Jewish state in Palestine (or anywhere else) solve any Jewish problem. Herzl saw the Jewish problem in the symbol of Dreyfus; but the wealthy and cultured Jews he approached for help were less historically sensitive and regarded the Dreyfus case as an aberration and by no means as a weather vane. Their reply to Herzl was to the effect of the Jewish people having only one major problem—the destiny of the millions of poverty-stricken and benighted Ashkenazim of eastern Europe, who were suffering and dying in the Czar's program of organized persecution and systematic murder.

Their thinking was most influenced by the great migration to the United States—which was at its height now—and they felt that the necessity would be to organize and put into operation similar mass migrations to underpopulated countries of the western hemisphere, such as Argentina and Brazil. Herzl countered that the United States could

not possibly hold all of the Ashkenazim, even if they all desired to go there, and that so far as the Ashkenazim were concerned, they had shown no desire to go to a Spanish- or Portuguese-speaking country, the very names of Spain and Portugal being symbols of consuming horror to them.

(Two incidents must be mentioned here—to demonstrate
that ancient symbols, such as the Jewish horror of Spain, retain force and meaning only so long as they fit the current
situation. In 1898, in New York City, when Spain was seen
as a colonial oppressor, the Ashkenazi young men—who
had come to America as small children in the first immigration—organized several regiments of volunteers to fight in
Cuba against Spain, and thereby take revenge for the suffering Spain had once visited upon the Jews. However, in
1937, when the Lincoln Brigade was recruited in the United
States to fight for Republican Spain against Franco and his
Moors, over half of its membership was Jewish—the children and the grandchildren of the Ashkenazi immigrants.)

All arguments, rational or not, failed to convince Herzl,
who proceeded to write a fervent declaration of his beliefs.
This book, titled *Der Judenstat* ("The Jewish State"), was
published in 1896 and almost immediately translated. It put
forth all of Herzl's arguments about the senselessness of demanding or expecting assimilation of all of the Jews into
the body of Christian society, and it called for the establishment of a Jewish homeland. Hoping still to get the support
of certain wealthy Jews who were committed to the idea of
migration to South America or Africa, Herzl allowed for a
non-Palestinian territory, but only if that territory were the
choice of the Jewish people. For himself, his decision after
much thought was that such a homeland must be in Palestine and could hardly be successful anywhere else.

Herzl was a gracious and charming man, so much so that
the owners of the Vienna *Neue Freie Presse* were willing to
pay his salary and retain him in the rather undemanding
job of literary editor, which would leave most of his time
free for his own mission, which had already found a label—a
word coined a few years before by Nathan Birnbaum, a

writer—*Zionism*. Though the word was used in contempt, Herzl liked the word and grasped it. So far as he was concerned, for the rest of his life, he would be a Zionist, and only this word and cause would have meaning for him. At this time, in 1896, Herzl was thirty-six years old and already sick with heart disease. He had eight years left to live, and for those eight years he drove himself unsparingly.

Literally, he sought to move the earth. He knew the Duke of Baden, exceptional among German nobility in his liberalism and liking for Jews, and he convinced him of the justice of his cause. The Duke agreed to help, and opened many doors for Herzl, particularly in Turkey. Palestine was then a part of the Turkish Empire, which was key to all of Herzl's dreams, and after a rather nebulous promise of help from German-Jewish financiers, who could not resist his dedication, Herzl went to Turkey. He saw many people in Turkey, among them the Sultan's grand vizier, but then and later, the Sultan refused any grant of land in Palestine, although he told Herzl that he would not be opposed to mass immigration of the Jews into Turkey itself, where he would grant them a self-governing area. But neither Herzl nor his associates were enthusiastic about this kind of thing. Again and again, on various subsequent occasions, Herzl was offered land, once on the Sinai peninsula and again in Africa, but nothing short of Palestine was acceptable.

By the sheer power of his personality Herzl turned his scheme from an "unrealistic dream," as Baron de Hirsch called it, into "a sober demand of the times," as the British Prime Minister characterized it. By 1897, Herzl had enough adherents to be able to call the First Zionist Congress, which was convened in Basel in Switzerland in August of that year. At this Congress, the World Zionist Organization was founded, and Theodor Herzl was elected president and served in that capacity until his death seven years later.

Howsoever one regards the creation of the state of Israel in our time, one must accept the fact that the seed for it was planted by Theodor Herzl. What might have happened without Herzl, we don't know; possibly the result would

have been much the same; but he was unique and important in that he arrived at a historic moment of coincidence
and accepted the challenge it offered him.

＊＊＊＊

After Herzl's death in 1904, the Zionist movement grew
slowly but with a curious firmness. A trickle of Jews into
Palestine began, single young men and single families,
mostly from the great Ashkenazi area in eastern Europe, some
of them young men of physical strength and massive deter-
mination, who made their way on foot across Russia, into
Turkey, and thence into Palestine. In Palestine—which
then was a bare, bleak, and almost uninhabited land—there
were several Jewish agricultural colonies, struggling for an
existence very alien to them, since they were mostly Russian-
Jewish students, and helped somewhat by funds provided
by Baron de Rothschild. But neither funds nor organization
made the difference that began to turn Jews toward Palestine; it was the triumph of an idea whose time had come.
It was a new whisper on the wind, which Jews everywhere
heard. For twenty-five hundred years, since Babylon, the
Jew at Passover had cried out softly: "Leshonoh haba ah
Birusholayim!" Hebrew for "Next year in Jerusalem." It was
ritual; what meaning could it conceivably have on the cold
windswept prairies of the Pale of Settlement in Russia?
The Jews who closed the shutters of their sod huts against
the driving snow dreamed of a myth that had been without
concrete meaning for two thousand years. Once there had
been a white and golden city called Jerusalem, but God in
his wisdom had removed it; not even on earth was its presence.

Yet here and there, the sons of these same Jews filled their
pockets with bread, tied clay jugs of water to their belts, repeated the name of Herzl like an invocation, kissed their
weeping parents, and set off eastward across the prairie. On
the American prairie, the pioneers had traveled a thousand
miles in wagon trains, and were properly honored. These
Jews, in the years between 1898 and 1914, walked over

three thousand miles to Palestine. Many died along the way; others turned back in despair; but still others made the journey and came to Palestine, and it was their children and grandchildren who made up a part of the Haganah, Palestine's secret Jewish defense organization.

And what a journey it was—down through the Pale of Settlement to Odessa, where they could rest in the Jewish community and find food for the next stage; then on the shore of the Black Sea to Rostov, and then southward along the coast to Sochi and then Batumi, and then across the wild, almost uninhabited mountains of Turkey, a chore as gigantic as crossing the American divide, and then through Syria to Damascus and down from Damascus into Palestine.

Not too much in terms of numbers should be made out of this; it was just a trickle, a few hundred; but even if one Jew had made this journey, it would be an achievement of note and not without glory; and many of them made it.

Jews were returning to Palestine. Few at first, very few, but they were returning. To begin with, there had never been a time since Moses led the Jews into the hills of Judea that Palestine was without Jews—not a year or a month or a day when there were not Jews living somewhere in Palestine, a few families here, a tiny community there, a group of people in Jerusalem where they hid, lied, dissembled, but somehow survived the passage of centuries. We noted earlier how unreliable Jewish population statistics are, and no one can say with any accuracy what the Jewish population of Palestine was at any given point in history, but we are not without trustworthy partial information.

I dwell on this because there is all too much talk—most of it as uninformed as loose talk usually is—about the Jews returning to Palestine as utter strangers, as if their presence there were purely mythological. Without going back to actual antiquity, let us see what we can make of a more recent Jewish presence in Palestine. In 1495, there were over two hundred Jewish families in Jerusalem, and there were functioning synagogues in half a hundred other spots in

Palestine. In 1520, in Safed alone there were two thousand Jewish families. (We are not seeing a continuity here, but simply noting the Jewish population at various dates. Oppression and war always kept it in serious flux.) By 1600, we have varying reports, and in attempting to distill some modest truth out of them, we must conclude that somewhere between 100,000 and 200,000 Jews were resident in Palestine. Closer than that, we cannot really come. During the eighteenth century, the Jewish population dwindled, as did the population of the Samaritans, who, you will recall, were the descendants of the Beni-Yisrael, the northern kingdom of Israel. By 1837, the Jewish population of Jerusalem had been reduced by war, disease, and emigration to 3,000, although a steady if small flow into the country was increasing this. By 1892, the Jewish population in Jerusalem was over 25,000 and by 1895, we have an absolute and reliable head count. That year there were 30,794 Jews in the holy city, out of a total Jerusalem population of 51,000. And of the 20,000-odd non-Jews, less than half were Arabs.

(Non-Jewish non-Arabs included Samaritans, Druzes, and Christians. Subsequently, the very fact of the Jewish influx and the Jewish desire to buy property increased the Arab influx. The Jews paid higher wages than were paid anywhere else in the region, and the Jews, through medical and sanitary measures, decreased the Arab infant mortality in Jerusalem and of course throughout Palestine. The Jewish residents of Palestine during the pre-Zionist period were not in the majority farmers. In 1881, we estimate that the Jewish population of Palestine was about 40,000, of whom perhaps half lived in Jerusalem.)

After the Zionist Congress of 1911, which agreed that only in Palestine could a Jewish homeland be established, concrete measures were taken to aid immigration. A Palestine Office was opened in Jaffa, and the Zionist movement itself began the process of establishing agricultural settlements and assuming the responsibility for their continuation. What little the Ashkenazi Jews knew about farming was in terms

of Russian and Polish peasant husbandry; the swampy, ma-
larial valley bottoms and rocky bare hills of Palestine would
have presented a problem to the most advanced scientific
agronomists; to these Jews, strange to the semitropical climate and to the kind of farming it required, agriculture was
a combination of heartbreak and disaster.

Not, it must be noted, that the Arab population fared better. In 1910, when a handful of Jews began to dig foundations on a bare sandspit outside of Jaffa, Palestine was as
wretched and inhospitable a wasteland as could be found
in the Middle East. These Jews had a crazy dream of a city
that they would put up on the land behind the sandy beach.
Fittingly, they named it Tel Aviv, in honor of a fellow Jew
whose own dreams had been appropriately mad—Theodor
Herzl. Herzl had written a novel about Palestine, which he
called *Altneuland*—"Old-new land"—and when the book
was translated into Hebrew, the Hebrew publisher titled it
Tel Aviv, Hebrew for "Spring-dale." To name a city with the
title of a book was no more impractical than for a group of
nearsighted Russian-Jewish students to decide to put up a
city on a bare beach and backland.

But throughout history, the Jew had never been deterred
by either the unreasonable or the impossible. If he had an
idea, the very fact that the idea existed in his mind was proof
enough for him that it could be carried out; but he had never
before nurtured an idea so unreasonable as the reconstitution of the dead land of Palestine. Once, long ago, as we
noted, Jewish Palestine had been a garden, every foot of
land coddled, used, blessed, and stimulated to a degree of
productivity that was the wonder of the ancient world.
Rome itself was capitalized by the wealth of Judea, and the
Judean hills were mantled with greenery, terraced, and laced
with the silver-green of countless olive trees. In harvest time,
"the grapes on the vine beaded it with jewels, like a brides-
maid," to quote from the Talmud.

But after that, for two thousand years up to our own time,
Palestine had been drained and destroyed. Anyone who has

witnessed the havoc wreaked upon the fertile valleys of Southern California during the past twenty years understands the process. The Romans destroyed the olive groves and the cedar stands, and began the process of breaking the terrace walls. The soil in the terraces washed away, as did the mountain soil once the trees were removed. Invasion by Bedouin tribesmen and their goats prevented any timber stands from returning, for goats eat the shoots of trees reseeding, and thus for centuries the topsoil left the hills. The eroded soil choked the stream beds, and thus the hard seasonal rainfall piled up and created swamps that became the breeding grounds for the malaria mosquitoes. Constant invasion and unrest prevented fruit and olive orchards from coming to fruition, and this kind of fruit culture vanished for the most part. Ancient forms of irrigation were destroyed, the conduits broken, the channels clogged with the neglected refuse of the ages. Removal of tree stands and low growth tended to change the climate, and each century the desert area of the country increased and the amount of acreage in farmland decreased. More and more was the country used as semi-badland grazing country, and when the Zionist Congress convened in 1911, the entire population of Palestine, including the Jews, was about a half million— in a land which once, as Jewish Palestine, held perhaps five million inhabitants.

Yet from 1911 to the onset of World War I, a period of only four years, Jewish immigration was large beyond the dreams of the most enthusiastic Zionists, and when the war halted the immigration, there were over a hundred thousand Jews in Palestine—not only idealistic Ashkenazim from Russia and Poland, but Yemenites, Syrians, Moroccans, Maghrebians, Kurds, Persians, Bokharans, Babylonians— and American and Canadians and Germans and French, all of them Jews and attempting to submerge their babble of tongues to the resurrection of an ancient language, a language that had ceased to be spoken even by the time of Jesus, the old, holy tribal language of the fierce Yehudim, the tribe that Moses had led into the promised land.

World War I temporarily halted the Ashkenazi immigration into Palestine, if for no other reason than that Russia and Turkey were at war—as were England and Turkey. All other immigration out of the Ashkenazi lands came to a virtual halt, but with the defeat of the Central Powers, control of Palestine passed from the Turkish Empire to the British Empire. In Britain, during the war years, there had been considerable quiet negotiation between important and influential Jews, who were joined closely with Britain's war effort and the British Government, and this led to a letter, written by Lord Arthur James Balfour and addressed to Lord Walter Rothschild, who was asked to convey it to the Zionist Federation. It expressed the sympathy of the British Government for the Zionist aspirations of the Jews, and it said, in part, "His Majesty's Government view with favor the establishment in Palestine of a national home for the Jewish people and will use their best endeavors to facilitate the achievement of this object. . . ."

This was written at a time when the war was still undecided, by an emotional man who had fallen under the spell of Herzl, and who was one of a group of British Judophiles; yet it established the first legal and modern position for Zionism, and importantly associated the Jewish cause with British victory. However, the blessing was mixed, and while thousands of Jews poured into Palestine after the end of World War I, doubling and then tripling the population in fifteen years, the British impeded rather than helped the immigration process—wishing, no doubt, that Lord Balfour's letter could be called back into the vault of history. Using typical empire tactics of the time, the British detached from Palestine its natural and historical hinterland, set it up as a separate colonial entity, arbitrarily named Transjordan, and used it as a training and recruiting ground for an elite Arab army which was subsequently hurled against the Jews to prevent their actual independence.

By 1936, the Jewish population in Palestine was very close to four hundred thousand, but already the Nazis and the Italian Fascists were training and supplying Arab terrorist

groups. A virtual war in Israel between Jews and German-
stimulated and German-supplied Arab terrorists began and
continued intermittently, now small, now quiescent, now
flaring hot and bitter, over the next twelve years. Even during the war years, Palestine was a minor battleground, yet
never did the reclamation and development of the country
by the Jewish settlers come to a halt. These men and women,
coming of the one people on earth who had put away war and
violence as unbefitting to man, now found themselves standing guard day and night in their ancient homeland, that
they might not be wiped out even before they had sunk their
feet into the earth.

When Britain succeeded in making the immigration of
Jews into Palestine almost impossible, the Jews already there
set up underground, illegal avenues of immigration, which
immigration they managed to continue all during World
War II.

———•—◆—•———

Leading up to the Nazi holocaust which consumed over
six million Jews, more than one third of the whole Jewish
population of the earth, the question of immigration and
responsibility cannot be avoided. The entrapment of the
Ashkenazi masses in eastern Europe was not the doing of
any single power, and it was five million of these same Ashkenazi Jews, gentle, pious people to whom violence was unthinkable, who perished in the Nazi murder camps. Many
of them could have escaped if the great powers had not been
so obsessed by their own games of oil and death.

(Much of the Russian Revolution in 1917 and the Civil
War that followed raged across the Jewish Pale of Settlement, those areas where the eastern European Ashkenazi
Jews were most thickly settled. The current callous attitude
of the Russian Government toward Soviet Jews, their
needs, desires, religion, and will—on the part of many—to
go to Israel, has led people to forget the ghastly pogroms that
the White, antirevolutionary forces had perpetrated against
the Jews. Linking the Jewish masses to the Revolution, the
White armies slaughtered and murdered Jews, over a hun-

dred thousand perishing. In the early days of the Soviet Union, anti-Semitism was considered a crime against the Soviet state, and so punished, and in those years, the Russian universities and professions were wholly open to the Jews. The Soviet reaction against the Jews came only in the thirties, with Stalin's assumption of total power—and of course continued in the post-World War II years—but in spite of this, the Russians removed the Jews from the path of the German invading armies and from that part of Poland which Russia occupied. Thus, by a gigantic effort of organization, the Soviets transported almost a million Jews out of Poland and the Ukraine into southeastern Russia. It is quite true that these Jews suffered many privations. They rarely had enough to eat—neither did anyone else in Russia then—and they lived under poor conditions, but they received adequate medical attention and *they survived*. Which, after all, was the single most important factor.)

Who can say how many more would have escaped if England had opened the gates of Palestine to them and had facilitated their journey there? One Jew? One hundred? One thousand? One hundred thousand? In the Talmud, in the Mishnah Sanhedrin, it is said: "One man alone was brought forth at the time of creation, in order to teach us that he who destroys one human soul is regarded as though he had destroyed a whole world; while he who preserves one soul within humanity is regarded as though he had preserved the whole world."

And what of the United States? Few acts in the history of mankind match the generosity and nobility of the United States of America in taking into itself whole nations of the oppressed, the homeless, the most wretched of the human race; and then nurturing them and caring for them and giving back to them that most precious possession, human dignity. Whatever the future for America, this will be remembered; but it must also be noted that in 1921, America began to close her gates with the imposition of the quota system—and then the subsequent National Origins Act, limiting all European immigration to 150,000 a year.

In the six years between 1933 and 1939, a sensible and humanistic attitude toward immigration on the part of the United States Department of State could have saved the lives of a million Jews. There are few shoddier incidents in American history than the State Department's reaction to the German ship *St. Louis*, which sailed into Havana Harbor in Cuba in 1939 with 907 Jewish refugees. If the passengers were refused permission to land, the ship would have to return them to death in Germany. The Cubans, under Batista, refused to allow the Jews to land, and when the ship approached Miami, the State Department instructed the Coast Guard to prevent any landing—even by people leaping overboard and swimming. (A similar incident took place in 1940, where only the personal intervention of Mrs. Eleanor Roosevelt saved the passengers on the 1940 refugee ship from death.) The *St. Louis* sailed back to Europe, where Belgium, Britain, the Netherlands, and France gave the passengers refuge.

But this whole period that preceded the Nazi decision to put to death all the Jews in the lands they controlled was an era of shame in the annals of the United States and of Great Britain too. Every quiet, polite, and well-placed anti-Semite in the governments of both countries got into the act, dressing their hatred of Jews in legal technicalities, the legal technicalities that prevented England from allowing the Jews to go to Palestine, the legal technicality expressed by Representative Karl E. Mundt, of the United States Congress, who said blandly (as quoted by *Look* Magazine, November 14, 1967, in a copyrighted article by Arthur D. Morse), "As a general policy for this country it is not good practice for us to establish a precedent or if the precedent is already established, to emphasize it, whereby we pass legislation which singles out groups of people by their religion, or by their color or their faith, or their political affiliations, either for special consideration or for special penalties."

I quote this, not because it is singular to Representative Mundt, but because it was so typical of the reaction of the entire Department of State under Cordell Hull and Sumner Welles—as well as numerous men in Congress and in the Executive branch of the Government. Even a plea to accept twenty thousand children and save them from the ultimate gas ovens fell uselessly on the heartless and mindless bureaucrats, who crouched behind their "technical" defenses and whispered in polite circles that "the damned Jews wanted everything." And since most of everything is the fact of being alive, that was to a large degree true.

The facts as naked statistics are rather dreadful. Even under the "race and nation" quota system of the United States Department of Immigration, during the ten years between 1933 and 1943, the year the ultimate slaughter of Jews began, the United States could have admitted 1,500,000 aliens. There were actually admitted only 476,930 aliens, of whom 165,756 were Jews. Thus, six million Jews died, while the United States admitted only about 16,000 a year to refuge. As a government—and we must exempt the people of both nations from these judgments—the British were no better, and, unlike the United States, they were not asked to take the Jews into their own country but only to allow them entrance to Palestine, where Jewish private funds and organizations would accept the responsibility of sheltering them and feeding them.

When the Jews' moment of supreme crisis came, when the Ashkenazim faced the end of their existence on earth, almost all governments had closed their doors to them. If the gauge of civilization in a given land were its treatment of the Jews, then we could only speak of a handful of tiny nations as being civilized, the Scandinavian lands, Holland, Switzerland—and where could these countries have sheltered such a population? Perhaps nations cannot be measured as individuals, but perhaps nations as well as people do precisely what they desire to do.

———•—•—•———

Certainly, this was the case with Germany. No one forced Hitler and National Socialism (Nazism) upon the German people. They took both to their bosoms, and the majority of

the population supported the repression—indeed the murder
—of the best and noblest souls in Germany, Jew and non-
Jew. Hitler and his Nazis exterminated six million Jews, but
they also murdered millions who were not Jewish (though
only the Gypsies were chosen with the Jews for genocide)
and they put to death the best and bravest of their own—
Germans who remained to fight Hitler and who perished,
mainly because there was no shelter for them or any real
underground in the bosom of the German people.

When the United States ended its open-door immigration
policy and established the quota system, the Jews in eastern
Europe (that is, in Poland) were trapped, so to speak, and
in their desperate struggle against the walls of misery that
encompassed them, a trickle of them managed to make their
way into Germany. German hatred of the Jew is, as we have
seen, ancient and endemic, and the sight of these poverty-
stricken Ashkenazi Jews, in their ragged caftans and their
skullcaps, bearded, their faces framed in their long hair and
earlocks, speaking their medieval German-Hebrew Yiddish
(a language which appears to irritate and even enrage so
many Germans, perhaps because the Jewish tongue has the
same origin as their own), was enough to arouse old hatreds.
During the late 1920's and the beginning 1930's anti-Semitism exploded in Germany. But it was a restrained explosion,
since the democratic Weimar Republic forbade it, restrained
it, and opened the doors of government to a great many
Jews. Thus the extreme anti-Semitism became the ideology
of the right-wing German forces that were grouping around
Adolf Hitler and his National Socialist Party.

We are still far from understanding why in Germany
an unreasonable, mindless, and brutal hatred of a people
could become the focal point of a national movement that
would eventually enlist the support of the overwhelming
majority of the people. After all, the German Jews were less
than 1 percent of the German population. Most of them were
thoroughly integrated, and in speech, dress, and culture,
indistinguishable to any casual observer from the Christian
German. Indeed, over the hundred-year period since their

liberation from the ghetto and the granting to them of certain civil rights, the German Jews had intermarried very widely with the Christian population, and hundreds of thousands of Germans had some amount of Jewish intermixture. And surely the few thousand Ashkenazi refugees were not sufficient to throw so much of the German population into what can only be described as a lunatic frenzy of Jew-hatred. Nor can this be explained—as many try to explain it—by the fact that so many of the German Jews were doctors, lawyers, writers, jurists; men of talent, success, and position. There were far more non-Jews in the same category; nor is the envy of talent considered in other countries to be so pathological as to turn a normal, decent citizen into a ravening madman, bent on murder.

We have already seen the origin of that most nonsensical of all pseudo-scientific gibberish, the Aryan theory of the superman, and the super-superman, who is the blond, blue-eyed German. (Incidentally, Freud—a non-Aryan, non-superman—in his brilliant study of paranoia in a German magistrate, notes the fact that the paranoiac sees himself, subjectively, as god or superman.) Soon after the Nazis took power in Germany, on April 11, 1933, they issued the "Aryan Decree," which defined as non-Aryan any person having a non-Aryan—which meant Jewish—parent or grandparent. So from the very beginning, the Nazis began to enforce the center of their program, the destruction of the Jews.

On September 15, 1935, the Reichstag adopted the Nuremberg Laws, which formalized and established legal procedure for anti-Semitism, persecution of Jews, and arrest and incarceration in concentration camps without due process and without any recourse to habeas corpus or any other legal protective right that civilized nations observe as basic to modern life. This legalized the national license—granted to the German people by implication in 1933—to rob, beat, rape, and even kill Jews with impunity. Of course, this kind of national hoodlumism does not run rampant through a population as disciplined and law-abiding as the Germans traditionally have been, and it was not until after the occupation of Austria, in March of 1938, that both organized and inspirational violence against the Jewish population became literally an everyday, every-hour occurrence.

Later that same year, in November of 1938, a Jewish boy in Paris, half-mad with what was happening to the Jews in Germany, assassinated Von Rath, a Nazi consular official. This let loose in Germany the kind of sadistic bloodlust that had been so common in the Middle Ages. Synagogues and Jewish houses were burned, Jews were driven into buildings and burned alive, Jews were murdered, beaten to death on the streets by hoodlum gangs. Infants were killed, small children beaten to death. This outburst of savagery, throughout Germany, shocked and horrified the world, and protests poured in to the German Government from every land.

Nothing loath, Herman Goering proceeded immediately to levy a punitive fine of a billion marks upon the Jews of Germany, and with this and confiscation and specific penalties which he levied as he saw fit, he eliminated the Jews from the economic body of Germany almost in one group of actions.

From the moment Hitler took power, Jews began to flee from Germany and those areas which Germany occupied before World War II. Between 1933 and 1941, when Jews were forbidden to leave Germany and the final decision was taken to exercise genocide against the Jewish population of Europe, putting them all to death, almost a quarter of a million Jews managed to escape from Germany, as well as one hundred thousand from Austria and perhaps thirty-five thousand from Czechoslovakia.

There is some difference of opinion as to when the Germans made a clear decision to engage in genocide against the Jews, but it is generally accepted that in a conference in Hitler's private railroad car in 1939, it was agreed by Hitler and his close companions that all the Jews of Europe should be put to death. At that point, the Nazis fully believed they would conquer all of Europe, and thus they made plans for the entire European Jewish population. Writing of these things almost thirty years later, one is so shocked that disbelief must be inserted between the mind and the horror.

In this case, six million corpses proved that the most monstrous decision in all the history of mankind had actually taken place. One cannot characterize the German leadership during this period because man has never before faced the necessity to create words descriptive of such an action.

In order to carry out this "final solution to the Jewish problem," ghettos were set up in the major cities of conquered Poland, so that the Jews might be herded together to make the ultimate German task easier. Corrals were built at major railroad depots, and extermination camps were built in Belzec, Sobibor, Treblinka, and Maidanek. Everything was done well and every detail was considered with German thoroughness; but the German engineers who were assigned to grapple with this problem informed Heinrich Himmler that these camps could not process the Jews quickly enough, nor could the fertilizer plants that Hitler had ordered constructed process the amount of Jewish flesh and bones that would result from the procedure. They told Himmler that a more massive slaughter center must be set up, and that certain Jewish bodies would have to be reduced to ashes and still others buried without benefit to German agriculture or the German soap industry. (Later, Germans protested that they could not enjoy washing with the soap made from dead Jews, and so the soap was for the most part used by forced labor. Bars of this soap were exhibited in New York in 1946.)

In order to satisfy this final need, Himmler gave the orders to build the enormous concentration-extermination camp in Auschwitz.

Reinhard Heydrich was the head of the Nazi Security Police, and Hitler praised him as the only man cool enough to see the whole human race eliminated without a tremor of emotion. He was given the responsibility by Hitler of creating a master plan for the elimination of the Jews, and in pursuit of this duty, he called the Wannsee Conference on January 20 of 1942. The agenda of this conference bore one major item— the need for a systematic pattern for Jewish extermination. As always, German method, organization, and thoroughness were brought to bear. The conference was a success, and a few

months later the master plan went into action and the death
chambers began to function; nor did this well-constructed
German network of factories for mass murder cease to function until six million Jews had died.

The Jews for the first great killing came from the Warsaw
Ghetto, where three hundred thousand were processed from
the ghetto into the Treblinka death machine and scientifi-
cally murdered. Then, ghetto after ghetto was systematically
processed. Since not all Jews could be processed, a select detachment of elite Nazis, the Einsatzgruppen, were trained to
dispatch Jews swiftly and expertly wherever these Jews
were, and they were sent into the cities and villages of Soviet
Russia that the Nazis had occupied to find any Jews who had
not managed to escape, to separate them from the rest of the
population, and to put them to death. Auschwitz proved to be
everything Himmler said it would be, for in sixty-seven days,
three hundred and fifty thousand Hungarian Jews were put
to death in its gas chambers. To go through the entire list is
unbearable, but Adolph Eichmann testified that over four
million Jews were put to death in the murder camps and
better than two million more in other ways.

The notion that all these Jews supinely and stupidly went
to their deaths is far from the truth. The question has been
asked: Why didn't the Jews fight back? Some did, and we will
come to that, but the majority did not—and for the following
reasons:

For a hundred years, the Ashkenazi Jew of Poland had
regarded the German Jew, and therefore Germany, as the
epitome of civilization. The Ashkenazi Jews who came to
America shared this attitude toward the German Jews, and
in the cities of Poland, particularly, the notion that the Germans could have planned and carried through the prepara-
tions I describe above, was unthinkable and unbelievable.
Even though again and again the Jews in the ghettos of Warsaw and Vilna and Bialystok were told precisely what was
going on in the Treblinka death factory, they refused to believe that people so civilized as the Germans would permit
this. This tragic misjudgment on the part of the Jews as to

what constituted civilization stemmed from the very core
of their own culture. Rabbinical Judaism places a higher
value on human life than any other religion or philosophy known to mankind. The Talmud is filled with expres-
sions sanctifying human life, and in the Jewish home, this
reverence for life and repugnance to inflict any hurt on another is central to family existence. The deeply Orthodox
and the Hasidic Jews believe that in the eyes of God, all human life is equally cherished, wherefore the taking of another
life in defense of your own is no less culpable than murder of
another human being.

Another reason lies in the fact that those who can fight
best are the most mobile, the young men between eighteen
and thirty—and these were the Jews who to a large degree
managed to escape. Jewish fathers and mothers, hopeless in
their own situation, persuaded thousands of the young and
strong to leave, to make their way into the forest and join
the partisans, to Russia, to Palestine when that was possible—
to any place where they might survive. So that a majority of
those who went to the death camps were very old and very
young, the small children, the infants, and the middle-aged
and the old.

Still another reason lies in the weakened condition of the
Jews. For months, they had been literally starving to death.
People so weak that they can barely drag one foot after an-
other are not good candidates for an uprising.

And finally, the Jews were not armed.

Yet, in spite of this, they fought back.

———•◦•———

Jews are very tough-minded people, and man is beginning
to learn that it takes more courage to die for a belief in nonviolence than it does to die for a belief in violence. The Ashkenazi Jew was very steadfast in his belief in nonviolence,
and for a thousand years he was not shaken in that belief.
Surrounded by a world that measured nobility, courage, and
honor in terms of butchery, he looked upon the gentile without envy and maintained his position that a human being

does not take human life and then dissolve the horror of the deed in a rationale of necessity. In America, he became an American and changed his outlook for reasons we have seen; yet I know of few intelligent Jews who take any real pride in the fact that the Israelis are as good as any soldiers on earth. They admit the necessity but do not welcome it.

So did the Ashkenazi Jews feel after they accepted the fact that a death machine was functioning to destroy them. It took indescribable horror to turn them to violence, but once they made the decision, their last, dying moment left an example to all of mankind. There had been almost a half million people jammed into the Warsaw Ghetto; on April 19 of 1943, when the Jews began their battle against the Germans, only forty thousand were left. But of the forty thousand fewer than five thousand had the strength to bear arms and there were arms for only a few hundred, a few pistols, a few rifles. The Jewish fighting groups in Warsaw raided Nazi barracks and installations to obtain arms, and during the fighting they took more arms from the Nazi dead. But they never had enough ammunition to sustain any sort of firepower, and the grenades, mines, and Molotov cocktails—fused bottles of gasoline—they made themselves.

For forty-two days, they stood off the Nazi attacks. The Nazis threw everything they had against these handfuls of half-armed Jews—heavy artillery, tanks, even dive bombers, and they had sufficient machine-gun firepower literally to churn anything in the ghetto into dust—yet the Jews fought them for forty-two days, teen-age boys and girls, old men without the strength to move from where they fought and died, and bold determined men who lived through the fighting until the ghetto was utterly destroyed, and then escaped through the sewers, made their way to Israel, and five years later fought for Israel in the War of Independence. And they took their toll of the Germans and perhaps taught the Germans some facts about the human spirit.

Not only in Warsaw was there resistance. Revolts broke out in the ghettos of Cracow and Vilna, gallant and tragic battles that matched the Warsaw revolt in courage and defiance. At the Konin labor camp, the Jewish inmates revolted in 1944, and there was a Jewish revolt in 1943, in the concentration camp of Sobibor; and there were revolts at Trabnik and Treblinka. But never was the great death that the Germans had devised halted, and in the end two-thirds of the Ashkenazi Jews in Europe perished.

Three million survived in the Soviet Union and perhaps two million more outside of Russia, and with those in Israel and in the United States, perhaps eleven million Jews in the whole world. In their long journey through history, the Jews had been able to endure all except Germany. If the Jew moved through history in some attempt to prove that man could put away the sword and teach his neighbors to love, then Germany confounded him.

The war ended finally, in 1944 in Europe, and those monuments to German efficiency, the death factories, ceased to operate. Russian, American, and British troops opened the gates of the concentration camps, and the whole world looked with horror and disbelief at the living and the dead, the feeble, emaciated survivors whom the Germans had not had sufficient time to destroy, and the mass graves where the dead in the tens and hundreds of thousands were piled; for the killing had outrun the fertilizer and soap factories.

The world over, men of conscience were numb and speechless, for what could be said? Somewhere in the dark soul of Germany, God had died, and this sense of the death of God spread across the face of the earth. Nazis were brought to trial, and in the dock, they were mundane and stupid men, afraid now that their time had come—among them no prince of darkness but only dreadful, shabby little men, without soul or mind or imagination, who trembled as the witnesses accused them.

A handful of elderly Jews who had hidden in the ruins of Warsaw and so escaped, were asked whether they were pleased to be alive. They shook their heads, and one of them said slowly: "We did not hide to live. We hid to have time to sanctify ourselves."

That is not easily explained or understood, but among

the Jews there are some—as among the gentiles—who are as
old as time and who remember. It was easier for Jews than
for Christians to look at what had happened with open eyes
and to appraise it and to accept it, while most of the Christian world pretended that it had never happened. The Pope
expressed his opposition to Jewish settlement in Palestine,
and the British Government tightened every control it could
exercise to limit Jewish immigration into Palestine. The
United States stood quietly behind its quota system, and the
Jews who had survived lived in the refugee camps and settlements from day to day and waited.

There was current then the story of the Jew who had survived, losing wife and children and mother and father to the
gas chambers, and he was asked by a resettlement worker:

"And where would you like to go?"

"New Zealand," he replied.

"But it's so far."

"From where?" the Jew asked.

Recha Freyer was forty years old in 1932, a Jewish school
teacher in Germany, and already there was death in the air.
She did a direct and merciful thing; she assembled a group
of teen-age children, fifteen to seventeen, trained them to
live and work in Palestine—and got them there. They lived.
It was the definition of Jewish Palestine—a place where
people could live instead of dying. Taking up this same work,
Henrietta Szold, a most remarkable woman who subsequently organized the Women's Zionist Organization of
America, organized and thereafter worked with a remarkable
movement called Youth Aliyah, the Jewish child-rescue
movement. Through this movement, over seventy-five thousand children, many of them orphans and waifs, were brought
to Palestine. *They lived.* There is no other way to understand
the history of the Jew in modern Palestine, the creation of the
State of Israel, and subsequent events there—except to dwell
on the meaning of life itself.

There is no division of guilt in the world that calls itself

Christian, and unless Christians finally come to understand the bitter and almost inadmissible truth, that the murder of six million Jews by the Germans was the final, hideous outcome of a Christian ideology that had spent two thousand years teaching mankind to hate the Jew—then the crucifixion of the Jews and the connected inhumanity of the Christian will continue, on and on, until finally mankind, in the name of that gentle Jew Jesus, who died without ever hearing the word *Christian* or knowing what agony his own people would suffer in his name, destroys itself.

The meaning of Israel is clear. The Jew had experienced too much death, and a portion of the Jewish people decided that they would die quietly no more. So it is; and no arguments, no clever political talk, no logic, no parading of right and wrong can change this fact. The Jews returned to Israel because it was their ancient land. From 1810 onward, Jews in Palestine had been murdered by Arabs. The pious Jews of Safed, who would raise no hand in their defense, had been robbed and murdered and burned out again and again by Arabs—as the Jews in Jerusalem and Tiberias had been robbed and slain and burned out. Bedouin Arabs passed through Palestine at will—and killed and robbed Jews as a profitable thing. In the nineteenth and twentieth centuries, Arab feudal lords in Palestine organized pogroms precisely as the Czar had organized pogroms. Palestine was a blighted and relatively empty land until the Zionist movement returned it to life, and it is worth remembering that it was not the Jew but the gentile who created the situation that made Zionism a fact without an alternative.

In 1939, the British Government saw the face of Nazism very clearly—yet that same year they decreed that Jewish immigration into Palestine be limited to fifteen thousand persons a year. And even when the German abattoirs had gone into production, even when England was fighting for her very existence against the fleets of Nazi bombers and their firebombs, the British found the time and the men and the ships to hunt down every ship that attempted to bring Jewish refugees to Palestine. Even the fact that thirty thousand

Palestinian Jews had joined the British army as volunteers and were fighting and dying in Africa did not dent the hard nugget of anti-Semitism that certain sections of the British ruling class cherished; and the United States Department of State, ridden with its own logical anti-Semitism, remained discreetly quiet.

The S.S. *Patria*, loaded with refugee Jews, reached to within sight of Haifa before the British halted it. Though they were at war with Hitler, the British refused to allow the seventeen hundred Jews on board to land. An explosion on board ship killed two hundred of them. The S.S. *Struma* was turned away by the British—a ship with no other place to go or dock, out of Rumania in 1941, when it was death for the 769 Jews aboard to return there—and finally she foundered in the Black Sea. All on board were lost.

One could go on and on. The thousands of Jews who perished in the Mediterranean or on its shores because the doors to Palestine were closed will never be counted or named. Yet the thousands of incidents where the Jewish underground and various Jewish organizations brought immigrants in would fill volumes. For the Jews, there was no alternative, and by 1948, the Jewish population in Palestine had passed 650,000.

———— •◦•◦• ————

The role of the British during all of this is hardly pleasant to recall. The empire-mongers, the "white man's burden" lot in British government circles wanted desperately to hold Palestine as a key to the Middle East and Middle Eastern oil. They fomented Jewish-Arab strife, set up provocations, armed the Arabs, and spared no effort to disarm the Jews. And when hostilities erupted, that incredible relic of the Empire-Kipling idiocy, Glubb Pasha, the British commander of Jordan's Arab Legion, watched with delight as his Arabs spread-eagled and tortured and mutilated dead and dying Jewish soldiers.

But not Britain nor the Arab threats could stand against the desperation of the Jews, and on April 2, 1947, the British were forced to ask for a special session of the General Assembly of the United Nations. Having no government as such, the Jewish settlers in Palestine were represented by the Jewish Agency, and its spokesmen, Dr. Chaim Weizmann, David Ben-Gurion, Dr. Abba Hillel Silver, and Moshe Sharett.

To the amazement of most of those present, the Russian delegate to the United Nations, Andrei Gromyko, supported the Jewish cause, and on May 15, speaking at the United Nations, he said:

"The aspirations of an important part of the Jewish people are bound up with the question of Palestine, and with the future structure of that country. This interest is comprehensible and completely justified."

Today, with the Russians as senselessly arming and then rearming the Arabs for the destruction of Israel as their precursors, the Czars, senselessly organized the murderous pogroms over and over again, this quote from Gromyko has a particularly bitter and pointless taste. In their forgetfulness of Jewish suffering and sacrifice and their callous betrayal of Jewish hopes, the Russians can proudly take their place alongside of the dreariest of their capitalist contemporaries—oil holding infinitely more allure than either morality or the pledges of socialism.

A special committee was set up by the United Nations to examine the question, and the result was a recommendation for the partition of Palestine into a Jewish, an Arab, and a neutral sector, each a separate self-governing entity. To this the spokesmen for the Jewish Agency agreed; and Britain let it be known that she would terminate her military occupation of Palestine on May 15, 1948.

On April 10, 1948, the United Nations Palestine Commission reported to the General Assembly as follows:

The Jewish Agency for Palestine cooperated with the Commission in its task of implementing the Assembly's resolution. The governments of the Arab States and the Arab Higher Committee not only withheld their cooperation from the commission but actively opposed the Assembly's resolution. Armed

Arab bands from neighboring Arab states have infiltrated into the territory of Palestine together with local Arab forces defeating the purposes of the resolution by acts of violence.

On May 15, after sparing no efforts to complete the disarmament of the Jews, the last of the British military forces withdrew from Palestine. A day before this, Radio Tel Aviv had announced at 4:06 P.M. the creation of an independent Jewish State in Palestine, and that this state would be called Israel. Almost immediately, five Arab countries began the invasion of Israel.

———•◆•——

There is no natural point where such a story as this ends; there is only a moment when one feels that he has allowed himself to be drawn wholly into the drama around him, and at that moment he loses an objective viewpoint. Yet with the creation of the State of Israel, one comes to a turning point in Jewish history, and it is as well to end the story here as at any other point.

Anyone who has read my story this far will realize that the situation of the Jews among the peoples of the earth has undergone a qualitative change during the twentieth century. The two great blocks of the world's Jewish population in the Diaspora are in the Soviet Union and in the United States. The anti-Jewish measures taken after World War II in the Soviet Union were political attitudes on the question of the orientation of Soviet Jews toward the State of Israel and also as part of the great power struggle for the rich Arab oil resources. Along with this, a vicious historical Russian anti-Semitism survives as a part of the social-cultural fabric of the Soviet Union. It is to be hoped that a growing sophistication and liberalism—slow but nevertheless growing—in the Soviet Union will finally control and eventually eradicate this anti-Semitism, if only as something unworthy of an intelligent population. But as yet, such hope is unfulfilled.

The political question, however, is quite different. Israel is unfortunate in the fact that vast reserves of oil lie in the Arab states around her but not under her own soil, and these reserves of oil are the area of contention among the great powers of the earth. This contention is far too active and confused at this moment for anyone to make predictions; but if sanity and a will toward peace prevail, Israel will survive and flourish and make her own contribution to the future of the human race. And while no one can now assess such a contribution, one can say with some certainty that at any time in history, the Jewish contribution to mankind has been neither dull nor without value.

As for the United States—there as much as elsewhere, the Jew's future is uncertain. Surely the forces for assimilation are greater than ever before, yet there are other forces at play as well. In the open society of the United States, the Jew has flourished as never before. He has added a richness, an excitement and viability to American life that have left no one in America untouched. So far, America has been singularly free of the European disease of anti-Semitism. Native hates and resentments have been constantly opposed and rejected by important Christian elements in American society, and there is in America an acute consciousness of racial and religious hatred as perhaps a mortal danger to the national entity itself.

What direction the future will take, no one knows, but it is hardly to be expected that in the foreseeable future as in the remembered past, the story of the Jew will ever be without excitement, creativity, and passion. Being a Jew is not a cause for despair or depression; such despair and agony as the Jewish people have had to endure over the past thousand years is the result, not of what they are, but of what the Christian world has inflicted upon them; and since so many Jews stubbornly remained Jewish in spite of that, the fact of being Jewish must hold an enticement in itself.

I think there will always be Jews—if only because the fact of being a Jew is a special kind of wonder, not a condition of superiority and neither a condition of inferiority, but rather a condition of civilization, of being a little bit of an outsider with the outsider's point of view, so that at least some of those who are Jews see things more clearly because they are apart. The world needs its outsiders, Jew or not; and being a Jew—and indeed being anything else in the family of man— is a special kind of experience. So many Jews savor with delight what they are, that one who talks of their demise talks out of a lack of knowledge. Mankind will just have to get used to the fact that the Jews are here to stay, and once he is relaxed on that score, he might enjoy them.

BIBLIOGRAPHICAL NOTE

Twenty-eight years ago, Mr. Isadore Werbel, of the Hebrew Publishing Company, asked me whether I would like to write a very short history of the Jews for teen-agers. My reply to this was that the only qualification I possessed was that I happened to be Jewish. Aside from this fortunate accident of birth, I had only the fuzziest notion of Jewish history and could not imagine anyone less qualified. But he felt that I might bring to the subject a fresh point of view, and as for knowledge—well, he brought me to the Hebrew Publishing Company's bookstore on Delancey Street, where it still is today, and told me to help myself to whatever books I felt I might need. Those were Depression times, and he said that the books might compensate for the limited financial reward.

I think the books overcompensated. Faced with the enormous wealth around me, I made only two choices; but these were basic, and have remained basic throughout my life, to my understanding of Jewish history.

The first was the gigantic twelve-volume edition of the *Jewish Encyclopedia*, the original edition beginning with the 1901 Volume I, under the editorial guidance of Dr. Isadore Singer. Not only do I consider this the most exciting and rewarding work of Jewish scholarship ever put together, but its nine thousand or so pages constitute one of the grandest works of scholarship ever conceived and carried out in any culture. I have read in it for almost thirty years, yet it contains untouched treasures that ask for more than a man's lifetime. I still have this original edition, its fine paper hardly yellowed by the years and its binding surviving constant handling.

My second choice at the Hebrew Publishing Company was their

own edition of Professor Graetz's *A Popular History of the Jews,* in six volumes, translated by Rabbi A. B. Rhine. This eloquent work—unmatched, for all of its shortcomings—remains a basic beginning for the study of the history of the Jews. The edition I have, published in 1935, is an excellent piece of bookmaking, and the paper and binding remain in almost perfect condition.

These two choices enabled me to write my small story of the Jews that was published almost thirty years ago; they also helped to begin an investigation of my own heritage and being that has lasted until today.

After the publication of my first history—whose only virtue was readability—I began a conscious collection and study of Judaica. It would be pointless to list the books I read over the years, even if I could remember all of them; they serve simply as a background. For the reader who would like to dig more deeply into any part of the story I tell here, I list the major works that I used, read and reread, during the time I worked on the manuscript, including of course the *Jewish Encyclopedia* and Graetz's history.

For the Bible, I consulted both the King James Version and the Jewish Publication Society's new translation. I have read the King James Version in the Oxford edition several times, and many parts of it in comparison with the Jewish translation, and while it is superb literature, I prefer the Torah (the first five books) in the 1962 edition of the Jewish Publication Society. All the quotes from the Torah are taken from the 1962 edition. As background to this, I used Louis Ginzberg's *Legends of the Bible, The Life and Works of Flavius Josephus* in William Whiston's translation, and the Apocrypha in the King James Version of 1611.

In connection with the above, I used the following historical material: *The Culture of Ancient Egypt* by John A. Wilson, *The Religion of the Semites* by W. Robertson Smith, *The History of Herodotus* in the Rawlinson translation, *The Art of Warfare in Biblical Lands* by Yigael Yadin, Oskar Seyffert's *Dictionary of Classical Antiquities, Herod* by Samuel Sandmel, *Schechem* by G. Ernest Wright, *The Archeology of Palestine* by W. F. Albright, *The Birth of Civilization in the Near East* by Henri Frankfort, *Hebrew Origins* by T. J. Meek, and *An Introduction to Literature of the Old Testament* by S. R. Driver.

In a special category—I consider it a most unusual work—is

Jacob de Haas' *History of Palestine,* a book I have read and re-read with the greatest of profit and pleasure, and which I feel is one of the best histories of Palestine. For an informative, overall one-volume history of the Jews, I referred to *The History of the Jewish People* by Margolis and Marx, a thorough and scholarly book, if somewhat dated and meticulous.

All too little has been written about that remarkable aspect of the Jewish people, the sea and mercantile shipping. I read and can recommend *They Took to the Sea* by Samuel Tolkowsky. Otherwise, my information on this subject had to be pieced together from a variety of sources.

On Christianity and Christian origins, aside from the *Catholic Encyclopedia,* I used the following books: *Harper's Bible Dictionary* by M. S. and J. L. Miller, *The First Christian* by A. Powell Davies, *The Dead Sea Scriptures,* edited and translated by Theodore H. Gaster, *The Origins of Christianity* by Archibald Robertson, *The Foundations of Christianity* by Karl Kautsky, *The Mystery-religions and Christianity* by Samuel Angus, *The Death of Jesus* by Joel Carmichael, and *The New Testament* in the new translation of 1961.

Of course, I include here only those specifically directed works, leaving out general histories, encyclopedias, and atlases consulted constantly for reference. I consulted the Everyman's eighteen-volume *Talmud.* I read in it, but would not dare to assert that I have read it. I used both Hyman E. Goldin's translation of the *Pirke Abot* and Judah Goldin's translation of the *Abot de-Rabbi Nathan.* I used my father's old prayerbooks, published long ago by the Jewish Premium Publishing Company, and the modern Union Prayerbook of the Central Conference of American Rabbis —my Hebrew being such that I could not use one without a translation. To bolster my inadequate Hebrew, I used Blumberg and Lewitte's *Modern Hebrew* and Harkavy's *Hebrew and Chaldee Dictionary.* For modern Orthodox practice, I used the *Kitzur Schulchan Aruch (Code of Jewish Law),* compiled by Rabbi Solomon Ganzfried, in Hyman E. Goldin's translation. I used the *Zohar* and Jiri Langer's *Nine Gates to the Chassidic Mysteries.* As a one-volume reference work, I used the Doubleday *Jewish Encyclopedia,* which is edited by Cecil Roth—by far the best one-volume encyclopedia available.

For more modern developments, I used S. M. Dubnow's *History of the Jews in Russia and Poland,* in the three-volume Friedlander translation, *The Ghetto* by Louis Worth, *The Documentary History of the Jews in the United States* by Morris U. Schappes, *The Fighting Ghettos* by Meyer Barkai, *The Rise and Fall of the Third Reich* by William L. Shirer, and *Essays on Antisemitism,* edited by Koppel S. Pinson. Three other general books, while not dealing with the modern scene, have been of such value in the preparation of my manuscript that I must mention them: *The Ancient City* by Fustel de Coulanges in the 1873 translation by Willard Small, a book I consider basic to an understanding of ancient society; *The Ancient Mariners* by Lionel Casson; and *Carthage* by B. H. Warmington.

In addition to the books mentioned above, I have drawn directly from a number of other books which are listed in the Bibliography which follows.

BIBLIOGRAPHY

Abot de-Rabbi Nathan, trans. by JUDAH GOLDIN. New Haven, Conn., Yale University Press, 1955

ABRAHAMS, ISRAEL, *Jewish Life in the Middle Ages,* Cecil Roth, ed. London, E. Goldston, 1948

ADLER, E. N., ed., *Jewish Travellers.* London, Routledge, 1938

ADLER, MORRIS, *The World of the Talmud,* 2d ed. New York, Schocken, 1963

AGUS, JACOB B., *Evolution of Jewish Thought.* New York, Abelard, 1960

ALBRIGHT, WILLIAM F., *The Archeology of Palestine.* London, Penguin, 1960

ANGUS, SAMUEL, *The Mystery-religions and Christianity.* New York, U. Books, 1967

BARKAI, MEYER, ed., *The Fighting Ghettos.* Philadelphia, Lippincott, 1962

BARON, SALO WITTMAYER, *The Jewish Community; its history and structure to the American Revolution.* Philadelphia, Jewish Publication Society, 1942

—————— *A Social and Religious History of the Jews,* 12 v. New York, Columbia University Press, 1952–67

BARR, STRINGFELLOW, *The Mask of Jove.* Philadelphia, Lippincott, 1966

—————— *The Will of Zeus.* Philadelphia, Lippincott, 1961

BLUMBERG, H., and LEWITTE, M. H., *Modern Hebrew,* 2 v. New York, Hebrew Publishing Co., 1946–52

BUBER, MARTIN, *Tales of the Hasidim,* 2 v. New York, Schocken, 1947–48

CARMICHAEL, JOEL, *The Death of Jesus.* New York, Macmillan, 1961

CASSON, LIONEL, *The Ancient Mariners.* New York, Macmillan, 1959

The Catholic Encyclopedia, CHARLES G. HERBERMANN AND OTHERS, eds. New York, R. Appleton, 1907–12

DAVIES, A. POWELL, *The First Christian.* New York, New American Library, 1959

DE HAAS, JACOB, *History of Palestine.* New York, Macmillan, 1934

DRIVER, SAMUEL R., *An Introduction to the Literature of the Old Testament.* New York, Meridian, 1967

DUBNOW, S. M., *History of the Jews in Russia and Poland,* 3 v., trans. by I. Friedlander. Philadelphia, Jewish Publication Society, 1916–20

FRANKFORT, HENRI, *The Birth of Civilization in the Near East.* New York, Doubleday, 1959

FUSTEL DE COULANGES, NUMA DENIS, *The Ancient City,* trans. by Willard Small. Gloucester, Mass., Peter Smith, 1959

GANZFRIED, SOLOMON, ed., *Kitzur Schulchan Aruch (Code of Jewish Law),* trans. by Hyman E. Goldin. New York, Hebrew Publishing Co., 1961

GASTER, THEODORE H., ed., *The Dead Sea Scriptures.* New York, Doubleday, 1956

GINZBERG, LOUIS, *Legends of the Bible.* New York, Simon & Schuster, 1956

GRAETZ, HEINRICH, *A Popular History of the Jews,* 6 v., trans. by A. B. Rhine. New York, Hebrew Publishing Co., 1935

HARKAVY, ALEXANDER, ed., *Students' Hebrew and Chaldee Dictionary to the Old-Testament.* New York, Hebrew Publishing Co., 1914

The History of Herodotus, trans. by G. RAWLINSON. New York, Tudor, 1967

The Holy Bible, KING JAMES VERSION. London, Oxford University Press

The Holy Bible, KING JAMES VERSION OF 1611

JAMES, E. O., *Myth and Ritual in the Ancient Near East.* New York, Barnes & Noble, 1961

KAUTSKY, KARL, *The Foundations of Christianity.* New York, International, 1925

LANGER, JIRI, *Nine Gates to the Chasidic Mysteries,* trans. by Stephen Jolly. New York, McKay, 1961

The Life and Works of Flavius Josephus, trans. by WILLIAM WHISTON. New York, Holt, Rinehart & Winston, 1957

MARCUS, JACOB RADER, *Memoirs of American Jews, 1775–1865,* 3 v. Philadelphia, Jewish Publication Society, 1955–56

MARGOLIS, M. L., and MARX, A., *The History of the Jewish People.* Philadelphia, Jewish Publication Society, 1938

MEEK, T. J., *Hebrew Origins*. New York, Harper, 1936

MILLER, M. S. and J. L., *Harper's Bible Dictionary*. New York, Harper, 1961

MOORE, GEORGE FOOT, *Judaism in the First Centuries of the Christian Era*, 3 v. Cambridge, Mass., Harvard University Press, 1966–67

The New English Bible: New Testament. London, Oxford University Press, 1961

PHILIPSON, D., *The Reform Movement in Judaism*, rev. ed. New York, Ktav, 1967

PINSON, KOPPEL S., ed., *Essays on Antisemitism*. New York, Conference on Jewish Social Studies, 1946

Pirke Abot, trans. by HYMAN E. GOLDIN. New York, Hebrew Publishing Co., 1962

ROBERTSON, ARCHIBALD, *The Origins of Christianity*. New York, International Publishers, 1962

ROTH, CECIL, ed., *The Standard Jewish Encyclopedia*. New York, Doubleday, 1959

ROTH, CECIL, *The History of the Jews*, rev. ed. New York, Schocken, 1961

SAMUEL, MAURICE, *The World of Sholom Aleichem*. New York, Knopf, 1943

SANDMEL, SAMUEL, *Herod*. Philadelphia, Lippincott, 1967

SARTRE, JEAN-PAUL, *Anti-Semite and Jew*. New York, Schocken, 1965

SCHAPPES, MORRIS U., ed., *The Documentary History of the Jews in the United States, 1654–1875*. New York, Citadel Press, 1950

SCHOLEM, GERSHOM, ed., *Zohar: Book of Splendor*. New York, Schocken, 1949

SCHURER, EMIL, *History of the Jewish People in the Time of Jesus*, N. N. Glatzer, ed. New York, Schocken, 1961

SCHWARZ, LEO W., *Memoirs of my People*. New York, Schocken, 1963

SEYFFERT, OSKAR, *A Dictionary of Classical Antiquities*. New York, Meridian, 1967

SHIRER, WILLIAM L., *The Rise and Fall of the Third Reich*. New York, Simon & Schuster, 1960

SINGER, ISADORE, ed., *Jewish Encyclopedia*, 12 v. New York, Funk & Wagnalls, 1901–1906

SMITH, W. ROBERTSON, *The Religion of the Semites*. New York, Meridian, 1956

Talmud, L. Epstein, ed., trans. by E. W. Kirzner. 18 v. New York, Bloch Publishing Co., 1960

TOLKOWSKY, SAMUEL, *They Took to the Sea*. New York, Thomas Yoseloff, 1964

Torah: A New Translation. Philadelphia, Jewish Publication Society, 1962

The Union Prayerbook for Jewish Worship, 2 v. Cincinnati, The Central Conference of American Rabbis, 1894–95

WARD, C. OSBORNE, *The Ancient Lowly*. New York, B. Franklin, 1967

WARMINGTON, B. H., *Carthage*. London, Penguin, 1965

WILSON, JOHN A., *The Culture of Ancient Egypt*. Chicago, University of Chicago Press, 1951

WORTH, LOUIS, *The Ghetto*. Chicago, University of Chicago Press, 1956

WRIGHT, G. ERNEST, *Schechem*. New York, McGraw-Hill, 1964

YADIN, YIGAEL, *The Art of Warfare in Biblical Lands*. New York, McGraw-Hill, 1963